PRE-INTERMEDIATE BUSINESS

ENGLISH TEACHER'S RESOURCE BOOK

NEW EDITION

MARKET
LEADER

Bill Mascull

with

Lizzie Wright

www.longman.com

FINANCIAL
TIMES

Pearson Education Limited
Edinburgh Gate, Harlow,
Essex CM20 2JE, England
and Associated Companies throughout the World

First published 2002

New edition 2007

ISBNs
Book   978-1-4058-1307-5
Book for pack 978-1-4058-1308-2
Pack   978-1-4058-1344-0

Set in 9/12pt MetaPlus

Printed in Spain by Mateu Cromo, S.A. Pinto, Madrid

www.market-leader.net

Acknowledgements

We are grateful to the following for permission to reproduce the following copyright material:

Claire Adler for an extract adapted from 'Tried and tested or tired formula?' by Claire Adler published in *The FT* 5th June 2006 © Claire Adler; Richard Donkin for an extract adapted from 'Understand your team and the rest is plain sailing' by Richard Donkin published in *The FT* 27th July 2006 © Richard Donkin, author of 'Blood Sweat and Tears, The Evolution of Work' www.richarddonkin.com; The Financial Times for extracts adapted from 'Kraft gives products healthy makeover' by Jeremy Grant published in *The FT* 12th March 2003, 'Mere mortals and the genesis of great ideas' by Simon London published in *The FT* 18th April 2005, 'Cost effective route to create future managers' by Andrew Taylor published in *The FT* 13th July 2005, 'Investors are turning up the heat on stress' by Alison Maitland published in *The FT* 18th January 2006, 'Business and the ultimate pleasure' by Jill James published in *The FT* 13th February 2006, 'Raymarine to launch 12 new products' by David Blackwell published in *The FT* 28th February 2006, 'Misunderstanding and mistrust bedevil contracts' by Andrew Baxter published in *The FT* 12th April 2006, 'Bonds that keep workers happy' by Alison Maitland published in *The FT* 18th May 2006, 'How golf's integrity appeals to blue-chip sponsors' by Jill James published in *The FT* 24th May 2006, 'Investors adapt to consumer trends' by Jenny Wiggins published in *The FT* 13th June 2006, 'GE keeps innovation in harness' by Francesco Guerrera and 'Freedom or slavery' by Alan Cane, both published in *The FT* 12th July 2006, 'The gains from growing pains' by Alicia Clegg published in *The FT* 20th July 2006, 'Online advertising' by Lex Column published in *The FT* 27th July 2006, 'Amazon goes to Hollywood with film deal' by Joshua Chaffin and Jonathan Birchall published in *The FT* 28th July 2006, 'Hippychick completes baby steps and braces for critical growth spurt' by Jonathan Moules published in *The FT* 29th July 2006, 'Secrets of the maverick cobbler' by James Wilson published in *The FT* 3rd August 2006, 'Tesco plans to open Las Vegas supermarkets' by Jonathan Birchall and Elizabeth Rigby published in *The FT* 9th August 2006, 'Ford restructuring plan shifts up a gear (Ford to unveil accelerated restructuring plan)' by Doug Cameron published in *The FT* 10th August 2006, 'A foreign way to avoid dying at home' by Jonathan Moules published in *The FT* 12th August 2006 and 'HP beats forecasts and raises outlook for year' by Kevin Allison published in *The FT* 17th August 2006; and Clare Gascoigne for an extract adapted from 'Appeal of the softer side of the business' by Clare Gascoigne published in *The FT* 17th October 2005 © Clare Gascoigne.

Layouts by Jennifer Coles and HL Studios
Project managed by Chris Hartley
Edited by Catriona Watson-Brown
Produced for Pearson Education by Phoenix Publishing Services

Photocopying

Contents

Contents

Resource bank

Introduction

1 Course aims

Market Leader is an extensive new Business English course designed to bring the real world of international business into the language teaching classroom. It has been developed in association with the *Financial Times*, one of the world's leading sources of professional information, to ensure the maximum range and authenticity of business content.

The course is intended for use either by students preparing for a career in business or by those already working who want to improve their English communication skills.

Market Leader combines some of the most stimulating recent ideas from the world of business with a strongly task-based approach. Role-plays and case studies are regular features of each unit. Throughout the course, students are encouraged to use their own experience and opinions in order to maximise involvement and learning.

An essential requirement of Business English materials is that they cater for the wide range of needs which students have, including different areas of interest and specialisation, different skills needs and varying amounts of time available to study. *Market Leader* offers teachers and course planners a unique range of flexible materials to help meet these needs. This book makes suggestions on how to use the unit material extensively or intensively and indicates how the material in the Practice File integrates with the Course Book. There are optional extra components, including *Business Grammar and Usage*, videos and a series of special subject books to develop vocabulary and reading skills. This book contains extensive extra photocopiable material in the Text bank and the Resource bank.

2 The main course components

Course Book

This provides the main part of the teaching material, divided into 12 topic-based units, plus four revision units. The topics have been chosen following research among teachers to establish the areas of widest possible interest to the majority of their students. The Course Book provides input in reading, speaking and listening, with guidance for writing tasks as well. Every unit contains vocabulary development activities and a rapid review of essential grammar. There is a regular focus on key business functions, and each unit ends with a motivating case study to allow students to practise language they have worked on during the unit. For more details on the Course Book units, see Overview of a Course Book unit below.

Practice File

This gives extra practice in the areas of grammar and vocabulary, together with a complete syllabus in business writing. In each unit, students work with text models and useful language, and then do a writing task to consolidate the learning. Additionally, the Practice File provides regular self-study pronunciation work (with an audio CD and exercises), and a valuable survival language section for students when travelling.

Audio materials

All the listening activities from the Course Book (interviews with business practitioners and input for other activities such as role-plays and case studies) and the Practice File (pronunciation exercises) are available on cassettes and audio CDs, depending on the user's preference.

Teacher's Resource Book

This book provides teachers with an overview of the whole course, together with detailed teaching notes, background briefings on business content, the Text bank (24 optional extra reading texts) and the Resource bank (photocopiable worksheets practising communication skills).

Test File

Six photocopiable tests are available to teachers and course planners to monitor students' progress through the course. There are an entry test, four progress tests and an exit test, which reviews the work done throughout the course.

3 Overview of a Course Book unit

A typical unit consists of the following sections:

Starting up

Students have the opportunity to think about the unit topic and to exchange ideas and opinions with each other and with the teacher. There is a variety of stimulating activities such as answering quiz questions, reflecting on difficult decisions, prioritising options and completing charts. Throughout, students are encouraged to draw upon their life and business experience.

Vocabulary

Essential business vocabulary is presented and practised through a wide variety of creative and engaging exercises. Students learn new words, phrases and collocations, and are given tasks which help to activate the vocabulary they already know or have just learnt.

There is further vocabulary practice in the Practice File.

Discussion

There are a number of discussion activities in the book. Their main purpose is to build up students' confidence in expressing their views in English and to improve their fluency.

Reading

Students read interesting and relevant authentic texts from the *Financial Times* and other business sources. They develop their reading skills and acquire essential business vocabulary. The texts provide a context for language work and discussion later in the unit.

Listening

The authentic listening texts are based on interviews with business people and experts in their field. Students develop their listening skills such as prediction, listening for specific information and note taking.

Language review

These sections develop students' awareness of the common problems at pre-intermediate level. They focus on accuracy and knowledge of key areas of grammar. If students already know the grammar point, this section works as a quick check for them and the teacher. If they need more explanation, they are referred to the Grammar reference at the end of the Course Book.

There is further grammar practice in the Practice File and in *Business Grammar and Usage* (see Extending the course below).

Skills

This section helps learners to develop their communication skills in the key business areas of presentations, meetings, negotiations, telephoning and social English. Each section contains a Useful language box, which provides students with the support and phrases they need to carry out the business tasks in the regular role-play activities.

Case studies

Each unit ends with a case study linked to the unit's business topic. The case studies are based on realistic business problems or situations and are designed to motivate and actively engage students. They use the language and communication skills which they have acquired while working through the unit. Typically, students will be involved in discussing business problems and recommending solutions through active group work.

All of the case studies have been developed and tested with students in class and are designed to be easy to present and use. No special knowledge or extra materials are required. For teaching tips on making the best use of the case studies, see Case studies that work below.

Each case study ends with a realistic writing task. These tasks reflect the real world of business correspondence and will also help those students preparing for Business English exams. Models of writing text types are given in the Writing file at the end of the Course Book.

4 Using the course

Accessibility for teachers

Less experienced teachers can sometimes find teaching Business English daunting. They may be anxious about their lack of knowledge of the business world and of the topics covered in the course. *Market Leader* sets out to provide the maximum support for teachers. The Business brief section at the beginning of each unit in the Teacher's Resource Book gives an overview of the business topic, covering key terms and suggesting a list of titles for further reading and information.

Authenticity of content

One of the principles of the course is that students should deal with as much authentic content as their language level allows. Authentic reading and listening texts are motivating for students and bring the real world of business into the classroom, increasing students' knowledge of business practice and concepts. Due to its international coverage, the *Financial Times* has been a rich source of text and business information for the course.

The case studies present realistic business situations and problems, and the communication activities based on them – group discussions, simulations and role-plays – serve to enhance the authenticity of the course.

Flexibility of use

Demands of Business English courses vary greatly, and materials accordingly need to be flexible and adaptable. *Market Leader* has been designed to give teachers and course planners the maximum flexibility. The course can be used either extensively or intensively. At the beginning of each unit in this book are suggestions for a fast route through the unit if time is short. This intensive route focuses mainly on speaking and listening skills. If the teacher wants to extend this concentration on particular skills, optional components are available in the course (see Extending the course below).

5 Case studies that work

The following teaching tips will help when using case studies.

1   Involve all the students at every stage of the class. Encourage everyone to participate.
2   Draw on the students' knowledge of business and the world.
3   Be very careful how you present the case study at the beginning. Make sure your instructions are clear and that the task is understood. (See individual units in this book for detailed suggestions on introducing the case study.)
4   Ensure that all students have understood the case and the key vocabulary.
5   Encourage the students to use the language and communication skills they have acquired in the rest of the unit. A short review of the key language will help.
6   Focus on communication and fluency during the case-study activities. Language errors can be dealt with at the end.

Make a record of important errors and give students feedback at the end in a sympathetic and constructive way. Note good language use, too, and comment on it favourably.

7 If the activity is developing slowly or you have a group of students who are a little reticent, you could intervene by asking questions or making helpful suggestions.

8 Allow students to reach their own conclusions. Many students expect there to be a correct answer. Teachers can give their opinions but should stress that there usually is no single 'right' answer.

9 Encourage creative and imaginative solutions to the problems expressed.

10 Encourage students to use people management skills such as working in teams, leading teams, delegating and interacting effectively with each other.

11 Allocate sufficient time for the major tasks such as negotiating. At the same time, do not allow activities to drag on too long. You want the students to have enough time to perform the task and yet the lesson needs to have pace.

12 Students should identify the key issues of the case and discuss all the options before reaching a decision.

13 Encourage students to actively listen to each other. This is essential for both language practice and effective teamwork.

6 Extending the course

Some students will require more input or practice in certain areas, either in terms of subject matter or skills, than is provided in the Course Book. In order to meet these needs, *Market Leader* provides a wide range of optional extra materials and components to choose from.

Teacher's Resource Book

The Text bank provides two extra reading texts per unit, together with comprehension and vocabulary exercises.

The Resource bank provides photocopiable worksheet-based communication activities, linked to the skills introduced in the Course Book units.

Business Grammar and Usage

For students needing more work on their grammar, this book provides reference and practice in all the most important areas of Business English usage. It is organised into structural and functional sections.

Video

Portfolio features four specially made films at pre-intermediate level. The films provide students with authentic and engaging examples of Business English in use.

The video is accompanied by a Video Resource Book containing photocopiable worksheets and a transcript.

Special subject series

Many students will need to learn the language of more specialised areas of Business English. To provide them with authentic and engaging material, *Market Leader* includes a range of special subject books which focus on reading skills and vocabulary development.

The first books in the series are *Banking and Finance, Business Law* and *International Management*. Each book includes two tests and a glossary of specialised language.

Longman Business English Dictionary

This is the most up-to-date source of reference in Business English today. Compiled from a wide range of text sources, it allows students and teachers rapid access to clear, straightforward definitions of the latest international business terminology.

Market Leader website: www.market-leader.net

This website offers teachers a wide range of extra resources to support and extend their use of the *Market Leader* series. Extra texts of topical interest will be added regularly, together with worksheets to exploit them. Links to other relevant websites are posted here, and the website provides a forum for teachers to give feedback on the course to the authors and publishers.

The Test Master CD-ROM

The Teacher's Resource Book includes a Test Master CD-ROM which provides an invaluable testing resource to accompany the course.

- The tests are based strictly on the content of the corresponding level of *Market Leader* Advanced and New Editions, providing a fair measure of students' progress.
- An interactive menu makes it easy to find the test you are looking for.
- Keys and audio scripts are provided to make marking the tests as straightforward as possible.
- Most tests come in A and B versions. This makes it easier for you to invigilate the test by making it harder for students to copy from each other.
- The audio files for the listening tests are conveniently located on the same CD.

Types of test

The Test Master CD contains five types of test.
- Placement Test(s)
- Module Tests
- Progress Tests
- Mid-Course Test
- End-of-Course Test

Flexible

You can print the tests out and use them as they are, or you can adapt them. You can use Microsoft® Word to edit them as you wish to suit your teaching situation, your students or your syllabus.

Levels

Test Master CDs are available for *Market Leader* Advanced and all levels of *Market Leader* New Edition.

1 Careers

At a glance

	Classwork – Course Book	Further work
Lesson 1 *Each lesson (excluding case studies) is about 45–60 minutes. This does not include administration and time spent going through homework.*	**Starting up** Ss talk about their level of ambition and say what makes for a successful career. **Vocabulary: Career moves** Ss look at typical word combinations and verbs used with *career*. **Reading: Ten ways to improve your career** Ss read an article giving tips on how to get ahead.	*Practice File* Vocabulary (page 4)
Lesson 2	**Listening: Improving your career** Ss listen to two people talking about the best ways to improve your career. **Language review: Modals 1: ability, requests and offers** Ss look at modals used for ability, requests and offers (*can*, *could* and *would*) and do exercises based around a job interview.	**Text bank** (pages 114 and 115) *Practice File* Language review (page 5) *Business Grammar and Usage*
Lesson 3	**Skills: Telephoning: making contact** Ss listen to some calls and learn how to get through to who they want to speak to, leave messages, etc.	**Resource bank** (page 146)
Lesson 4 *Each case study is about 1 to 1½ hours.*	**Case study: Fast-Track Inc.** Ss choose the right candidate for an internal promotion within an international training company.	*Practice File* Writing (page 6)

For a fast route through the unit focusing mainly on speaking skills, just use the underlined sections.

For 1-to-1 situations, most parts of the unit lend themselves, with minimal adaptation, to use with individual students. Where this is not the case, alternative procedures are given.

Business brief

Reports of the death of the traditional career have been greatly exaggerated. Despite the growth of **outsourcing** (buying in services that were previously performed by a company's employees from outside the organisation) and **teleworking** by freelancers working from home communicating via the Internet, most professional people still go to what is recognisably a job in a building that is recognisably an office. The average **tenure**, the length of time that people spend in a particular job, has remained unchanged (at about seven years) for two decades.

From the point of view of the **human resources department (HRD)** of a large company, managing people's careers can still be seen in the traditional activities of **selection procedures** and **recruitment**, managing **remuneration** (how much people are paid) and working with department managers on **performance reviews**: annual or more frequent meetings with employees to tell them how well they are doing and how they may progress further on the career ladder. The HRD will also be involved with **training** and **professional development** of the company's staff.

A company's HRD may also be involved in making people **redundant**. Redundancies may be the result of an economic downturn with reduced demand for the company's goods or services, but they may follow a decision by a company to **de-layer** (to reduce the number of management levels) and **downsize**. It may offer **outplacement services**, advice to people on how they can find another job, perhaps after some **retraining**.

A manager made redundant in this way may become what Charles Handy calls a **portfolio worker**, offering their services to a number of clients. But there are also reports that many such managers describe themselves as **consultants** when in fact they would prefer to be working in a salaried job in an organisation like the one they have been forced to leave.

Others may enjoy their new-found freedom and embrace the **flexibility** that it offers. (Companies too may talk about flexibility when they use the services of freelancers in this way, rather than relying on salaried employees.) Freelancers have to maintain their degree of **employability** by keeping up with the latest trends and skills in their profession or industry, for example by attending short courses. They may complain that working outside an organisation gives them fewer opportunities to learn these new skills. For many salaried employees, on the other hand, developing one's career in an (enlightened) organisation is a process of give-and-take – the environment they work in allows them to keep their skills up to speed.

Read on

The section on Careers, jobs and management on FT.com is a good up-to-date source of information on this area: http://ftcareerpoint.ft.com/ftcareerpoint

Charles Handy: *The Elephant and the Flea*, Hutchinson, 2001

Institute of Management: *Personal Effectiveness and Career Development*, Hodder & Stoughton, 1999

Tricia Jackson: *Career Development*, Chartered Institute of Personnel and Development, 2000

Lesson notes

Warmer

- Write the word *career* in big letters at the top of the board.
- Ask Ss to suggest different stages in a typical career using expressions such as *go to school, go to university, get qualifications in ..., get a job in a company, move to another company, retire,* etc. Do this as a quick-fire activity – don't spend too long on it.

Overview

- Ask the Ss to look at the Overview section on page 6. Tell them a little about the things you will be doing, using the table on page 8 of this book as a guide. Tell them which sections you will be covering in this lesson and which in later lessons.

Quotation

- Write the quotation on the board and ask Ss to discuss it briefly in pairs. Make sure Ss understand the dual meaning of *work*.
- With the whole class, ask pairs for their opinions. (They may point out that some things can be achieved with not much work, and vice versa.)

Starting up

Ss talk about their level of ambition and say what makes for a successful career.
If this is your first lesson with the group and they have done a needs analysis, this is a good opportunity to get more background information about people's jobs and their English-learning needs in relation to their future careers. You may have students whose careers depend on improving their level of English.

- For each activity, get Ss to discuss the points in groups of three or four. Circulate, monitor and assist if necessary, especially with career-related vocabulary.
- After the groups have discussed each point, get a spokesperson for each group to give the views of the group. Relate each group's points to those of other groups. Deal tactfully with the non–career-orientated students.
- Praise good language points and work on some areas that need it, especially in relation to career-related language.

> **1 to 1**
> If this is your first lesson with a one-to-one student, this will be a good opportunity to get to know them better and to supplement the information in the needs analysis, if there was one.

Vocabulary: Career moves

Ss look at typical noun combinations (collocations) with *career*, verbs used with the word and verbs used with other career-related nouns (operating verbs).
If it's the first lesson with the group, point out that memorising blocks of language – typical word combinations – is an important part of the learning process.

- Do this as a quick-fire activity with the whole class.

> 1 c 2 d 3 b 4 a

- Get Ss to do this exercise in pairs or small groups. Tell them they can use a good bilingual dictionary or a monolingual one such as the *Longman Dictionary of Contemporary English*. Circulate, monitor and assist if necessary.

> 1 have
> 2 take
> 3 make
> 4 offer
> 5 decide

Ⓒ

- Again, have Ss do the exercise in pairs or small groups. Circulate, monitor and assist if necessary.

> *Odd items out:*
> 1 a training course
> 2 progress
> 3 a part-time job
> 4 a mistake
> 5 a pension
> 6 an office job

- Ask Ss to do this activity in pairs or small groups.

> 1 take early retirement
> 2 work flexitime
> 3 get a promotion
> 4 do research
> 5 earn a bonus

Reading: Ten ways to improve your career

Ss read a list of tips giving advice on how to get ahead in your career and decide which are the most important.

 A

◎ You may prefer to discuss the first question with the whole group, making two lists (personal and workplace) on the board, before asking Ss to work on the second question in pairs.

◎ Draw their attention to the Vocabulary file at the back of their books, where they will find useful vocabulary for their discussion.

◎ Bring the group together to compare Ss' lists.

B

◎ The idea behind this type of exercise is to get Ss to scan the article without trying to understand everything at the first attempt and to spot similar concepts, even if they are expressed differently. They can do this individually or in the same pairs as in Exercise A.

C

◎ This requires closer reading of the text to link the ideas. Get Ss to read through the article again and identify any words they don't understand. If you have time, encourage them to guess at the meaning by looking at the context or look the words up themselves in a dictionary.

◎ Go through the example with Ss, explaining why the sentence fits at the end of tip 4 (i.e. *These* refers back to *professional development seminars*, which are places where you can network with people).

◎ Remind Ss that they only need to look at the three tips given as options in each case.

◎ Ss can work individually or in pairs. When they have finished, get Ss to explain which words/structures gave them clues to the answers.

> **a** 4 **b** 6 **c** 8 **d** 5 **e** 2 **f** 7

 D

◎ This is a simple matching exercise that can be done orally. See if Ss can do it without looking back at the article first.

> **1** c **2** d **3** e **4** a **5** b

E

◎ Ss work in pairs to rank the tips in the article. This leads in to the Listening section, so follow up with a whole-group discussion to see if everyone chose the same three tips; if not, get Ss to explain their choices.

Listening: Improving your career

Ss listen to two women, Debbie and Nikola, discussing the article in the Reading section.

A 🎧 1.1

◎ Before playing the conversation, get Ss to read the article again quickly to remind themselves of the tips.

◎ Play the conversation through once. Debbie gives her answers first, so you may want to pause after she says *You can't make progress if you don't take risks sometimes* to check Ss answers. Note that Debbie also makes a comparative assessment of their answers at the end.

◎ Once Ss have decided on their answers, play the whole conversation again, pausing after each answer to elicit the correct tip number.

	Debbie	Nikola
1	Tip no 6	Tip no 6
2	Tip no 1	Tip no 4
3	Tip no 7	Tip no 7

 B

◎ The discussion is probably best done as a whole group, inviting suggestions from Ss. Ask them to justify their opinions.

◎ The relationship between the two speakers is not specified, but the conversation is informal and they obviously know each other (Debbie shortens Nikola's name to 'Nik'), but they work for different companies (Nikola says *Some companies – like mine, for instance*).

◎ Their ages and nationalities are not specified either, but Debbie has an Irish accent and Nikola an Eastern European one.

C 🎧 1.2

◎ Play the three extracts from the conversation. Ss have to listen closely to fill in the gaps. Make sure that Ss understand that each gap needs between two and four words.

◎ Check answers quickly with the class.

> **1** what you're good at **2** work on **3** take it on
> **4** into a routine **5** what you've already got

 D

◎ Read out the quote (*If you always do what you've always done, you'll only get what you've already got*) and ask Ss what they think it means.

◎ Ask Ss whether they agree with it, giving reasons for their opinion.

Lesson notes

Language review: Modals 1: ability, requests and offers

Ss look at modals used for ability, requests and offers, and do exercises.

◎ Check that Ss know about modal verbs and their characteristics.

> Modals are verbs like *may*, *might*, *can*, *could*, etc. They don't change with different persons (for example, *I can*, *you can*, *he can*).
> The ones they will see here are *can*, *could* and *would*.

◎ Get Ss to fill in the gaps in the Language review box.

> • Making a request • Describing ability
> • Making an offer

◎ Instruct Ss to work in pairs on rearranging the words. Circulate, monitor and assist if necessary.
◎ Then get them to work out whether they are requests, offers or asking about ability.

> 1 Can I get you anything? – making an offer
> 2 Could I confirm your contact details? – making a request
> 3 Can you use this software package? – asking about ability
> 4 Can you speak any other languages? – asking about ability
> 5 Could you tell us more about your present job? – making a request
> 6 Could you tell me your current salary? – making a request
> 7 Would you let us know your decision as soon as possible? – making a request
> 8 When can you start? – asking about ability
> 9 Would you like some more coffee? – making an offer

◎ Discuss Ss' answers, clarifying any difficulties.

(B)

◎ Get Ss in pairs to match the questions and answers.
◎ Circulate, monitor and assist if necessary, for example by explaining *currently* and *notice period*.

> **a** 6 **b** 3 **c** 7 **d** 1 **e** 2 **f** 9 **g** 5 **h** 4 **i** 8

◎ Get Ss in pairs to practise reading the exchanges with pleasant intonation. Circulate, monitor and assist if necessary.
◎ Point out that the politeness in the requests is in the intonation: none of them involve *please*.
◎ Then get some performances from individual pairs for the whole class.

(C)

◎ Have Ss complete the sentences in pairs. You may want to write the positive and negative forms of *can*, *could* and *would* on the board as a reminder. Circulate, monitor and assist if necessary.
◎ Discuss Ss' answers, clarifying any difficulties.

> **1** wouldn't **2** couldn't **3** can; can't **4** would **5** couldn't

(D)

◎ Go through the five sentences to ensure that Ss understand them, then allow Ss to work in pairs to discuss whether they are true or not for them.
◎ Ss may need help in rewriting sentences to make them true, as some sentences require more than the verb changing from positive to negative (or vice versa). For example, the first sentence might change to *I would like to work overtime, especially if the pay was very good, as I'm saving to go on holiday.*

Skills: Telephoning: making contact

Ss discuss how they use the telephone in English, then listen to three telephone calls, do exercises based on them and role-play a telephone call themselves.

(A)

◎ Point out that the focus of this section is on making contact and getting through.
◎ With the whole group, get Ss to discuss the calls they make and receive. Ask them what they find particularly difficult and bring their attention to points from the following activities that will help them.
◎ Write the telephone expressions Ss come up with on the board, preferably organising them into groups, such as *getting through* or *asking for someone*.

(B) 1.3, 1.4, 1.5

◎ Get Ss to listen to the calls once or twice, stopping after each call. Get them to describe the purpose of each call and say in complete sentences whether the callers know each other.

> Conversation 1: Christophe Boiteaud phones about a job advertisement in a magazine called *Careers Now*. He wants Carmen Diaz to send him an application form for the job. The callers do not know each other.
> Conversation 2: Jacques from Intec phones Andrea, but she is not there. He leaves a message to say that he will not be at a training course. Jacques implies that speaker B knows who he is, even if they do not know each other personally. (Point out to any puzzled Italian Ss that Andrea is normally a woman's name in the English-speaking world, unlike in Italy.)
> Conversation 3: Dave phones John, whom he knows, to get the fax number for Workplace Solutions because he can't get through on the phone.

Ⓒ 🎧 1.3

◎ Get Ss to listen again to the first call. Play it several times if necessary, stopping after each utterance to give them time to note it down. Circulate, monitor and assist if necessary.

---

1 I'd like to speak to …
2 Thank you. Hold on.
3 I'll put you through.
4 Hello. Is that Carmen Diaz?
5 Speaking.
6 Yes, I'm phoning about your advert …
7 Could you give me your name and address?

◎ Go round the class and ask individual Ss to say these expressions with friendly, polite intonation.

Ⓓ 🎧 1.4

◎ Play the second call again and get Ss to complete the phrases, making sure that they get the exact words – *Could I speak to Andrea …* rather than *Can*, etc.

---

1 Could I speak
2 I'm afraid
3 take
4 message
5 This is
6 Could
7 tell
8 make
9 call
10 back
11 on

Ⓔ 🎧 1.5

◎ Play the third call again and get Ss to choose the correct alternatives.

Dave   Hi, John. Dave here.
John   Oh, hello, Dave. / How are you?
Dave   Fine, thanks. Listen, just a quick word.
John   Yeah, go ahead.
Dave   Do you think you could let me have the fax number for Workplace Solutions? I can't get through to them. Their phone's always engaged.
John   I've got it here . It's 020 7756 4237.
Dave   Sorry, I didn't catch the last part. Did you say 4227?
John   No, it's 4237.
Dave   OK. Thanks. Bye.
John   No problem. Bye.

◎ Get Ss to read the conversation in pairs, using the underlined expressions. Then get one pair to read the conversation for the whole class.

◎ If time permits, get Ss to practise reading the conversation with the alternative expressions, those they did not underline, which are all correct usage. Then get another pair to read the conversation for the whole class.

Ⓕ

◎ Ask your Ss to practise, in pairs, the expressions in the Useful language box. Circulate, monitor and assist with pronunciation and friendly intonation if necessary.

◎ Then move on to the role-play. Get Ss to look at the job advertisement. Help with any difficulties of understanding and then explain the background to the role-play.

◎ Allocate roles. Make sure that Ss are looking at the correct page for their role. Check that Ss with the A role understand that they will play two different people in the two role plays: Laurie Thompson's colleague and then Laurie Thompson. Students with the B role card play themselves.

◎ Get your Ss to role-play the first call in pairs. Use telephone equipment if available; otherwise get Ss to sit back-to-back. Circulate, monitor and assist if necessary, especially with expressions relating to making telephone calls and applying for jobs.

◎ Bring the class to order. Praise strong language points and work on two or three points that require it, getting individual Ss to say the improved versions.

◎ Then get one of the pairs to do the role-play for the whole class, integrating the improvements.

◎ Get Ss to role-play the second call in pairs. Circulate, monitor and assist if necessary.

◎ Again, praise strong language points and work on two or three points that require it, getting individual Ss to say the improved versions.

◎ Then get one of the pairs to do the role-play for the whole class, integrating the improvements.

Case study

Fast-Track Inc.

Ss choose a candidate for an internal promotion within an international training company.

Stage 1: Background

◎ Instruct the Ss to read silently the sections entitled 'Background' and 'A new appointment', including the extract of the job description giving the qualities required of the successful candidate. Circulate and answer any queries.

◎ While Ss are reading, write the headings from the left-hand column of the table below on the board. With the whole class, elicit information to complete the column on the right.

Company	Fast-Track Inc.
Activity	Training videos and management training courses
Based in	Boston, US, with a subsidiary in Warsaw, Poland
Recent sales performance and reasons for this	Poor (30 per cent below target) because ◎ sales reps not motivated ◎ high staff turnover ◎ previous manager – no clear strategy ◎ only a few contracts with senior managers at client companies
Nature of new sales position	◎ developing sales and increasing numbers of customers ◎ managing sales team – more motivated, dynamic, effective
Number of candidates	3
Qualities required	◎ natural leader ◎ energetic, enthusiastic and determined ◎ confident, outgoing ◎ strong sales ability ◎ organisational and interpersonal skills ◎ good academic background and experience ◎ numeracy and admin skills ◎ languages ◎ must like travelling on business

◎ Without pre-empting the discussion to come in the task, clarify unfamiliar vocabulary and discuss some of the points above with the whole class. For example, ask students what it means to have *strong sales ability*.

Stage 2: Profiles of the candidates

🎧 1.6, 1.7, 1.0

◎ Divide the class into groups of three or four. Get each group to analyse the written information about *all* the candidates. Circulate, monitor and assist if necessary. Get each group to appoint a spokesperson who takes notes of the key points for each candidate, without getting into comparing the merits of the candidates.

◎ Play the recordings to the whole class, stopping at the end of the recording for each candidate and explaining any difficulties.

◎ Alternatively, if the room is big enough and if you have sufficient equipment, allocate one to each group and get the groups to specialise in a particular candidate, so, for example, one or two of the groups listen only to Barbara Szarmach's interview. Circulate, monitor and assist if necessary. Then ask a spokesperson for each group to summarise for the whole class the interview that they listened to.

Stage 3: Task

◎ The discussion in part 2 of the task does not, strictly speaking, need a chairperson, but if you think this would be useful to help structure the discussion, appoint a chair. If this is the first role-play you have done with this class, choose a self-confident student to run the meeting. Do this while the group discussions below are still going on and brief the chair on what they should do – invite contributions, make sure everyone has a chance to speak, make sure that each candidate is given proper consideration, etc.

◎ Working in groups, Ss discuss the relative merits of each candidate for the job. Appoint a different spokesperson in each group (i.e. not the same person as in stage 2 above) to note down the main points of the discussion and the reasons for the choice of candidate. Circulate, monitor and assist if necessary.

◎ Then get the whole class to discuss who should be chosen for the job, under the direction of the chair if you have decided to appoint one.

◎ While the discussion is going on, note down strong language points plus half a dozen points that need improvement. Come back to them when a candidate has been selected and the discussion is over. You may want to concentrate on the language used to

– describe people in the context of job interviews, such as *calm*, *relaxed*, *gets on well with others*.

– make contrasts, for example *Szarmach was rather aggressive at the interview **whereas** Rheinberger seemed nervous*.

> **1 to 1**
> Use the points above as the basis for discussion with your student. If there is time, you could go on to ask them how recruitment is done in their own organisation, whether internal promotion is favoured over looking for external candidates, etc.

Stage 4: Writing

◎ The Ss write up the decision of the meeting in e-mail form as if they were the head of the interviewing team. This can be done for homework. Make sure that each student knows that they have to
  – say who was chosen
  – describe briefly the strengths of the candidate.

 Writing file page 133

Selling online

At a glance

	Classwork – Course Book	Further work
Lesson 1 *Each lesson (excluding case studies) is about 45–60 minutes. This does not include administration and time spent going through homework.*	<u>**Starting up**</u> Ss talk about traditional shopping versus buying online and goods typically bought online. **Vocabulary: Shopping online** Ss work on words related to buying and selling. **Listening: Multi-channel retail** Ss listen to the Head of E-Commerce of Argos talk about how to succeed in online selling.	*Practice File* Vocabulary (page 8)
Lesson 2	**Reading: Worry for retailers** Ss read an article about the impact that online shopping has had on traditional retailing. **Language review: Modals 2:** *must, need to, have to, should* Ss apply modals for obligation, necessity and prohibition (*must, need to, have to* and *should*) in the context of rules for an online book club and in an interview.	**Text bank** (pages 116 and 117) *Practice File* Language review (page 9) ***Business Grammar and Usage***
Lesson 3	<u>**Skills: Negotiating: reaching agreement**</u> Ss discuss tips for successful negotiating, listen to a negotiation and then role play one themselves.	**Resource bank** (page 147)
Lesson 4 *Each case study is about 1 to 1½ hours.*	<u>**Case study: Lifetime Holidays**</u> A traditional package holiday company wants to team up with an online business. Ss role play negotiations between the two companies.	*Practice File* Writing (page 10)

For a fast route through the unit focusing mainly on speaking skills, just use the underlined sections.

For 1-to-1 situations, most parts of the unit lend themselves, with minimal adaptation, to use with individual students. Where this is not the case, alternative procedures are given.

Business brief

The world of **e-commerce** moves fast. The **dotcom frenzy** of the late 1990s, with companies raising vast amounts of money from investors, for example just to sell dog food over the Internet, came and went, and some organisations removed the dotcom suffix from their names, so much did it become a synonym for failure.

E-commerce courses in business schools are no longer oversubscribed and no longer preaching that 'everything has changed'. Companies look more at how e-commerce can be used in conjunction with other methods of selling: in retailing this means **clicks and mortar**, combining traditional retail outlets with online operations, rather than **pure e-tailing**. Some **old-economy** companies, like the UK supermarket company Tesco, have made a success of e-commerce by combining it with their existing operations, rather than investing in a whole new expensive **infrastructure**. Webvan, a pure online groceries company in the US, fell down on the hurdles of logistics: **warehousing** and **delivery**.

Amazon is now almost the only **pure-play** (exclusively) online seller of *goods* that has any sort of brand recognition. The range of goods it offers is becoming ever broader, and its **e-fulfilment systems** (order processing and delivery) are renowned for their efficiency. But its long-term profitability is still not clear.

However, in *services*, low-cost airlines like EasyJet and Ryanair are reporting that more than 90 per cent of ticket purchases are now made online. This bears out the prediction made a few years ago that online sales would develop fastest where there are no goods that have to be **physically delivered**.

And then there is **business-to-business (B2B) e-commerce**. Competing companies, for example in the car industry, have set up networks where they can get suppliers to do this. Orders are placed and processed, and payment made over the Internet, hopefully with massive cost reductions through the elimination of processing on paper. An allied area is **business-to-government (B2G)**, where companies can bid for government contracts over the Net.

Read on

Timothy Cumming, Richard Branson: *Little E, Big Commerce*, Virgin Books, 2001

Michael J Cunningham: *B2B: How to Build a Profitable E-commerce Strategy*, Financial Times Prentice Hall, 2000

Jeffrey Rayport, Bernard J Jaworski: *E-commerce*, McGraw Hill, 2001

Lindsay Percival-Straunik: *E-commerce*, Economist Books, 2001

Business brief

Lesson notes

Special note

Some Ss may know a lot about online selling, otherwise known as e-commerce, with personal experience of buying online; others may have no experience of it at all. Bear this in mind when teaching the unit.

Warmer

◎ Write the words *selling online* in big letters on the board.

◎ Ask the Ss to say what this means to them, if anything. Ask if anyone has bought anything online, but do not pre-empt the discussion in Starting up below.

Overview

◎ Ask the Ss to look at the Overview section on page 14. Tell them a little about the things you will be doing, using the table on page 16 of this book as a guide. Tell them which sections you will be covering in this lesson and which in later lessons.

Quotation

◎ Write the quotation on the board and ask Ss to discuss briefly in pairs what they understand by it.

◎ With the whole class, ask pairs for their understanding of the quote. Compare and contrast different pairs' views.

> The main point here is that a bad business idea will not work any better just because it is being used as the basis for selling via the Internet. The technology will not, in itself, make up for any deficiencies.

Starting up

These questions introduce Ss to the subject of online sales and allow you to gauge their knowledge of, and interest in, the subject.

Ⓐ–Ⓒ

◎ Ask Ss to discuss the questions in pairs. Circulate, monitor and assist if necessary.

◎ Ask each pair to present its ideas on each question in turn. If they don't have experience of buying on the Internet, concentrate on shopping in general. Do they like it? Why or why not?

Exercise B

Some goods and services may be more suitable for selling online, for example holidays and travel, where no physical delivery of goods is involved – see Business brief.

Exercise C

Some of the problems of e-commerce are the same as those for mail order: for example finding that goods are not suitable when they arrive or getting things you did not order.

Otherwise, Ss may mention security problems with using credit cards online and the fact they actually enjoy shopping in real shops.

Vocabulary: Shopping online

Ss look at the vocabulary of buying, selling and payment.

Ⓐ

◎ Go through the meanings of the words with the whole class.

◎ Instruct Ss to work on the exercise in pairs. Circulate, monitor and assist if necessary.

◎ Check the answers with the whole class.

> 1 b 2 c 3 b 4 a 5 c 6 b

Ⓑ

◎ Point out the principle of this matching exercise to the whole class: there is sometimes more than one match, but you are looking for the matches that correspond to the definitions 1–7.

◎ Do the exercise as a quick-fire activity with the whole class. Explain any remaining difficulties.

> credit card details – 2
> cooling off period – 1
> money back guarantee – 6
> method of payment – 3
> interest-free credit – 4
> out of stock – 5
> after sales service – 7

Listening: Multi-channel retail

Indira Thambiah, Head of E-Commerce at Argos, talks about how the company successfully combines online and traditional retailing.

Ⓐ

◎ These sentences will prepare Ss for the listening activity. At this stage, they are predicting answers based on context, so don't confirm or deny them.

◎ Once each pair has decided on their answers, move on to Exercise B.

Ⓑ 🎧 2.1

◎ Play the recording and allow Ss to check their answers to Exercise A.

◎ Ask if anyone had different answers – if so, discuss whether they were valid alternatives, or whether they were incorrect.

> 1 online; telephone   2 website; identical; store
> 3 enquire; order; channel   4 run; integrated

Ⓒ 🎧 2.2

◎ Have Ss read the four points and make sure they understand them.

◎ Play the recording. You may prefer to ask Ss to listen once to get the gist of what Indira says, then again to put the points in order.

> 1 d 2 c 3 a 4 b

Ⓓ

◎ Ss work in pairs to discuss the three questions.

◎ If time is limited, you may wish to divide Ss into three groups and allocate one question to each group.

Ⓔ 🎧 2.3

◎ Play the recording for Ss to listen to Indira's views. You may want to warn them that what she says is continuous speech, and is not broken down into the three questions.

> 1 True   2 False   3 True

◎ If Indira's answers differed from the answers Ss gave in Exercise D, you may want to discuss Ss' reasons for their answers.

Reading: Worry for retailers

Ss read an article about how traditional retailers are coping with the competition from Internet shopping.

Ⓐ

◎ This initial discussion should get Ss thinking about the relationship between traditional and online retailing. You may prefer to do this as a whole-class activity if Ss are struggling.

Ⓑ

◎ Get Ss to do the matching activity, then check their answers.

> 1 e   2 g   3 a   4 c   5 f   6 d   7 b

Ⓒ

◎ Set a time limit (e.g. one minute) for Ss to find the answer to the question. The skill of skimming for specific information is a useful one, and a time limit discourages Ss from trying to read and understand every word.

> Many traditional retailers are worried about the rise of online shopping and some of its consequences, e.g. the number of people shopping online is increasing; a lot of customers compare prices online; Internet retailers can offer very competitive prices; etc.

Ⓓ

◎ Ss should now read the article again in more detail before answering the questions. Allow them to work in pairs if they want.

> 1 Firstly, online sellers, unlike their bricks-and-mortar competitors, do not have the fixed costs of running a physical shop. Secondly, shoppers know how to get the best deals by visiting price comparison websites.
>
> 2 Because running a physical store is more expensive than a website, but the goods sold are the same. So, in order to make a profit, those retailers sometimes have a different price in store and online for the same product.
>
> 3 Because, according to some experts, consumers will become better at surfing the Internet. As a result, online and offline prices will have to be the same eventually.
>
> 4 One way is for businesses to integrate both their online and offline operation, for example by offering customers a multi-channel approach to shopping via stores, through the website and over the telephone.

Lesson notes

Language review: Modals 2: *must, need to, have to, should*

Ss apply these in the context of the rules for an online book club and in relation to the interview that they listened to earlier.

◎ This is a difficult area. Go slowly and adjust the material to the level of the class. Go through the different examples and relate them to the article that Ss read and discussed in the Reading section.

◎ Point out that *need to*, *should* and *must* are of increasing 'strength' in the order mentioned. Point out the difference between *don't have to* and *mustn't*. Try to get Ss to see the 'logic' of the different modals in context rather than get bogged down in the terminology of *obligation*, *necessity*, etc.

Ⓐ
◎ Ask Ss to work on the activity in pairs. Circulate, monitor and assist if necessary.

◎ Check the answers with the whole class.

1 no	2 no	3 no	4 no	5 no	6 no	7 yes

◎ Ask your Ss if any of them belong to a book club or music club, even if it is not an online one. Get them to explain what the rules are, using modals.

Ⓑ
◎ Ask Ss to work on the activity in pairs. Circulate, monitor and assist if necessary.

◎ Check the answers with the whole class.

1 f	2 g	3 e	4 b	5 c	6 d	7 h	8 a

Ⓒ
◎ If there's time, play the interview again (recordings 2.1, 2.2 and 2.3). (If you didn't do the Listening section, it is probably better to get Ss just to look at the script.) Ask Ss to work on the activity in pairs. Circulate, monitor and assist if necessary.

Possible answer
You need to treat your customers as individuals.
You must understand what your customers want.
Operations need to be intergrated.
It's important that you understand customers use websites for different reasons.
You have to provide good images and good information.
* This is not a modal of course, but Ss may come up with it. Ask them to express the same idea using a modal, for example 'You must have an excellent customer service team ...'

◎ Go through the exercise with the whole class, discussing the answers.

Skills: Negotiating: reaching agreement

Ss discuss negotiating tips, listen to a negotiation between a website designer and the manager of a bookstore chain and look at the language of agreement and disagreement. They then role-play the negotiation of a maintenance contract for a website.

Ⓐ
◎ Divide the class into two groups – A and B. (If there are more than about ten Ss, divide the class into four groups – two group As and two Bs.)

◎ Get the groups to look at the negotiating tips for their group, choosing the five most important. Circulate, monitor and assist if necessary.

◎ When Ss have made their short lists, form the same number of new groups.

◎ Get the new groups to make a short list of what they consider the five most important tips. Circulate, monitor and assist if necessary. (The idea here is that deciding the most important tips is itself a negotiating process.)

Ⓑ 🎧 2.4, 2.5, 2.6
◎ Before you play the recordings, establish the situation – a negotiation between the manager of a bookstore chain (Michelle) and a website designer who is bidding to design her website. Ask Ss to look at the chart and say what they think they will hear in the recording. For example, Michelle will probably want a shorter lead-time than two months for setting up the website, the designer will want more than $6,000, etc.

◎ Play each part of the negotiation for the whole class and get Ss to complete the points in the chart.

◎ Go through the various points with the whole class, if necessary playing parts of the negotiation again.

Negotiating point	What Michelle wants	What the designer wants	What they agree
Schedule for setting up the website	One month, by the end of July	*Two months*	One month, fewer pages
Payment terms	*Fixed amount: $6,000*	$50 an hour	$6,000 (half in advance)
Website design	A large number of covers on every page	One big image	*Two covers per page*

Ⓒ 🎧 2.4, 2.5
◎ Play parts 1 and 2 of the negotiation again and ask Ss to complete the gaps in the script. Circulate, monitor and assist if necessary.

◎ Work on the points that have caused the most difficulty.

1 will you agree
2 priority
3 agreed
4 normal fee
5 we'd prefer
6 offer
7 mind If I
8 as long as
9 How about
10 agree to

D 🎧 2.6

◎ With the whole class, get your Ss to listen to part 3 of the negotiation in its entirety. Then play the recording again, several times if necessary. Stop after each key expression so that Ss can note them down.

◎ Ss work in pairs to 'score' each expression, noting if it is a) strong, b) polite or c) shows hesitant agreement or disagreement.

◎ With the whole class, ask for the answers. If necessary, play the recording again to help clarify any difficulties.

D Now, the design of the website. Will we have book covers on it?
M Absolutely[1]. I'd like to display a large number of book covers on every page. They'd really attract people's attention. What do you think?
D It's a bit too much, I'd say[2]. A lot of pictures take too long to download. I'd prefer one big image. How about that?
M Mmm, I don't know[3]. People like to see the book covers. It draws them into the website, believe me.
D Maybe you're right[4]. How about two covers per page, then?
M OK, that sounds reasonable[5]. Now, what else do we need to discuss before you get started?

1 strong agreement
2 polite disagreement
3 hesitant disagreement
4 hesitant agreement
5 polite agreement

E

◎ As with all role-plays, ensure that the Ss understand the general situation: a representative of a website maintenance company meets a company manager to negotiate a maintenance contract for the company's website. Explain if necessary that websites need maintaining and updating if they are to function properly.

◎ Before asking Ss to look at their role cards, get them to look at the Useful language and practise the expressions, asking individual Ss to read them after you with appropriate intonation. Insist on correct pronunciation of the contractions *We'd* and *I'll*.

◎ Allocate the roles. Give Ss plenty of time to assimilate the information and prepare their roles. Circulate, monitor and assist if necessary.

◎ When the Ss are ready, get them to start the role-play in pairs.

◎ Circulate and monitor. Note language points for praise and correction afterwards, especially negotiation language.

◎ When Ss have finished, ask one or two pairs to explain what happened in their negotiation and what the final outcome was.

◎ Praise strong language points that you heard and discuss half a dozen points that need improvement, getting individual Ss to say the correct forms.

◎ Ask individual pairs to re-enact short parts of their negotiation containing the forms you have worked on, getting them to put the correct forms into practice.

1 to 1
This role-play can be done between teacher and student. Don't forget to note language points for praise and correction afterwards. Also point out some of the key language you chose to use. Ask the student about their negotiating plan, the tactics they were using, etc.

Case study

Lifetime Holidays

A traditional package holiday company wants to team up with an online business. Ss study the background and role-play negotiations between the two companies.

Stage 1: Background

◎ Ask Ss to look at the background information. Meanwhile, write up the headings on the left of the table below on the board, but don't put in the other information.

◎ Answer any questions about vocabulary or other difficulties.

◎ Then elicit information from the whole class to complete the table. (The points followed by question marks below show information that can reasonably be inferred, even if it is not specifically stated. Ask Ss if they agree with these points.)

	Lifetime Holidays	DirectSun
Type of holiday	package holiday (all prices?)	low-budget
Product range	large catalogue of package holidays (wide range of destinations?)	small range of destinations, arranges flights, accommodation, car hire, insurance
Sales outlet(s)	many high-street shops	website
Existing customers	mainly over 50	'good' customer base (wide range of age groups?)
Aims	appeal to wider age group (especially 30–50), join with an online company	bigger catalogue of holidays to offer, join with a bigger organisation
State of business	falling demand	good customer base

Stage 2: Task

◎ Divide the class into two groups, or if it is very large, into four or six groups for parallel negotiations. You could also appoint an observer for each negotiation. The observer does not take part but notes down key points from the negotiating process – how and when each side makes concessions, points they do not concede, etc.

◎ Make sure each group understands which side it will be negotiating for. You could also appoint a lead negotiator in each team if you think this will help.

◎ Circulate, monitor and assist Ss in preparing for the negotiation. Get them to write down key expressions they will use, like the ones in italics under 'Length of contract' on the role cards. Check that they look at the agenda for the meeting, as well as the information on their role cards.

◎ When the groups are ready, tell them to begin. Circulate and monitor. Note language points for praise and correction afterwards, especially negotiation language.

◎ Warn groups when they only have ten, then five, minutes left, hurrying them to reach an agreement.

◎ When groups have finished, ask a member of each group to describe the negotiating process and the final agreement. If you appointed an observer, get them to describe the process.

◎ Praise strong language points that you heard and discuss half a dozen points that need improvement, getting individual Ss to say the correct forms.

◎ If there is time, ask pairs of Ss to re-enact short parts of the negotiation containing the forms you have worked on, getting them to put the correct forms into practice.

Stage 3: Writing

◎ The Ss write up the outcome of the meeting in the form of a letter to a member of the other side. Point out that it should cover all five points on the agenda. This letter can be done for homework.

 Writing file page 130

UNIT 3 Companies

At a glance

	Classwork – Course Book	Further work
Lesson 1 *Each lesson (excluding case studies) is about 45–60 minutes. This does not include administration and time spent going through homework.*	**Starting up** Ss talk about the type of company they would most like to work for and the business sector they work in now. **Vocabulary: Describing companies** Ss look at vocabulary used to describe companies and that used in company reports to describe performance. **Listening: A successful company** Ss listen to IKEA's UK Deputy Country Manager talk about the factors that make his company successful.	*Practice File* Vocabulary (page 12)
Lesson 2	**Reading: The world's most respected companies** Ss look at tables showing the world's top ten companies in an FT survey. **Language review: Present simple and present continuous** The two tenses are compared and contrasted. Ss then complete a job advertisement with the correct tenses.	**Text bank** (pages 118 and 119) *Practice File* Language review (page 13) ***Business Grammar and Usage***
Lesson 3	**Skills: Presenting your company** Ss look at some advice for making presentations, listen to a presentation about a fashion company and then make a presentation about a company they invent.	**Resource bank** (page 148)
Lesson 4 *Each case study is about 1 to 1½ hours.*	**Case study: Valentino Chocolates** A maker of fine chocolates is in difficulty. Ss propose a strategy for revival and growth.	*Practice File* Writing (page 14)

For a fast route through the unit focusing mainly on speaking skills, just use the underlined sections.

For 1-to-1 situations, most parts of the unit lend themselves, with minimal adaptation, to use with individual students. Where this is not the case, alternative procedures are given.

At a glance

Business brief

Multinationals are the most visible of companies. Their **local subsidiaries** give them sometimes global reach, even if their **corporate culture**, the way they do things, depends largely on their country of origin. But the tissue of most national economies is made up of much smaller organisations. Many countries owe much of their prosperity to **SMEs** (small and medium-sized enterprises) with tens or hundreds of employees, rather than the tens of thousands employed by large **corporations**.

Small businesses with just a few employees are also important. Many governments hope that the small businesses of today will become the multinationals of tomorrow, but many owners of small companies choose to work that way because they find it more congenial and do not want to expand.

And then of course there are the **sole traders**, one-man or one-woman businesses. In the professional world, these **freelancers** are often people who have left (or been forced to leave) large organisations and who have set up on their own, taking the expertise they have gained with them.

But in every case the principle is the same: to survive – the money coming in has to be more than the money going out. Companies with **shareholders** are looking for more than survival – they want **return on investment**. **Shares** in the company rise and fall in relation to how investors see the future profitability of the company; they demand **shareholder value** in the way the company is run to maximise profitability for investors, in terms of increased **dividends** and a rising **share price**. **Publicly quoted companies**, with their shares **listed** or **quoted** on a **stock exchange**, come under a lot of scrutiny in this area. Some large companies (often family-owned or dominated) are **private**: they choose not to have their shares openly bought and sold, perhaps because they do not want this scrutiny. But they may have trouble raising the capital they need to grow and develop.

Profitability is key. Formulas for success are the subject of thousands of business courses and business books. Of course, what works for one person may not work for others. See below for books on two styles of running a company that might be hard to imitate!

Read on

Michael Brett: *How to Read the Financial Pages*, 5th edition, Random House, 2000

David Carson et al.: *Marketing and Entrepreneurship in SMEs*, Financial Times Prentice Hall, 1995

Jack Welch: *Jack: What I've Learned Leading a Great Company and Great People*, Headline, 2001

Richard Branson: *Losing My Virginity: How I've Survived, Had Fun, and Made a Fortune Doing Business My Way*, Virgin Books, 2000

Business brief

Lesson notes

Warmer

◎   Write the word *company* on the right of the board.

◎   As a quick-fire activity, ask Ss to say which adjectives and verbs could come in front of the word *company*. You may end up with something like this, depending on their level. You could give the initial letters of the words on the left as clues.

family-owned multinational small medium-sized profitable failing bankrupt work for a stay with a change	**company**

Overview

◎   Ask the Ss to look at the Overview section on page 22. Tell them a little about the things you will be doing, using the table on page 24 of this book as a guide. Tell them which sections you will be covering in this lesson and which in later lessons.

Quotation

◎   Write the quotation on the board. Ask Ss to discuss briefly in pairs what they understand by it.

◎   Bring together the pairs' findings with the whole class. If they haven't mentioned it, ask if it's really possible to 'be everywhere and do everything'.

Starting up

Ss talk about the type of company they would most like to work for and, for those at work, the business sector they work in now.

◎   Get Ss to discuss the question in pairs. Obviously, in-work Ss will approach this differently to those not in work. Circulate, monitor and assist if necessary. Then ask each pair to present its ideas to the whole class.

◎   Alternatively, you could do the activity as a class discussion and provide a number of points for Ss to think about for each type of company by presenting a table like the one below. Write the headings from the left-hand column on the board. Then discuss what to put in each box in the right-hand column. Of course, these are just suggestions. People in different places will have different ideas about the merits of working for each type of company. The answer in many

cases will be 'It depends'. Teach this expression, and then ask Ss to say what it depends on. Your Ss may mention other issues in addition to the headings given in the table.

Work environment	May be more friendly in a small family business. But some family-owned businesses are multinationals with thousands of employees, and the environment may not be that different to working in an ordinary multinational. Self-employed people working on their own sometimes complain about feeling isolated. You may feel more in control running your own company, but there again, if you have employees to look after, this can be a big responsibility.
Pay	Small family companies may or may not pay good wages and salaries. One issue here is that when multinationals come to an area with low unemployment, they may make it more expensive for firms in the area to employ people in office or factory jobs. On the other hand, some multinationals are well known for paying very low wages to people in places such as fast-food outlets. The pay of self-employed people, of course, varies enormously.
Promotion possibilities	There will be fewer opportunities for promotion in family companies, especially if family members are in key positions. Multinationals will probably offer more scope – the fast-food worker may become a branch manager and possibly go even further, but examples of top managers who have risen all the way from shop-floor level are rare.
Job security (= probability that you will keep the job)	Family companies may hesitate longer before laying people off (explain this expression) out of a feeling of responsibility towards their employees. Multinationals have had different attitudes towards laying people off, but companies in general are probably quicker to lay people off than before.

◎   Before working on the activity itself, check that Ss know what the different industries are.

◎   Then practise stress and pronunciation of the names of the industries. Write them up on the board, putting the stressed syllable in capitals:

TelecommuniCAtions

EnginEERing

REtailing

- Get Ss to repeat the names with the correct stress.
- Then get Ss to discuss the questions. If you did the previous activity as a whole-class activity, do this one as pair work, and vice-versa.
- If doing this as pair work, circulate, monitor and assist if necessary. Ss may need help with naming companies in each sector, especially if there are no well-known 'national champions' in their own country/countries.
- If there is interest and your Ss have access to the Internet, get them to look at the industries section on FT.com (click on 'Industries' on the FT.com home page) and see which companies are currently in the news in each industry. Ss should not try to read the articles, just spot company names in the headlines. You could ask them to do this for homework.

Vocabulary: Describing companies

Ss look at the vocabulary used to describe companies and that used in company reports to describe performance.

 A

- Tell Ss to do the exercise in pairs. Circulate, monitor and assist if necessary.

> 1 turnover (Point out that this is only used in *BrE*. Americans just talk about 'sales'.)
> 2 profit
> 3 subSIDiary (Point out the stress.)
> 4 workforce
> 5 market share
> 6 head office
> 7 share price

- Go through the exercise with the whole class, asking for the answers and explaining any remaining difficulties.

B

- Get Ss to do the exercise in pairs. Circulate, monitor and assist if necessary. Make sure Ss read the whole extract before trying to complete it. Explain any difficult vocabulary, for example *loyal*.

> 1 Turnover
> 2 profit
> 3 market share
> 4 share price
> 5 head office
> 6 subsidiary
> 7 workforce

- Go through the exercise with the whole class, asking for the answers and explaining any remaining difficulties.

 C

- Before doing the exercise, check comprehension and pronunciation of the words in the exercise, for example *chemical*.

- Write the table from the Course Book on the board and get Ss to call out the answers to fill the gaps.

Company	Main activity	Nationality
Cisco Systems	Internet equipment supplier	American
Peugeot	Car manufacturer	French
Bacardi Martini	Drinks supplier	Spanish
American Express	Travel and financial services provider	American
Bayer	Drug and chemical maker	German
Benetton	Clothing manufacturer	Italian
Sony	Electronic goods maker	Japanese
AP Møller-Maersk	Container ship operator	Danish

- Go round the class and get Ss to talk about particular companies, following the model *Cisco Systems is an American IT company which supplies Internet equipment.*

 D

- Ask Ss to work in pairs in describing a company they know well. Circulate, monitor and assist if necessary.
- With the whole class, ask three or four Ss to say which companies they talked about.

Listening: A successful company

Ss listen to the UK Deputy Country Manager of the Swedish furniture company IKEA talk about what makes the company so successful.

A

- Go through the six points to ensure that Ss understand them, focusing on difficult vocabulary, e.g. *market share, user-friendly, workforce*.
- Get Ss to work in groups of three or four and discuss which factors they think contribute most to a company's success.
- Give the groups five minutes to reach agreement, then ask a spokesperson from each group to list the three factors they have chosen. If the groups have chosen different factors, have a short debate on the reasons for their choices. Can you reach a class consensus?

B 🎧 3.1

- Before playing the recording, ask Ss if they have heard of IKEA and, if so, whether they have ever visited an IKEA store. If they haven't, explain that IKEA is a Swedish furniture store that specialises in low-cost furniture with simple, modern designs. It manages to keep its costs down by supplying many of the items as 'flat pack', i.e. customers have to put the furniture together themselves.

Lesson notes

◎ Play the recording, then ask Ss to identify which factors from Exercise A that Peter Jelkeby mentions. If necessary, play the recording again for Ss to put the factors in the right order.
◎ Check answers with the class.

> 1 starting with a simple business idea that is easy to understand
> 2 having a strong company culture
> 3 having good designers who also understand production
> 4 having user-friendly packaging

Ⓒ 🎧 3.2

◎ Have Ss read the notes and predict what words might fill the gaps (you can tell them that gaps 1–3 need one word and gap 4 needs two). Even if they don't guess the correct words, they should be able to predict that they need a verb in the –*ing* form for gap 1, the second half of a compound noun for gap 2, a plural noun for gap 3 and a verb phrase in the –*ing* form for gap 4.
◎ Play the recording for Ss to complete the notes, then check their answers. Play the recording a second time if necessary.

> 1 understanding   2 needs   3 competitors
> 4 offering solutions

Ⓓ 🎧 3.3

◎ Have Ss read the four questions and make sure they understand them.
◎ Play the recording and ask Ss which question they think Peter is answering. This is quite tricky, so you may need to play the recording several times.

> Question 3

Reading: The world's most respected companies

Ss do information-gap exercises with the results of an FT survey, then read articles on either Toyota or Microsoft and swap information.

Ⓐ

◎ Get Ss to read the information box first, as this gives the background to the survey. Go through the vocabulary, especially terms such as *criteria, ranking, shareholder value, community commitment*, to ensure that Ss understand.
◎ Ss work in pairs and turn to relevant pages. Make sure they understand that they have to ask the appropriate questions to complete the gaps in their tables.
◎ When they have finished, allow them to look at their partner's table to check that they have the right answers.
◎ Discuss the tables with the class. Were they surprised at the results? Were there any companies that they expected to see, but didn't? Or companies that they were surprised to see?

Ⓑ

◎ In the same pairs, Ss read one of the two articles on page 25 and make notes on the key information. Remind Ss that notes do not have to be complete sentences, and should not be lifted verbatim from the text.

Ⓒ

◎ Ss then expand on their notes to explain in their own words what they have learned about Toyota/Microsoft, and make notes about their partner's company in the table.
◎ This practises the skills of talking from notes and taking notes from a talk, both of which are extremely useful in business.

Language review: Present simple and present continuous

The two tenses are compared and contrasted. Ss then complete a job advertisement with the correct tenses.
◎ Go through the examples with the whole class, then have Ss complete the rules with the phrases provided.

> 1 factual information
> 2 routine activities and habits
> 3 ongoing situations and actions
> 4 temporary situations
> 5 future arrangements

◎ The main thing to underline with the present simple is that it is for 'general truths': factual information about companies is one example of this. You could also give the example *Paris stands on the Seine*.
Point out that *Paris is standing on the Seine* is very strange, implying perhaps that yesterday it was standing somewhere else, for example on the Loire.
◎ The present simple is also used for routine activities, with *always* as in the Course Book example, and also *never, sometimes, generally, often*, etc.
◎ The main thing to underline with the present continuous is that it is for temporary or changing situations, even if they are not taking place at the moment of speaking. A company marketing director can say '*We're constantly improving the way we sell our products*' even when she is not at work.
◎ The present continuous can also be used for future arrangements, especially fixed plans (as in the third example in the Course Book).

Ⓐ

◎ Tell Ss to work on the sentences in pairs. Circulate, monitor and assist if necessary.
◎ Go through the exercise with the whole class, working on any difficulties.

1 hold; are holding
2 are using; use
3 takes
4 raise; are raising
5 deals
6 recruit; are advertising
7 are renting
8 wants

B

◎ Tell Ss to work in pairs. Circulate, monitor and assist if necessary.

◎ Go through the exercise with the whole class, working on any difficulties.

1 are
2 offer
3 have
4 are growing
5 employ
6 are considering
7 are preparing
8 are looking
9 need
10 offer/are offering

Skills: Presenting your company

Ss look at some advice for making presentations, listen to a presentation about a fashion company and then make a presentation about a company they invent.

A

◎ Ask Ss what experience they have of giving presentations both in their own language and in English. What did they find most difficult in each case? (Surveys show that speaking in front of an audience is the activity that most managers fear above all else, even in their own language. As a language trainer used to speaking in front of groups, don't lose sight of how difficult this is for most people.)

◎ With the whole class, go through the points one by one. See if your Ss agree with the following points:

1 Find out as much as possible about your audience and adapt your presentation accordingly, using this information. Don't just give the presentation you were going to give anyway.
2 Good idea. Make sure your in-work Ss know their job titles as they really would be in English rather than an anglicisation of the titles in their own language.
3 Humour is used very differently in different places. Some cultures see it as a lack of seriousness. If in doubt, leave it out.
4 Point out that in the English-speaking world, this is a fairly normal procedure. It certainly helps language learners to structure their presentations in this way.

5 You could ask Ss what they understand by *tone*. It could be taken to include stress (putting emphasis on particular syllables and words), volume (loudness) and intonation (rise and fall of the voice). These should be varied but, at the same time, don't overdo it!
6 Don't bury your nose in your notes and don't write out a complete script.
7 Good idea, but don't overdo it and use too many. Don't overcrowd the visuals with too much information.
8 Related to point 4 and very useful.

B 🎧 3.4

◎ Prepare Ss for what they are going to hear by getting them to look at the chart. Explain any difficulties in the headings, for example *net* profit is profit after tax.

◎ Play the recording two or three times as necessary, stopping after key pieces of information, and get Ss to complete the chart.

Tara Fashions	
Where is the head office?	Córdoba, Spain
What does it sell?	Clothes (practise pronunciation)
Who are its customers?	Fashion-conscious men and women aged 20–35
Annual turnover?	€260 million
Annual net profits?	€16 million
Number of stores: in Spain? in other European cities?	15 14 (5 new stores next year)
Strengths?	Can bring out new designs very quickly Designs sold at right price
Future plans?	New store in New York next year

C 🎧 3.4

◎ Play the recording again once or twice, this time getting Ss to concentrate on the language of presentations. Get them to tick the suggestions from Exercise A that the speaker uses.

The speaker uses suggestions 2, 4 and 5. She may also use 1 and 6, but you can't tell from the recording.

D

◎ Go through the phrases in the Useful language box with Ss. Have them read the phrases aloud and encourage them to think about the intonation.

◎ Give Ss a short time (e.g. five minutes) to prepare a few notes on their company (or a company they know), then ask them to make their presentation to their partner. Remind Ss that these can be very short – they only have to speak for a minute or two – but that what they say should be clear and well structured.

Case study

Valentino Chocolates

A maker of fine chocolates is in difficulty. Ss propose a strategy for revival and growth.

Stage 1: Background

◎ Instruct Ss to look at the background information. Meanwhile, write up the headings on the left of the table below on the board, but don't put in the other information.

◎ Answer any questions from the Ss about vocabulary difficulties, etc.

◎ Then elicit information from the whole class to complete the table.

◎ Ask one student to summarise the table in their own words for the whole class.

Company	Valentino
Products	Fine chocolates, packaged chocolates, Classic Bars, drinks, biscuits and cakes
Based in	Turin
Employees	300
Shops	75
Sales problems	Falling demand; rising costs; falling profits

Stage 2: Listening 🎧 3.5

◎ Tell Ss that they will hear three people speaking.

◎ You may need to play the recording several times, as the information does not come in the same order as presented in the table.

◎ Copy the table onto the board while Ss are listening. After each playing of the recording, ask Ss if they can supply any more information. Continue until the table is complete.

Reasons for falling profits	
Prices	Higher than competitors' prices due to price-cutting
Production	Delays due to old machinery breaking down
Demand	Falling demand for new products (biscuits and cakes) and Classic Bar
Staff morale	Sales team and production staff demotivated

Stage 3: The future

◎ Tell Ss to read the text about the future and the investment options (Chart 2) in pairs. Circulate, monitor and assist if necessary.

◎ With the whole class, get Ss to say what the options are, using different expressions, for example:
  – One option is to buy new machinery this would cost

€200,000 and it would end the delays caused by the old machines breaking down.

Valentino could invest in more research and development. This would cost €200,000, but they could develop new products such as a low-fat chocolate drink or new biscuits and cakes.

Stage 4: Task

◎ Put Ss in pairs again and tell them that they will weigh up the different options. Warn them that one member of each pair may have to present the findings of the pair, so one member of each pair should note down the main points from the discussion and what their final choice of options is.

◎ Circulate and monitor. Note down language points for praise and correction afterwards, especially those relating to planning and growth.

◎ When the pairs have drawn up their plans, call the whole class to order, praise some of the good language you heard and work on half a dozen points that need improving. Get individual Ss to say the correct forms.

◎ Get two or three pairs to present their investment plans. Try to choose pairs whose ideas are different in order to give variety and stimulate discussion. Note down language points for praise and correction afterwards, this time concentrating on presentations language.

◎ Praise some of the good presentations language you heard and work on half a dozen points that need improving. Get individual Ss to say the correct forms.

◎ Get Ss to discuss the different plans as one group. If the class is very large, divide it into two or three groups. Circulate and monitor. Note down language points for praise and correction afterwards, perhaps ones related to some you noted earlier.

◎ Call the class to order. Work on half a dozen language points that require it.

◎ Rather than have another presentation of the final choice of investment options now, ask a representative of the group (or of each group) to prepare one for the following session. If you do this, don't forget to allow time for the presentation(s) in a future session. This will also allow you to recap key language from this session.

---

1 to 1

This case study can be done as a discussion between teacher and student and then as a basis for a presentation by the student. Don't forget to note language points for praise and correction afterwards. Also point out some of the key language you chose to use.

Stage 5: Writing

◎ The Ss write up the final selection of investment options as a proposal document to the CEO of Valentino. Make it clear whether the memo should reflect the opinion of the group as a whole or the opinions of the student writing it. This proposal can be done for homework.

 Writing file page 131

Revision

This unit revises and reinforces some of the key language points from Units 1–3, and links with those units are clearly shown. Point out these links to your Ss – in some cases, they will need information from the original activities to do the exercises here.

These exercises can be done in class individually or collaboratively, or for homework.

For more speaking practice, see the Resource bank section of this book beginning on page 141.

1 Careers

Vocabulary

◎ This relates to the Vocabulary section on page 7. Ss should try to do the exercise without referring back first.

> **1** b   **2** a   **3** c   **4** c   **5** c   **6** a   **7** b

Modals

◎ This practises the modals on page 10. Go through the example with Ss to make sure they understand why the answer is 'a'. They can then work individually or in pairs.

> **1** a   **2** b   **3** b   **4** c   **5** c   **6** b   **7** b   **8** a   **9** c   **10** a

Skills

◎ Once Ss have matched the sentences, have pairs of Ss read them aloud.

> **1** d   **2** a   **3** b   **4** e   **5** c

Writing

◎ This exercise can be done without reference to the case study, but it is useful to ask Ss to reread this for background knowledge.

◎ Explain that the phrases in the box are set out in pairs and that Ss should choose the correct phrase from each pair for each gap.

> **1** With reference   **2** would like   **3** In addition   **4** As regards   **5** Finally   **6** look forward
> **7** faithfully

◎ Ss should use Tadeusz's letter as a model, substituting either Barbara or Eva's details.

2 Selling online

Vocabulary

◉ This relates to the vocabulary on pages 14–15. All the words appear in either Exercise A or B; Ss may find it easier to complete the sentences, then find the words in the grid, or to look for words in the grid and then complete the sentences.

> **1** stock **2** discount **3** details **4** return **5** refund **6** bargain **7** cancel **8** credit **9** bulk
> **10** service **11** despatch **12** purchased

Modals

◉ These modals were featured on page 17. Get Ss to reread the Language review box if necessary before tackling this exercise.

◉ Go through the answers with the class. Where more than one answer is correct, ask Ss to explain the difference in meaning between the two answers.

> The incorrect options are:
> **1** a, c **2** a **3** b, c **4** b, c **5** c **6** a, b **7** a, c

3 Companies

Vocabulary

◉ This relates to the vocabulary from pages 22–23.

> **1** performance; Turnover; per cent; profit
> **2** competitive; share; share price
> **3** subsidiary; workforce

Present simple and present continuous

◉ Tell Ss to look again at the rules for the present simple and present continuous on page 26 before doing this exercise.

> **1** own **2** want **3** are opening **4** am/'m interviewing **5** employ **6** is growing

4 Great ideas

At a glance

	Classwork – Course Book	Further work
Lesson 1 *Each lesson (excluding case studies) is about 45–60 minutes. This does not include administration and time spent going through homework.*	**Starting up** Ss talk about how new ideas are found and nurtured. **Vocabulary: Verb and noun combinations** Ss look at and use typical verb and noun combinations in relation to new ideas, opportunities, etc., and hear them used in context. **Listening: The Innovation Works** Ss listen to a description of a place designed to encourage innovation, and opinions on new ideas.	*Practice File* Vocabulary (page 16)
Lesson 2	**Reading: Three great ideas** Ss read about three good business ideas and exchange information about them. **Language review: Past simple and past continuous** The two tenses are compared and contrasted. Ss then use them in the context of an article about the inventor of Post-it notes.	**Text bank** (pages 120 and 121) *Practice File* Language review (page 17) ***Business Grammar and Usage***
Lesson 3	**Skills: Successful meetings** Ss look at what makes for successful meetings and listen to a meeting in progress. They then study meetings language.	**Resource bank** (page 149)
Lesson 4 *Each case study is about 1 to 1¹⁄₂ hours.*	**Case study: Fabtek** A small company has developed a new fabric. Ss representing another firm suggest new products using the material and how they can be marketed.	*Practice File* Writing (page 18)

For a fast route through the unit focusing mainly on speaking skills, just use the underlined sections.

For 1-to-1 situations, most parts of the unit lend themselves, with minimal adaptation, to use with individual students. Where this is not the case, alternative procedures are given.

Business brief

Resistance to new ideas is well known. In organisations, the best way of killing an idea may well be to take it to a meeting. The very things that make companies successful in one area may prevent them from developing success in new activities. Early work on personal computers at Xerox was dismissed by its senior managers because they considered that the company's business was copying, not computing. Company leaders talk about **corporate venturing** and **intrapreneurship**, where employees are encouraged to develop **entrepreneurial** activities within the organisation. Companies may try to set up structures in such a way that they do not stifle new ideas. They may put groups of talented people together in **skunk works** to work on **innovations** – development of the PC at IBM is the most famous example. Skunk works are outside the usual company structures and are less likely to be hampered by bureaucracy, in-fighting and so on.

When innovators go to large companies with new designs for their products, they face similar problems. The inventor of the small-wheeled Moulton bicycle could not persuade Raleigh to produce it, so he set up his own company. But a single innovative **breakthrough** is not enough. There has to be **continuous improvement** and **market response**. The current winners in bicycle innovation are producers of mountain bikes, who have taken the original bicycle design and eliminated its irritations, revolutionising an old concept by providing relative comfort, easy gear changes, a 'fun' ride and so on.

The initial idea for a car will be turned into a series of **prototypes** and tested. In software development, the final 'prototype' is the **beta version**, which is **beta-tested**. Pharmaceuticals go through a series of **trials**. Even the most brilliant entrepreneurs will not have the resources to go it alone in industries like these, as the investment and experience required are enormous. Cars, software and pharmaceuticals are examples of industries dominated by giants. The 'rules of the game' are well established, and newcomers are rare, unless they can find a small **niche** unexploited by the giants. There may be more opportunity for innovation where the rules of the game are not yet established. This may involve selling and delivering existing products in new ways: think, for example, of selling books and airline tickets on the Internet.

One thing is certain: business will continue to benefit from the creativity of individuals and organisations who can develop great ideas and bring them to market.

Read on

Tom Peters: *The Circle of Innovation*, Coronet, 1999

Joe Tidd, John Bessant, Keith Pavitt: *Managing Innovation*, 2nd edition, Wiley, 2001

James M Utterback: *Mastering the Dynamics of Innovation*, Harvard Business School Press, 1996

Lesson notes

Warmer

- Write the words *an idea* in big letters on the right of the board. Work on the pronunciation of *idea* if necessary.

- Invite Ss to suggest verbs that can come in front of it. Some possibilities are given below.

have suggest think of like develop …	**an idea**

- Then, without pre-empting the material in the unit too much, get Ss to make complete sentences using these combinations.

Overview

- Ask Ss to look at the Overview section on page 34. Tell them a little about the things you will be doing, using the table on page 34 of this book as a guide. Tell them which sections you will be covering in this lesson and which in later lessons.

Quotation

- Write the quotation on the board and ask Ss if they have heard of this exclamation before, and if they know the context in which Archimedes was supposed to have uttered it. (The story goes that he was in the bath when he suddenly understood the concept of volume displacement; *eureka* is Greek for 'I have found it'.)

- Ask Ss if they think most great ideas are the result of a 'eureka' moment like this, or of a lot of little ideas that develop over time.

Many scientists, inventors and entrepreneurs have a number of ideas before coming up with the Big One. But some inventors are famous for not bringing their ideas to fruition. Leonardo da Vinci is often cited in this context – he drew tantalising pictures of parachutes and helicopters but did not develop them. It could be argued that the technology, materials, etc. for parachutes existed in his day, and he could be accused of not developing their potential – perhaps he was just not interested in this part of the process. However, the technology for helicopters certainly did not exist, and he cannot really be blamed for not making one.

Perhaps your Ss will talk about an idea whose time has come, either in relation to an idea that depends on a particular technology taking off (literally or metaphorically!), or one that must wait for the right social and economic conditions to emerge. For example, the growth of supermarket chains depended on almost everyone who uses them having a car.

Another point your Ss may make is that some modern inventors can't see the money-making, business applications of their inventions or are not interested in developing them, even when these are pointed out to them.

Starting up

Ss talk about how new ideas are found and nurtured.

- Tell Ss to discuss the statements in pairs. Circulate, monitor and assist if necessary.

- With the whole class, ask different pairs to say what their findings were.

- Discuss this question with the whole class.

Ss may come up with anything from a suggestions box to the R&D (research and development) department. Try to keep the discussion concrete by talking about how new ideas are encouraged in the organisations that your Ss work for or the schools they go to.

Vocabulary: Verb and noun combinations

Ss look at typical verb and noun combinations in relation to new ideas, opportunities, etc. and use them to complete the text of a talk by the head of a Research and Development Department.

 A

◎ Match the verb/noun combinations and their meanings as a quick-fire activity with the whole class and clarify meanings where necessary.

> **1** c **2** f **3** e **4** a **5** b **6** d

B

◎ Explain the context: Ss will later hear an extract from a talk by the head of a Research and Development Department. The text in the Course Book is the audio script with gaps. Instruct Ss to work on the exercise in pairs, using the phrases from Exercise A. Circulate, monitor and assist if necessary.

> **1** takes advantage of an opportunity
> **2** extend its product range
> **3** enter a market
> **4** make a breakthrough
> **5** meet a need
> **6** raises their status

 C 🎧 4.1

◎ Play the recording and tell Ss to check their answers. Assist with any remaining difficulties.
◎ Play the recording again for Ss to complete the remaining gaps in the text
◎ When they have finished, check their answers and get them to make a note of the featured collocations (e.g. *to reduce waste*).

> **7** reduces **8** protects **9** fills **10** win

Listening: The Innovation Works

Ss listen to Kate Pitts, Head of The Innovation Works, describe why it was developed and what she considers to be great new business ideas.

 A

◎ Ss start by focusing on some key vocabulary. They work in small groups, but they should not spend too long on this.

> **1** b **2** a **3** c

B 🎧 4.2

◎ Explain that Reading is a city in southern England. Ss may be interested in its pronunciation, which is 'redding', unlike the verb.
◎ Allow Ss a few minutes to read through the sentences, as they will give a feel for the content of the interview.
◎ Play the recording once and see how far Ss get with the exercise. Play it again if they are struggling.
◎ When they have all finished, go through the answers, clarifying any points of confusion.

> **1** False **2** True **3** False **4** False **5** True

C 🎧 4.3

◎ Play the second part of the interview and ask Ss to work in pairs to discuss the first question.
◎ Play it again for them to focus on the second question.
◎ Go through the answers as a whole class.

> **1** For one type of innovation, the great idea seems to come from nowhere. For the other type, the idea builds on something that existed before.
> **2** eBay took the old idea of auction and made something completely new out of it. In addition, it met a real need (*people wanting to get rid of things they did not use any longer, ... and to make money out of it*).

Lesson notes

Lesson notes

Reading: Three great ideas

Ss read about three good business ideas and exchange information about them.

◎ Get Ss to work in small groups to discuss these questions. Give them five minutes or so, then have a spokesperson from each group present their ideas to the class. Encourage Ss who don't normally say much to act as spokesperson.

◎ Divide the class into groups of three and ensure that each student knows if they are Student A, B or C.

◎ Ask Ss to read the correct article. Circulate, monitor and assist if necessary.

◎ Get Ss to complete the relevant box with the answers to the five questions relating to the article they have just read.

Sample answers

Penske-Wynn
1. car dealership
2. Charging people an entrance fee to come into the car showroom
3. People do not usually pay to visit a car showroom.
4. There were far too many visitors, and only a few of them intended to buy a car.
5. This idea brings in about $100,000 a month in admission fees, and the dealers sell 20–30 cars a month.

PepsiCo
1. food and beverages
2. Growing oranges in India
3. This is the first time oranges from Florida have been grown in India; farmers from the Punjab traditionally grow wheat and rice.
4. The underground water level went down, and the soil got poorer because of intense cultivation of wheat and rice. Farmers were earning very little money, so it was important to diversify.
5. For PepsiCo: fruit available locally for their beverages, and long-term competitiveness in a huge market; for India: a good source of agricultural revenues; for local farmers: higher income.

Million Dollar Homepage
1. Internet advertising
2. Making a million dollars from selling pixels on a web page
3. It comes from a young person with entrepreneurial ideas, rather than from an experienced business person or a well-established company.
   Also, to start it, Tew just needed some web space and a domain name.
4. Tew very quickly earned enough money to finance his university studies. (Incidentally, he chose to postpone them and work on a new business venture instead.)
5. A lot of money for the entrepreneur, obviously. Possibly a source of inspiration for other young entrepreneurs, as it showed that original ideas can succeed on the Net. Finally, a cheap and apparently effective way for businesses to advertise their products and services.

◎ Get Ss to work in their groups of three to exchange information about their articles and take notes on the two articles they didn't read.

◎ Question 1 relates to Article 1; Questions 2 and 3 relate to Article 2; Question 4 relates to Article 3. You may want to ask pairs of Ss to focus on the questions that relate to the article they read, or on those that they didn't.

◎ Have a brief class discussion on one or all of the questions to bring Ss ideas together.

Language review: Past simple and past continuous

The two tenses are compared and contrasted. Ss then use them in context.

◎ Focus Ss' attention on how the two tenses are used in the examples in the Language review box.

◎ Get Ss to read the three rules and ensure that they understand them.

(A)

◎ Instruct Ss to work on the story in pairs. Circulate, monitor and assist if necessary.

◎ With the whole class, ask for the answers.

> 1 was working
> 2 developed
> 3 was living
> 4 opened

(B)

◎ In the same pairs, Ss do a similar exercise on the next part of the story, but this time they have to produce the verb form themselves from the infinitive.

◎ Circulate, monitor and assist as necessary.

◎ Go through the answers and ensure Ss understand the reason for the choice of tense in each case.

> **1** noticed   **2** were performing   **3** appointed   **4** emigrated
> **5** created   **6** lived / was living   **7** introduced
> **8** were visiting

Skills: Successful meetings

Ss look at what makes for successful meetings and listen to a meeting in progress. They then study meetings language.

◎ Ask Ss to discuss the points in pairs or threes. Circulate, monitor and assist if necessary. Note down language points for praise and correction, especially those relating to the language of meetings.

◎ Discuss with the whole class.

> The following ideas may help to stimulate discussion. Be tactful about meetings in the Ss' own organisation(s) and culture(s).
>
> 1 It probably depends on the type of meeting. It's probably good to have at the meeting only those who really need to be there and to limit this number as far as possible. However, large meetings can be successful if they are well chaired.
>
> 2 Different companies and cultures deal with this in different ways. Coffee and water may be freely available, but snacks between meals are unknown in some places. The working lunch is a possibility in some places, with perhaps sandwiches in the meeting room or lunch in a restaurant.
>
> 3 Again, different cultures have different ideas about this. In some places, starting a 2 o'clock meeting at 2.20 may count as starting 'on time'.
>
> 4 Some companies are well known for having all their meetings standing up, in order to encourage quick decisions. (You could also discuss the shape of the table – for example whether round tables make for more 'democratic' meetings.)
>
> 5 Again, it probably depends on the type of meeting. This is a good opportunity to teach *chair* in the sense of *chairman* or *chairwoman*.
>
> 6 Organised turn-taking can be very clear in some cultures, with long pauses to show that consideration is being given to what has just been said, but overlapping is the norm elsewhere. Perhaps this is a good opportunity to teach *Please let me finish*.

Lesson notes

(B) 🎧 4.4

◉ Explain the situation to Ss before they listen to the meeting. Then play the recording once or twice and explain any difficulties, without pre-empting the questions, of course.

◎ Ask the whole class for the answers.

> 1 to talk about when to launch the goggles and the marketing strategy
> 2 She says that the goggles are technically advanced and that there is no reason to wait.
> 3 Katharina mentions February or March, Kenneth suggests May or June, and Nadia says that February is the best time.
> 4 Julia wants to target specialist sports stores.

(C) 🎧 4.4

◎ Play the recording again and get Ss to tick the expressions they hear.

> 1 Can we start, please? ✓
> 2 The purpose of this meeting is to decide the date of the launch.
> 3 Katharina, what do you think? ✓
> 4 OK, let's hear a few more views. ✓
> 5 Nadia, how do you feel about this?
> 6 You're right, Katharina. Let's get back to the point. ✓
> 7 OK everyone, I think on balance we agree … ✓
> 8 I want us to talk about sales outlets now.

(D) 🎧 4.4

◎ Play the recording again and get Ss to find the words and expressions.

> 1 favour
> 2 don't know
> 3 suggest
> 4 launch
> 5 Hold on
> 6 I think
> 7 do you mean

(E)

◎ Go through the expressions in the Useful language box, working on intonation. Tell Ss to be careful with *I don't agree,* which has to be said with 'softening' intonation.

◎ Explain the situation about the launch of the new tennis racket.

◎ Divide the class into groups of three to five. Nominate a chair (role A) and allocate the other roles.

◎ Circulate, monitor and assist if necessary with preparation of the roles. Make sure the chair is ready to use the chairing language and the participants are ready to use their language.

◎ When the groups are ready, they can begin to role-play the meeting. Circulate and monitor. Note language, especially meetings-related language, for praise and correction afterwards.

◎ When the discussions have reached some sort of conclusion, bring the class to order and ask some of the groups what their decision was and how the discussion went.

◎ Praise strong language points and work on half a dozen points that need improving, getting Ss to say the correct forms.

Case study

Fabtek

A small company has developed a new fabric. Ss representing another firm suggest new products using the material, and how they can be marketed.

Stage 1: Listening ⌒ 4.5

- With the whole class, quickly read the introductory text to establish the context.
- Explain to Ss that they are going to hear an excerpt from a company presentation about Protean.
- Get them to read the gapped fact sheet and have a quick brainstorming session to predict what the missing words might be. Remind Ss that there can be up to three words in each gap.
- Play the recording and see how many gaps Ss were able to fill. Play it again if necessary, then go through the answers.

> **1** similar to　**2** light pass　**3** strong and long-lasting
> **4** colour　**5** sales potential　**6** licensing　**7** Swiss firm
> **8** award-winning products

- Ask Ss to look at the three products using Protean made by another company under a licensing agreement. Work on difficult vocabulary and write up notes about the three products on the board.

> **Dazzle – shoes for young women**
> – light and comfortable
> – colour can be changed
> – shiny, smart, durable
>
> **Protean steering wheel**
> – better grip
> – safer
> – pleasant to touch
> – cheap to produce
>
> **Protean watch straps**
> – waterproof, easy to clean
> – non-allergic
> – attractive
> – light up in the dark

Stage 2: Task

- Go through the preamble quite quickly, explaining that the Ss are employees of Gadget, a company that is good at thinking of new products and marketing them. The idea of the three products above is to inspire Ss to find new uses for Protean.

- Divide the class into groups of four or five and appoint a chair for each. Tell the groups that their ideas must be *creative*, *exciting* and *innovative*. Get them to look through the points in the e-mail – they should remember that marketing considerations are very important.
- Make sure the chair is ready to use the chairing language and the participants are ready to use their language.
- When the groups are ready, tell them to start. Circulate and monitor. You may have to assist less imaginative groups with ideas. Note down language points for praise and correction afterwards, especially meetings-related language from the Useful language box on page 39.
- When each group has come up with a number of ideas, tell them to move on to choosing which three should be proposed to Fabtek.
- When the groups have done this, call the class to order. Ask a member of each group to say what its three chosen products are. Note them on the board.
- Concentrating on meetings language, praise strong language points that you heard in the group discussions and work on half a dozen that need improving, getting individual Ss to say the correct forms.

> **1 to 1**
> This case study can be done as a discussion between teacher and student followed by a presentation by the student. Don't forget to note language points for praise and correction afterwards. Also point out some of the key language you chose to use.

Stage 3: Writing

- Ss should write a short report in their capacity as a member of Gadget's Product Development Department to the CEO of Fabtek. They should recommend *one* of the products chosen by the group, outline its key features and say why it represents a commercial opportunity. This report can be done for homework.

 Writing file page 135

Stress

At a glance

	Classwork – Course Book	Further work
Lesson 1 *Each lesson (excluding case studies) is about 45–60 minutes. This does not include administration and time spent going through homework.*	**Starting up** Ss discuss stressful situations and ways of relaxing. **Listening: Dealing with stress** Ss listen to the director of a stress-management consultancy talking about stress at work. He then discusses how he helps companies deal with stress and different causes of stress in men and women. (If there is time left over, Ss could start looking at the Reading activity.)	
Lesson 2	**Reading: A career change** Ss read about a professional who chose to change to a less stressful job. **Vocabulary: Stress in the workplace** Ss look at stress-related vocabulary. **Discussion: Stressful jobs** Ss compare stress levels in different jobs and in their own job.	**Text bank** (pages 122 and 123) *Practice File* Vocabulary (page 20)
Lesson 3	**Language review: Past simple and present perfect** The tenses are compared and contrasted. Ss then do exercises to find the correct tense and use the correct tense with time expressions. **Skills: Participating in discussions** Ss listen to members of a personnel department talking about ways of improving the staff's health and then use these expressions in another context.	*Practice File* Language review (page 21) *Business Grammar and Usage* **Resource bank** (page 150)
Lesson 4 *Each case study is about 1 to 1½ hours.*	**Case study: Genova Vending Machines** Ss analyse and tackle problems of stress and low morale in the human resources department of a company that has recently merged with another.	*Practice File* Writing (page 22)

For a fast route through the unit focusing mainly on speaking skills, just use the underlined sections.

For 1-to-1 situations, most parts of the unit lend themselves, with minimal adaptation, to use with individual students. Where this is not the case, alternative procedures are given.

Business brief

People like work that is **rewarding** and gives them **satisfaction**. For this, a reasonable amount of pressure may be necessary: many employees want work that **stretches** them, to have the feeling that it can sometimes be difficult, but that it is also **stimulating** and **challenging**. This is necessary if one is to have pleasant feelings of **achievement**.

But when **pressure** builds up, it's easy to feel **overwhelmed** by work, and this can produce feelings of **stress**. It is possible to become **stressed out** through **overwork** or other problems. People **burn out**, so stressed and tired that they may never be able to work again. The general consensus is that most jobs have become more demanding, with longer hours and greater pressures.

More and more people want to get away from what they call the **rat race** or the **treadmill**, the feeling that work is too competitive, and are looking for **lifestyles** that are less **stressful** or completely **unstressful**. They are looking for more relaxed ways of living and working, perhaps in the country. Some people choose to work from home so as to be nearer their families. People are looking for a better **quality of life**, a healthier **work/life balance**. Perhaps they are looking for more **quality time** with their partners and children. Choosing to work in less stressful ways is known as **downshifting** or **rebalancing**.

A whole **stress industry** has grown up, with its **stress counsellors** and **stress therapists** giving advice on how to avoid stress and on how to lessen its effects. However, other experts say that stress levels today are lower than they used to be. They point to the difficult working conditions and long hours of our great-grandparents. Perhaps the answer is that the material advantages of modern times give us the illusion that we should have more control over our lives. Like lottery winners who quickly become accustomed to the idea of being rich, we become 'spoilt' by material comforts and start to worry when we think we are losing even a little control over events.

Whatever the truth, people love to talk about the stress of their work. In the language classroom there should be no shortage of students willing to talk at length about the stress they are under. This stress might even be part of their **job satisfaction**.

Read on

David Allen: *Getting Things Done: The Art of Stress-Free Productivity*, Viking, 2001

Martha Davis et al.: *The Relaxation and Stress Reduction Workbook*, 5th edition, New Harbinger, 2000

John D Drake: *Downshifting: How to Work Less and Enjoy Life More*, Berrett-Koehler, 2001

Steve Williams, Lesley Cooper: *Managing Workplace Stress – A Best Practice Blueprint*, Wiley, 2002

Lesson notes

Lesson notes

Warmer

- Write the words related to *stress* below on the board, followed by the nouns indicated. Ask Ss for examples of each, without pre-empting the content of the unit too much.

> a **stressed** person
> a **stress-free** job
> a **stressful** experience

Overview

- Ask Ss to look at the Overview section on page 42. Tell them a little about the things you will be doing, using the table on page 42 of this book as a guide. Tell them which sections you will be covering in this lesson and which in later lessons.

Quotation

- Write the quotation on the board and ask the Ss if they agree with it. Explain what the rat race is and that *rat* here is an informal term for an unpleasant person.

Starting up

Ss discuss stressful situations and ways of relaxing.

Ⓐ

- Before they do this exercise, brainstorm with Ss situations that they find stressful in everyday life.
- Then get them to complete the phrases describing stressful situations.
- Go through the list. Do Ss consider all these situations to be stressful? (For example, not all Ss may consider going to the hairdresser to be stressful.) If you have time, encourage Ss to rank the list from most to least stressful and ask them to explain why. Insist on the correct use of *stress, stressful,* etc. Do not accept *stressing*.
- Did Ss think of all the situations listed? Were there others that Ss thought of that aren't listed? If so, ensure they have the correct verbs to describe them.

> 1 going   2 queuing   3 being   4 finding   5 going
> 6 having   7 making   8 travelling

Ⓑ

- Get Ss in pairs to discuss the situations and the ways of relaxing. Circulate, monitor and assist if necessary.

Ⓒ

- Here, you could get all members of the class silently to rank the situations. While they are doing this, write the nine points up on the board, as below.
- Then ask for their scores and do an overall ranking for the whole class as shown in the first line of the chart below. If there are more than ten Ss, get them to do the ranking in pairs or threes and complete the table with scores given by each pair or three. (Of course, your Ss may not have to do these things. If not, ask them to imagine how stressful it would be if they did have to do them.)

	S1	S2	S3	S4	S5	S6	Total
Making a presentation to senior executives	5	8	3	4	4	6	30
Leading a formal meeting							
Telephoning in English							
Writing a report with a tight deadline							
Negotiating a very valuable contract							
Meeting important visitors from abroad for the first time							
Asking your boss for a pay rise							
Dealing with a customer who has a major complaint							
Being afraid of losing your job							

Listening: Dealing with stress

Ss listen to the director of a stress-management consultancy talking about stress at work. He then discusses how he helps companies deal with stress and different causes of stress in men and women.

 A

◎ Do this as a quick-fire activity with the whole class. Write Ss' ideas quickly on the board, for example long hours, deadlines, endless meetings, competition and conflict with colleagues. If your Ss are pre-work, ask them what is most stressful about being a student, for example essays and exams.

B 🎧 5.1

◎ Before playing the interview, ask Ss what they think Alan Bradshaw will mention.

◎ Then play the first part of the interview two or three times, explaining any difficulties. Ask Ss to complete the notes.

◎ Ask for the answers. Ask Ss if they agree with the causes Alan describes.

---

1 combination   2 one cause   3 pressure   4 control
5 depression   6 any difference

C 🎧 5.2

◎ Play the second part of the interview two or three times and get Ss to note the two ways. Check the answers with the whole class.

---

1 By investigating causes of stress ('stress risk assess-ment').
2 They train managers by raising their awareness of stress and giving them skills to prevent and reduce stress at work.

D 🎧 5.3

◎ Before playing the recording, ask Ss what they expect to hear.

◎ Then play the third part of the interview two or three times and get Ss to choose the correct answers.

---

1 Men
2 Women
3 Men
4 Men
5 Women

◎ Ask your Ss if they are surprised by these answers.

E

◎ Tell Ss to discuss the points in pairs or threes. Encourage them to give specific examples about each point. Circulate, monitor and assist if necessary. Note down language points for praise and correction afterwards, especially relating to the language of stress.

◎ Bring the class to order. Praise good language you heard and work on half a dozen points that need improving, getting individual Ss to say the correct forms.

◎ With the whole class, get the groups to give their opinions. Encourage discussion, especially on points where opinions differ.

Lesson notes

Lesson notes

Reading: A career change

Ss read about a professional who chooses to change to a less stressful job.

- Go round the class quickly and ask Ss whether they prefer a slow or fast pace of life. Encourage discussion.
- With the whole class, elicit answers to questions 2 and 3. Refer back to the quote at the beginning of the unit.

B

- Get Ss to read the article in pairs and decide if the statements are true or false. Circulate, monitor and assist if necessary.
- With the whole class, explain any common difficulties and elicit the answers.

1 F   2 T   3 T   4 T   5 F

C

- Do this as a quick-fire activity with the whole class.

1 make   2 spend   3 do   4 keep   5 do   6 make

D

- Get your Ss to discuss these questions in pairs.
- With the whole class, compare answers.

Vocabulary: Stress in the workplace

Ss look at stress-related vocabulary.

- Go through the pronunciation of the words 1–5. Point out the connection between *workaholic* and *alcoholic*. You could also mention *shopaholic*. (*Flexitime* is *flextime* in AmE, but don't raise this unless someone mentions it.)
- Ask Ss to do the two exercises. Circulate, monitor and assist if necessary.
- With the whole class, elicit the answers and clear up any difficulties.

Exercise A
1 c   2 d   3 e   4 a   5 b

Exercise B
1   deadline
2   workaholic
3   workload
4   lifestyle
5   flexitime

Discussion: Stressful jobs

Ss compare stress levels in different jobs and in their own job.

A–**B**

- Go through the table with the whole class, explaining the different jobs.
- Get your Ss to complete the table in pairs. Explain that they have to place the six professions – actor, hairdresser, etc. – in the correct position in the stress league.
- Circulate, monitor and assist if necessary. Note down language points for praise and correction afterwards, especially those relating to stress.
- Praise strong language points and work on half a dozen points that need improving, getting Ss to say the correct forms.
- Ask pairs for their findings. Then reveal the answers.

Actor 7.2; Teacher 6.2; Bus driver 5.4; Hairdresser 4.3; Banker; 3.7; Librarian 2.0
Point out to your Ss that it's interesting that, according to the survey, bankers are under less stress than bus drivers, despite what Ss read in the article. The banker who became a bus driver would probably say that it is a different kind of stress in each job.

- Discuss with the whole class the kind of stress in each job and what might cause it. For example, the stress felt by many actors might be related to finding work in the first place, teachers from aggressive students, etc.
- Continue the discussion and ask Ss where their own jobs should go in the table.

C

- Get the whole class to discuss these points. Some will be very willing to say how much stress they are under (see Business brief for this unit). Get them to talk about specific problems, for example deadlines. For question 3, you could say that some people are workaholics because they want to be seen to be working hard in order to get promotion, or because of insecurity. Get your Ss to suggest other ideas.

Language review: Past simple and present perfect

The tenses are compared and contrasted. Ss then do exercises to find the correct tense and use the correct tense with time expressions.

◉ This area is very difficult, and further complicated by the fact that the rules are different in *AmE* – the ones here are for *BrE*. Take things slowly and don't expect Ss to get things right first time.

◉ Go through the examples and elicit answers to the questions.

> These two examples are with time expressions: *for five years* and *for three years* respectively.
> 1 Present perfect. This particular example with the time expression *for five years* implies that she is still working in Warsaw now.
> 2 Past simple. This is in the past: 'finished time'. She doesn't work in London now.

◉ Go through the rules for the past simple. When you have a time expression referring entirely to the past ('finished time') – *last weekend, on Monday,* etc. – you must use the past simple.

◉ Go through the rules for the present perfect. When you have a time expression referring to 'time up to now' (*just, so far,* etc.), you must use the present perfect.

(A)

◉ Go through the examples with the whole class, eliminating the incorrect sentences and discussing with your Ss why they are wrong.

> 1 Stress levels have increased in recent years.
> ~~Stress levels increased in recent years.~~
> 2 ~~The role of women changed dramatically over the past 100 years.~~
> The role of women has changed dramatically over the past 100 years.
> 3 He has worked as a stress counsellor since 1999.
> ~~He worked as a stress counsellor since 1999.~~
> The first three sentences refer to a time leading up to now, so the present perfect must be used.
> 4 I resigned two months ago.
> ~~I have resigned two months ago.~~
> This is a time in the past, so the past simple is required.
> 5 Have you ever been to a stress counsellor before?
> ~~Did you ever go to a stress counsellor before?~~
> With *ever*, you use the present perfect, because no particular time in the past is mentioned.
> 6 ~~I have seen a stress counsellor last week.~~
> I saw a stress counsellor last week.
> This is a time in the past, finished time, so the past simple is required.

(B)

◉ Ask your Ss to work on the time expressions in pairs. Before they start, make sure they have understood the distinction between finished time and time up to now.

◉ Circulate, monitor and assist if necessary.

◉ With the whole class, ask pairs for their answers and discuss how they arrived at them.

◉ Encourage Ss to discuss events in their lives using the expressions. They can invent things if they wish.

Past simple (with expressions referring to finished time)	Present perfect (with expressions referring to time up to now)
two years ago	so far
in 1999	ever
yesterday	yet
last Monday	just
during the 1990s	for the past 2 weeks
when I was at university	already
	never
	over the last few years
	since 2001

(C)

◉ Ask the Ss to work in pairs on inventing the mini-dialogues. Circulate, monitor and assist if necessary.

◉ Bring the class to order and get individual pairs to read particular dialogues aloud for the whole class, for example:

> A Have you ever travelled abroad on business?
> B Yes, I have.
> A Where did you go?
> B (I went to) New York.

Skills: Participating in discussions

Ss listen to members of a human resources department talking about ways of improving the staff's health and then use these expressions in another context.

(A) 🎧 5.4

◎ Explain the situation and play the recording two or three times. Explain any difficulties and get Ss to write down the suggestions in note form.

> offer a free medical checkup every year
> have a no-smoking policy in the staff restaurant
> offer healthier meals
> set up a counselling service

◎ With the whole class, ask for the answers. Explain what counselling is if you think your Ss are not familiar with it.

(B) 🎧 5.4

◎ Play the recording again and get the Ss to complete the expressions.

> 1 could offer
> 2 How about
> 3 should improve
> 4 could change
> 5 What about

◎ Ask for the answers and explain any difficulties.

(C) 🎧 5.5

◎ Play the recording of the second part of the meeting once or twice and ask Ss to say if they hear the expressions or not, and to tick the ones they hear.

◎ Play the recording again and get Ss to say if the speakers are agreeing or disagreeing. Also get them to say whether the expressions they don't hear are agreeing or disagreeing.

> 1 Mm, I don't know. ✓ D
> 2 It sounds interesting, but it could be very expensive. ✓ D
> 3 I agree with you, Tanya. It'd cost a lot ... A
> 4 I don't agree at all. It's got a very good pool and sauna. D
> 5 Yes, it's worth checking out, I suppose. ✓ A
> 6 A sauna is very relaxing, I must admit. ✓ A
> 7 Maybe, but there are so many other things we could do. ✓ D

◎ Point out the tendency in British English to 'hedge' (without using this word). For example, *Mm, I don't know* is a way of disagreeing politely.

(D)

◎ Go through the expressions in the Useful language box with the whole class. Work on intonation and try to eliminate any tendency for Ss to say *I am agree* or *I am not agree*.

◎ Point out that the purpose of the exercise is to put into action the language in the Useful language box. Put Ss into pairs and tell them that they should treat the three points as an agenda for the discussion.

◎ Start the activity. Circulate, monitor and assist if necessary. Note down language points for praise and correction afterwards, especially language used for discussions.

◎ Bring the class to order and ask the pairs what conclusions they came to on each point. Praise correct use of the expressions in the Useful language box and work on points for improvement, getting individual Ss to say the correct forms.

Case study

Genova Vending Machines

Ss analyse and tackle problems of stress and low morale in the Human Resources Department of a company that has recently merged with another.

Stage 1: Background

◎ Instruct Ss to read the background information. Circulate, monitor and assist if necessary, clarifying any difficulties.

◎ Go round the class and elicit key points from the information, writing them on the board.

– GVM merged with another company 18 months ago
– workforce cut by 15 per cent
– open-plan offices introduced
– proposed that salary payments and staff recruitment should be done by outside companies instead of the HR Department. ➜ redundancies in the department
– job security worries
– low morale
– HR Department overworked and stressed
– high absenteeism
– several resignations

◎ Get Ss to read the consultants' findings. Circulate, monitor and assist if necessary, clarifying any difficulties.

◎ Again, go round the class and elicit the two key points from the information, writing them on the board in note form.

◎ Stress among HR staff caused by redundancies last year
◎ Rumours of further redundancies; possibility of strike action

Stage 2: Listening 🎧 5.6

◎ Tell Ss that they are going to hear interviews with six members of staff at GVM. Have them look at the headings in the second part of the report so that they know what topics to listen out for. With weaker Ss, you may like to point out that the first two speakers talk about heavy workloads, the next two discuss space problems, and the last two mention the new HR Director.

◎ Play the recording once or twice for Ss to make notes.

Heavy workloads
◎ Fewer people to do more paperwork; lots of meetings to attend
◎ Too much time spent on admin; too much control, stressful being monitored continuously
Space problems
◎ Not enough space/privacy; open-plan not popular; one area overcrowded with no window
◎ Noisy environment
New HR Director
◎ Difficult to talk to
◎ Won't listen, quick to criticise, never praises

Stage 3: Task part 1

◎ Keep the above points on the board for Ss to focus on while they do the task. Put Ss into groups of three or four and appoint a chair for each group. Point out that all the points are related, but that Ss have to come up with answers to the two questions in part 1 of the task. Write them on the board.

◎ Which problems do you think are the most serious?
◎ What should the management do to solve the problems?

◎ Circulate and monitor the discussions. Remind Ss that they should try to use expressions from the Useful language box on page 47. Note down language points for praise and correction, especially those relating to stress and language used in discussions.

◎ When the groups have finished, bring the class to order and praise strong language points. Work on half a dozen points that need improving, getting Ss to say the correct forms.

Stage 4: Task part 2

◎ If the class is very large have two or three groups rather than just one. Make it clear that the purpose of the task is to produce an action plan to reduce stress in the HR Department, rather than in the company as a whole.

◎ Appoint a chair for the group and get them to start the discussion. Circulate and monitor. Note down language points for praise and correction afterwards.

◎ When the group has produced its list of recommendations, bring the class to order. Praise strong language points and work on those points that need improving, getting Ss to say the correct forms.

◎ Ask for the recommendations, getting one member of the group to write key points on the board. If there is more than one group, do the same with the others.

◎ Point out that the subsequent writing task follows on from the points in the discussion and give your Ss time to write them down.

1 to 1
This case study can be done as a discussion between teacher and student followed by a presentation by the student. Don't forget to note language points for praise and correction afterwards. Also point out some of the key language you chose to use.

Stage 5: Writing

◎ Ss should write the final section of the report as if they were leader of the Stress Management Team of consultants. They should give recommendations for reducing stress in the HR Department. This can be done for homework.

 Writing file page 135

UNIT **6** | # Entertaining

At a glance

	Classwork – Course Book	Further work
Lesson 1 *Each lesson (excluding case studies) is about 45–60 minutes. This does not include administration and time spent going through homework.*	<u>**Starting up**</u> Ss look at different options for entertaining businesspeople. **Listening: Corporate entertaining** Two managers of a London hotel talk about corporate hospitality. **Vocabulary: Eating and drinking** Ss look at the language of food and describing restaurants.	*Practice File* Vocabulary (page 24)
Lesson 2	**Reading: Corporate entertainment** Ss read about the activities offered by companies to their clients. **Language review: Multi-word verbs** Ss look at the behaviour of multi-word verbs in the context of entertaining.	**Text bank** (pages 124 and 125) *Practice File* Language review (page 25) ***Business Grammar and Usage***
Lesson 3	<u>**Skills: Socialising: greetings and small talk**</u> Ss look at what to say in different situations, listen to people socialising and apply the language in a number of contexts, including a role-play.	**Resource bank** (page 151)
Lesson 4 *Each case study is about 1 to 1½ hours.*	<u>**Case study: Organising a conference**</u> Ss analyse the different possible venues for a company conference and choose the most suitable one.	*Practice File* Writing (page 26)

For a fast route through the unit focusing mainly on speaking skills, just use the underlined sections.

For 1-to-1 situations, most parts of the unit lend themselves, with minimal adaptation, to use with individual students. Where this is not the case, alternative procedures are given.

At a glance

Business brief

It has been said that when two American or European business people meet, they are there **to do a deal**, but in Asia they are there **to establish a relationship**. Entertaining in Asia is often used to 'size up' a potential **business partner** – partner in the sense of future supplier or joint venture associate. Asians will want to know more about their guest, their background and their contacts before going ahead and doing business. This is an essential part of the business process, not just polite **etiquette**.

Relationship building takes different forms in different places – invitations to karaoke evenings in Japan or the yacht on the French Riviera are not to be refused. The demand for **corporate hospitality** in the UK has been criticised for making events such as grand-prix racing or Wimbledon more expensive for ordinary people. But **corporate sponsorship** of sport and culture brings in large amounts of money, and many such events benefit from this overall.

Entertaining in the form of invitations to your host's home exists in some cultures but not others, where work and private life are kept entirely separate.

Cultural awareness of **norms** in these and other areas can lead to better communication and avoidance of misunderstandings. Companies are spending more time and money these days on **cross-cultural training**, often but not always in tandem with language training, in order to facilitate better **social interaction**.

Socialising in another language is not easy. There is more focus than in business discussions on the language itself. Learners, rightly, demand formulaic expressions for particular situations. This is often called **small talk**. But to refer to it as 'small' undervalues its importance. Language learners see it as a minefield of potential problems and, inevitably, **gaffes**. People have their favourite stories about such mistakes, perhaps ones they made themselves. Telling these stories can be a useful form of ice-breaking activity in the classroom when working on this much-demanded **social English**.

Read on

Judy Allen: *Event Planning: The Ultimate Guide to Successful Meetings, Corporate Events, Fundraising Galas, Conferences, Conventions, Incentives and Other Special Events*, Wiley, 2000

John Jenkins, Adam Jolly (eds): *The CBI Guide to the Corporate Sponsorship of Good Causes*, Kogan Page, 2000

Debra Fine: *The Fine Art of Small Talk: How to Start a Conversation, Keep It Going, Build Rapport – And Leave a Positive Impression*, Small Talk Press, 2002

Lesson notes

Warmer

◎ Write the word *entertainment* in big letters on the board. Invite Ss to suggest different forms of entertainment in general, rather than in a corporate context. Some examples are given below.

Entertainment	◎ shows – e.g. plays, musicals, films ◎ concerts – e.g. classical, rock, jazz ◎ (night) clubbing ◎ sports – e.g. football, tennis, rugby

◎ Ask if any of these would be suitable for corporate entertaining.

Overview

◎ Tell your Ss that they will be looking at the subject of corporate entertaining and the language that goes with it, including small talk.

◎ Ask the Ss to look at the Overview section on page 50. Tell them a little about the things you will be doing, using the table on page 50 of this book as a guide. Tell them which sections you will be covering in this lesson and which in later lessons.

Quotation

◎ Write the quotation on the board and ask Ss not if they know who Anonymous was, but what it means.

◎ Ask your Ss if they agree with the quotation, in a business context.

The idea is that someone may pay for your lunch but that something will always be expected from you in return. In business terms this might be a contract, better sales terms, a job or some other favour.

Starting up

Ss look at different options for entertaining business people.

◎ Get Ss in pairs to discuss the points. Circulate, monitor and assist if necessary.

◎ With the whole class, ask different pairs to say what their findings were, why they chose the things that they did and why they eliminated others.

◎ Discuss this question with the whole class.

You could ask what the purpose of these events is – to obtain immediate sales or to generate goodwill (teach this expression) in the longer run? You could point out that a company may not just invite clients and potential clients but other contacts as well.

Listening: Corporate entertaining

Two managers of a London hotel talk about corporate hospitality.

Ⓐ 🎧 6.1

◎ Ask Ss to look at the five gapped words in question 1 and see if they can guess any of them.

◎ Play the recording once for Ss to complete the words.

◎ Ask Ss to read the sentence in question 2. With weaker Ss, tell them that there is just one word missing from each gap. Then play the recording again for them to complete the sentence.

◎ Check their answers to both questions quickly.

> 1 a) exhibition   b) workshops   c) seminars
>   d) conference   e) AGM
> 2 client; achieve; objectives

Ⓑ 🎧 6.2

◎ Ask Ss to read the statements and ask them what they think the 'Five Senses Experience' might be.

◎ Play the recording once and ask Ss to say whether each statement is true or false.

◎ Check their answers, playing the recording again if necessary, and ask Ss if they would like to try the 'Five Senses Experience'.

> **1** False   **2** False   **3** True

Ⓒ 🎧 6.3

◎ Tell Ss to read the paragraph first to get the gist of it.

◎ Play the recording and ask Ss to delete the words that they *don't* hear. With weaker classes, you may want to tell them that there are six words to cross out.

◎ Go through the answers with the class.

> '... the great thing about the 'Five Senses' ~~programme~~ is that it gets ~~most~~ people talking ~~freely~~, it breaks down ~~cultural~~ barriers and it gives people a memorable shared experience. It can help them to communicate ~~successfully~~ with and work with ~~new~~ colleagues, clients and customers in ways that are much more effective.'

Vocabulary: Eating and drinking

Ss look at the language of food and describing restaurants.

- Look at the steps and assist with any difficulties, for example the pronunciation of *dessert* and the meaning of *aperitif* (a drink before the meal).
- Ask Ss to put the steps into the correct order as a quick-fire activity with the whole class.

> **a** 2 **b** 7 **c** 1 **d** 8 **e** 5 **f** 6 **g** 4 **h** 3
> (This is the 'standard' order. Your Ss may point out that it is possible to have an aperitif before you look at the menu or ask for the bill before you have the dessert, for example if you are in a hurry.)

B

- This activity tests common collocations used when describing restaurants. Ask Ss to look at the example and make sure that they understand that *restaurant* goes with each of the four article/adjective combinations.
- Tell Ss to complete the other collocations using the words from the box.
- Go through the answers quickly. You may want to ask Ss to copy each collocation into their vocabulary notebooks for future reference.

> **1** restaurant   **2** service   **3** atmosphere   **4** food
> **5** location   **6** prices

C

- Go through the five bullet points to make sure Ss understand each one. Then ask them to work individually to put them in order of importance. Remind them of the context, i.e. that they are taking a foreign visitor out to dinner.
- Ss work in pairs to compare and discuss their rankings. Circulate, monitor and assist if necessary, making sure Ss are using the phrases from Exercise B.
- Ask Ss if there was much difference in their choices and if so, why they think that was. Ask them if they would have ranked the factors differently if they were taking a friend or family member out to dinner.

D

- Have a quick brainstorming session to list four or five typical dishes. If Ss are from different countries, choose one dish from each country.
- Ask Ss to try to describe each dish. With strong classes, you may wish to do this first without reference to the phrases given in the book.
- Be prepared to supply additional vocabulary if Ss are having trouble describing their dishes, e.g. *It's made with ...*, *The ingredients are ...*
- If you have time, ask one or two Ss to describe a dish for the others to guess.

Reading: Corporate entertainment

Ss read about activities offered by companies to their clients.

- If your Ss are from different countries, ask them to work in same-country groups to discuss these questions. If they are all from the same country, ask them to work in pairs or small groups.
- If your Ss are not working, for question 1b, you could ask them if they have ever been invited to a corporate event and if so, whether they enjoyed it.

B

- Go through the list and check that Ss understand the vocabulary, e.g. *tank, hot-air ballooning, health spa, jet fighter*. Ask them if they have heard of the Wimbledon tennis tournament (one of the major tournaments that takes place in south-west London in June every year).
- Ask Ss to work in pairs or small groups to choose the activities that would appeal the most to business people in their country.
- Summarise as a whole class by writing the six activities on the board and asking Ss to vote for their favourites. Which activity do they think would be most popular?

C

- Give Ss five minutes to read the article and tick the activities in Exercise B that are mentioned.
- Quickly check their answers.

> All the points are mentioned except 1.
> They are mentioned in the following order: 3, 2, 6, 4, 5

D

- Ss work in pairs to complete their questions. Circulate, monitor and assist if necessary, making sure that Ss realise that the answers are given below each question to help them.
- They then ask their partner their questions, finding the answers in the text.

> **Student A**
> **1** do; companies; ideas   **2** does it cost
> **3** How much does; cost
> **Student B**
> **1** does it cost; in a tank   **2** How much does; cost
> **3** Why do; spend

E

- This exercise picks out multi-word verbs from the text, thus leading into the Language review section. Give Ss five minutes to complete the sentences before going through the answers.

> **1** up with   **2** set; back   **3** out for

Language review: Multi-word verbs

Ss look at the behaviour of multi-word verbs in the context of entertaining.

◎ Ss are often interested in, but confused by, these verbs, also known as phrasal verbs. Go through the examples with your Ss.

◎ With multi-word verbs that can be separated from their particles, point out that if the object is a pronoun, they cannot be separated. For example, you say

I turned it down.

not

I turned down it.

◎ Optionally, you could get your Ss in pairs to look up these multi-word verbs in a general ELT dictionary such as the *Longman Dictionary of Contemporary English*.

Ⓐ ◯ 6.4

◎ Play the recording once for Ss to listen.

◎ Tell Ss to read the questions, then play the recording again for them to note down their answers.

Sample answers
1 Because several visitors arrived unexpectedly.
2 They would like to look around the city.
3 They refused the invitation to attend their sales conference, which was a mistake.

Ⓑ ◯ 6.4

◎ Ss may be able to complete this matching task without listening to the recording again. Give them five or ten minutes to try before playing the recording, either to help them or to check their answers.

1 e   2 c   3 d   4 a   5 h   6 f   7 g   8 b

◎ Ss then work in pairs to practise the dialogue. Have them swap roles half way through.

Ⓒ

◎ Point out to Ss that all the multi-word verbs in Ana's sentences are paraphrased in Ben's answers, as shown by the italics. Some of these, like *taking care of* and *got involved in*, are multi-word verbs themselves.

◎ Where the paraphrases are normal verbs (e.g. *visit, refuse*), ask Ss if they think the multi-word versions are more or less formal than the simple verbs. (Multi-word verbs are usually less formal.)

Skills: Socialising: greetings and small talk

Ss look at what to say in different situations, listen to people socialising and apply the language in a number of contexts, including a role-play.

Ⓐ

◎ Ask two confident Ss to come to the front of the class and demonstrate how they would introduce themselves to each other if they did not know each other. Insist on the correct use of *Hello, I'm … /My name is … .*

◎ Then get a third student, C, to come up. A introduces C to B. Point out that *How do you do* is quite old-fashioned now. Say that *Hello, pleased to meet you* or even just *Hello* are adequate responses.

Ⓑ –Ⓒ ◯ 6.5

◎ Explain the exercise. Then play the recording once or twice and get Ss to match the people and say if they know each other.

◎ Then play conversations 2 and 4 again and get Ss to complete them.

Exercise B
1 d – yes
2 e – no
3 b – yes
4 c – no
5 a – no

Exercise C
1 have, met
2 Good, you
3 know
4 work
5 Give, regards
6 Pleased
7 hear
8 great
9 love
10 forward

◎ As an optional extra activity, get Ss to read the conversations in pairs. Circulate, monitor and assist if necessary, especially with natural intonation.

◎ Then get particular pairs to read the conversations for the whole class.

◎ As a further step, get Ss to do conversation 4 again, substituting names of other people, other places for Munich, and other adjectives for *great*.

(D)–(E)

◎ Go through the expressions and ask Ss to say who says
what. Then get them to match the utterances.

Exercise D
a) 1 2 4 5 7
b) 3 6 8 9 10

Exercise E
1–6; 4–8; 5–3; 7–10; 9–2

◎ Practise intonation with the whole class and get pairs to
read the different exchanges with feeling.

(F)

◎ Go through the Useful language box as consolidation,
again practising intonation.

◎ Explain the situation, allocate roles and get Ss to prepare
their roles. Circulate and assist if necessary.

◎ When pairs are ready, ask them to start the role-play.
Circulate and monitor. Note down language points for
praise and correction afterwards, concentrating particularly
on socialising expressions.

◎ When the Ss have finished, bring the class to order and
praise strong language points and work on half a dozen
points that need improving, getting Ss to say the correct
forms.

◎ If there is time, ask one of the pairs to give a performance
of their conversation for the whole class, integrating the
corrections you have made.

Case study

Organising a conference

Ss analyse the different possible venues for a company conference and choose the most suitable one.

Stage 1: Background

- Give the general topic of the case study and ask Ss to read through the background information. Meanwhile, write the headings on the left of the table below on the board.

- Elicit information from your Ss to complete the column on the right.

Company and its base	VMI, Valencia, Spain
Activity	Financial services
Aims of the conference	1 Allow managers to get to know each other – stronger team 2 Thank them for hard work 3 Discuss improvements to products and services
Who will attend?	CEO, senior managers from head office, 50 managers from overseas
Dates/duration	July; Friday evening – Monday a.m.
Budget	$2,000 per person

- Go round the class and ask individual Ss to use the notes on each hotel to give a full description of it in their own words, for example:

  The Long Beach Hotel in Casablanca is on the sea. It has five stars. There are two large conference rooms but, unfortunately, no seminar rooms ... .

- However, don't allow Ss to pre-empt the task by commenting on the hotels they describe. Just get them to talk about the advantages and disadvantages in different ways, for example:

  The good thing about the Long Beach Hotel is its very attractive beach. However, there are not many cultural sites to visit in the area.

Stage 2: Listening 6.6

- Do a quick brainstorm with Ss on the type of features that might be mentioned, e.g. size, facilities, location.

- Play the recording for Ss as many times as is necessary for them to list the four features.

- Check the answers with the whole class.

The venue must have:
- one large conference room
- preferably four or more seminar rooms
- reasonable access to an international airport
- a choice of activities outside the main conference programme.

- Ask Ss to look at the results of the questionnaire and ask them which is the preferred location (city).

Stage 3: Task

- Divide the class into groups of four or five. Make sure that each group understands the task it must perform: as members of VMI's Marketing Department, choose the hotel that best meets the requirements of the conference.

- When the situation is clear, the discussion can begin. Circulate and monitor. Note down language points for praise and correction afterwards, concentrating on the language of advantages and disadvantages.

- When each group has come to a conclusion, bring the class to order.

- Praise strong language points that you heard and point out half a dozen that need improving. Ask individual Ss to repeat the correct forms.

- Then get Ss to pool their findings in one group or, if the class is very large, in two groups, and discuss the final choice of venue. Circulate and monitor the language of advantages and disadvantages.

- Ask the group(s) for their final choice and why they chose it.

- Praise strong language points and work again on points that need improvement, getting individual Ss to say the correct forms.

1 to 1

This case study can be done as a discussion between teacher and student and then as a basis for a presentation by the student. Don't forget to note language points for praise and correction afterwards. Also point out some of the key language you chose to use.

Stage 4: Writing

- Ss should write an e-mail in their capacity as CEO of VMI, inviting the overseas sales managers to the conference and giving details of its purpose and the location. This e-mail can be done for homework.

 Writing file page 133

Revision

This unit revises and reinforces some of the key language points from Units 4–6, and links with those units are clearly shown. Point out these links to your Ss – in some cases, they will need information from the original activities to do the exercises here.

These exercises can be done in class individually or collaboratively, or for homework.

For more speaking practice, see the Resource bank section of this book beginning on page 141.

4 Great ideas

Vocabulary

◎ This exercise relates to the Vocabulary section on page 34. Ss should try to match the verb/noun collocations without referring back to Unit 4 if possible.

◎ Ss then use the collocations to complete the sentences.

> **1** to win an award   **2** to make a breakthrough   **3** to fill a gap   **4** to extend a range
> **5** to enter a market   **6** to meet a need
> **a)** entered; market   **b)** meet; need   **c)** won an award   **d)** extend; range
> **e)** make; breakthrough   **f)** fills a gap

Past simple and past continuous

◎ If necessary, ask Ss to reread the box on page 38 before doing this exercise.

> **1** were supervising   **2** moved   **3** was studying   **4** had   **5** created   **6** was doing   **7** came
> **8** modified   **9** improved   **10** gave   **11** hired   **12** offered   **13** were setting up

5 Stress

Past simple and present perfect

◎ If necessary, ask Ss to review the box on page 46 before doing this exercise.

> **1** Has; changed   **2** has/'s been   **3** did; stay   **4** heard   **5** have/'ve missed   **6** was; was
> **7** earned   **8** offered   **9** did; complain   **10** has/'s been

Writing

◎ First, go through the numbered gaps, asking Ss what kind of information is needed in each one (e.g. date, salutation, phrase for signing off) and ask for suggestions of suitable phrases.

> **Sample answers**
> **1** 20 May 2007   **2** Dear Mrs Belmaker   **3** I look forward to hearing from you.
> **4** Yours sincerely

◎ Ensure that Ss understand why *Yours faithfully* would not be appropriate for gap 4 (because you know the name of the person you are writing to).

◎ Ask Ss to write the missing paragraph. If necessary, they can refer back to the Case study on pages 48–49 (including the transcripts on page 149).

6 Entertaining

◉ This relates to the Vocabulary section on page 51 and the Skills section on page 54.

◉ Remind Ss that even if they can't work out all the words straight away, they should fill in the grid with the ones they do know, as this may help them with the missing ones.

---

1 host **2** course **3** lift **4** table **5** mind **6** tasty
Hidden word: hospitality

◉ This tests Ss' ability to recognise continuity markers and to read for context.

◉ Tell Ss to scan the article quickly and ask them if it is common practice in their country for doctors to be given gifts or entertainment by drug companies. If you have time, you may want to have a short debate on the ethics of this.

◉ Remind Ss that only four of the sentences are needed to complete the article.

---

1 f **2** e **3** b **4** c

UNIT 7 Marketing

At a glance

	Classwork – Course Book	Further work
Lesson 1 *Each lesson (excluding case studies) is about 45–60 minutes. This does not include administration and time spent going through homework.*	**Starting up** Ss look at the four Ps: product, price, promotion and place and talk about impressive marketing campaigns. **Vocabulary: Word partnerships** Ss look at combinations of words to do with marketing and then use them to talk about particular products. **Listening: Successful marketing** Ss listen to a managing consultant talking about marketing.	*Practice File* Vocabulary (page 28)
Lesson 2	**Reading: Selling dreams** Ss read an article about the film made by Chanel to market their perfume. **Language review: Questions** Ss look at how questions are formed in the context of a consumer questionnaire.	**Text bank** (pages 126 and 127) *Practice File* Language review (page 29) ***Business Grammar and Usage***
Lesson 3	<u>**Skills: Telephoning: exchanging information**</u> Ss listen to calls and note down specific information relating to numbers, names, etc.	**Resource bank** (page 152)
Lesson 4 *Each case study is about 1 to 1½ hours.*	**Case study: Kristal Water** Ss analyse the reasons for the failure of a new mineral water and propose corrective action.	*Practice File* Writing (page 30)

For a fast route through the unit focusing mainly on speaking skills, just use the underlined sections.

For 1-to-1 situations, most parts of the unit lend themselves, with minimal adaptation, to use with individual students. Where this is not the case, alternative procedures are given.

Business brief

'We must be smarter at devising packages of services that our customers want and pricing them attractively. Set the marketing department free to shape new packages. Don't confine it to coming up with cute names for offerings designed by engineers and accountants.'*

This sums up the position of marketing in many companies, where it is often seen as a fancy name for selling or advertising. But, as the quote shows, marketing people should be involved not just in promoting sales but in all aspects of the marketing mix:

- **product**: deciding what products or services to sell in the first place

- **prices**: setting prices that are attractive to particular groups of customers (**segments**) and that are profitable for the company

- **place**: finding suitable **distribution channels** to reach these customer groups and

- **promotion**: all the activities, not just advertising, used to support the product – everything from pre-sales information to after-sales service.

These are the **four Ps** of the marketing mix, the 'levers' of a company's marketing machine, levers that it can adjust in different ways for different products and different buyers.

Another way of looking at this is from the point of view of customers, with the **four Cs**. From this perspective, the marketing mix is expressed in terms of:

- **customer solution**: offering the right product to satisfy particular **customer needs**

- **customer cost**: the price paid directly by the customer to buy the product, including the 'price' involved in not buying another product of the same or another type

- **convenience**: distributing the product in the way most suitable for each type of customer

- **communication**: exchanging information with the customer. Customers are informed about products through advertising, sales literature and so on, but customers also communicate with the seller, for example through **customer helplines**. This is a good way for sellers to find out more about customers and their requirements and to change or improve their **offer**.

Thinking of the marketing mix in these terms helps sellers maintain a **customer orientation** – a focus on customer needs.

*Peter Martin, 'A second chance for telecoms', *Financial Times*, 18 December 2001

Read on

Philip Kotler: *Marketing Management: Analysis, Planning and Control*, Millennium edition, Prentice Hall, 2000

Robert Shaw: *Improving Marketing Effectiveness*, Economist Books, 1998

Economist Pocket Marketing: Hamish Hamilton, 1997

Lesson notes

Warmer

- Write the word *marketing* in big letters on the board.
- Ask Ss for the things that they think of when they see the word. They will probably come up with things like *selling, salesperson, advertising*. If they have trouble coming up with words, put hints on the board, for example for *selling*, you could write *s e l l _ _ _*, for *salesperson*, write *s a l e s p _ _ _ _ _*, and give definitions of the words you are looking for, for example 'This is what you call someone who sells things'.

Overview

- Ask Ss to look at the Overview section on page 62. Tell them a little about the things you will be doing, using the table on page 60 of this book as a guide. Tell them which sections you will be covering in this lesson and which in later lessons.

Quotation

- Write the quotation on the board and ask Ss to discuss it briefly in pairs.
- With the whole class, ask pairs for their opinions. (They may feel that there is much more to business than these two functions. If so, ask them why they think Peter Drucker focused on these.)

Starting up

Ss look at the four Ps: product, price, promotion and place, and talk about marketing campaigns that have impressed them.

Ⓐ

- Do this as a quick-fire activity with the whole class. (Again, refer to the Business brief for background on the four Ps.)

1 d **2** a **3** b **4** c

Ⓑ 🎧 7.1

- Tell Ss the general subject of what they are going to hear and play the recording right through once or twice and then again, stopping after each speaker in order to give Ss time to answer.

Speaker 1: Place
Speaker 2: Promotion
Speaker 3: Price
Speaker 4: Product

Ⓒ

- To give Ss the idea, tell them about something you bought recently. Make up a story if necessary. For example:

> I bought some cosmetics in a discount store near where I live. I'd seen some advertising in a women's magazine for a new luxury shampoo. There was a free sample sachet and I tried it and liked it. Of course, it's not as pleasant as buying in a department store, but I saved at least 30 percent on the usual price. Anyway, parking near the department store in my town is impossible and the discount store is just round the corner, so place was an important factor.

- Ask Ss to work in pairs. They think of a product that they have bought recently and note down the factors that influenced them in the buying process. Circulate, monitor and assist if necessary.
- With the whole class, get pairs to talk about some of the products. Refer them to the Vocabulary file if necessary.

Ⓓ

- With the whole class, talk about a marketing campaign that has been on TV, on hoardings/billboards (teach these words) or in the press recently. Then get Ss to suggest other campaigns and talk about them in pairs.

Vocabulary: Word partnerships

Ss look at combinations of words to do with marketing and then use them to talk about particular products.

Ⓐ

- Get Ss to work in pairs on the exercise. Circulate, monitor and assist if necessary.

1	market	research – b segment – c share – a
2	consumer	behaviour – b profile – a goods – c
3	product	launch – a life cycle – b range – c
4	sales	forecast – b figures – c target – a
5	advertising	campaign – c budget – b agency – a

- Work on the pronunciation of difficult words such as *behaviour, campaign*.

(B)

◎ With the whole class, ask your Ss to suggest brands that they will work on in pairs. (If they are short of ideas, suggest some for them.) Try to get a good range so that they do not all work on luxury products.

◎ Go through the Mercedes example to give them the idea. It's probably easier to get Ss to think of typical individual users, rather than groups of users.

> age : 25+
> sex: male
> job: executive
> income level: €70,000+
> other products: Hugo Boss suits, Rolex watches, diving holidays in the Seychelles

◎ Start the pair work. Circulate, monitor and assist if necessary. Note down language points for praise and correction afterwards.

◎ Praise strong language points and work on half a dozen points that need improving, getting Ss to say the correct forms.

◎ With the whole class, ask for some of the products and typical users that the pairs came up with.

(C)

◎ This may be difficult for Ss, as they will be competing with some of the best marketing minds around! Start by asking Ss to think of existing advertising campaigns for these brands (or their competitors), and discuss the pros and cons of them. Encourage them to think of things that would appeal to the typical consumer that they identified. This is quite an in-depth task, so you may choose to focus on just one brand, rather than all four.

◎ Ask Ss what other marketing techniques could be used to increase sales (e.g. special promotions).

Listening: Successful marketing

Ss listen to a managing consultant talking about marketing.

(A) 🎧 7.2

◎ Explain to Ss that they are going to hear an interview with Jonathan Turner, who works for a strategic management consultancy in the UK. Ensure that Ss understand what a management consultancy is.

◎ Ask Ss to read the notes on 'Keys to successful marketing' and ask them to guess what the missing words might be. (Even if they aren't sure, they should be able to work out whether they are nouns, verbs, etc.) You may want to tell Ss that all the gaps are single words, apart from gap 7, which has four missing words.

◎ Play the recording and give Ss a few minutes to try to complete the notes.

◎ Play it again for them to check their answers.

> **1** customer **2** needs **3** behaviours **4** data **5** research **6** sense **7** your company makes money

(B)

◎ Ss work in small groups to discuss the four points. Go through the points to ensure that Ss understand all the vocabulary (e.g. *threat, to face, campaign*). You may want to divide the class into four groups and allocate one point to each group, then have one member of each group make a brief presentation of their discussion to the rest of the class.

◎ Ask Ss which of the four points they think Jonathan Turner is likely to mention next. (This is really an exercise in identifying which point Ss think is most important, as there are no clues given in the recording.)

(C) 🎧 7.3

◎ Play the recording and ask Ss to identify which of the four points Jonathan mentions. This information is given in the first sentence, so you may wish to just play that part initially.

> good communication skills

◎ Jonathan does two other things in this recording. Play the recording all the way through and ask Ss if they can identify what they are.

> He gives an example of why he thinks communication skills are important, and he summarises his three main points.

◎ Check that Ss have understood by noting the three main points on the board. Then ask Ss if they agree that these are most important factors in successful marketing. You can ask Ss to discuss this in small groups, or hold a whole-class debate.

(D) 🎧 7.4

◎ Ask Ss to read the four questions and make sure they understand them.

◎ Play the recording and give Ss time to note down the answers. You may wish to pause the recording after each answer is given.

◎ Play the recording several times if necessary, especially the last part concerning question 4.

◎ Go through the answers with the class.

> **1** A major bank.
> **2** It groups similar types of people together, based upon their behaviours, their attitudes, where they live, etc.
> **3** They designed a questionnaire, commissioned it, and then analysed the research.
> **4** They found that there were about eight groups of customers that mattered in that particular market place, whereas before, the bank had just been looking at all customers as one single group.

Lesson notes

Reading: Selling dreams

Ss read an article about the film made by Chanel to market their perfume.

Ⓐ

◎ Read the two questions together as a class and ensure Ss understand them, especially vocabulary such as *endorse*. Point out the use of *ads* as a short form of *advertisements*. (You might also want to tell Ss that *BrE* also uses *adverts*.)

◎ Give Ss five or ten minutes to discuss the questions. You may prefer to ask half the pairs to discuss one question, and the rest the other question.

◎ Ask two or three pairs to tell the class what they discussed.

Ⓑ

◎ This exercise is grammatical in function, but introduces Ss to the topic of the article.

◎ Ask Ss to quickly do the matching exercise and check their answers. If necessary, ask Ss which words enabled them to match the questions and answers (e.g. *When* + time phrase, *How much* + price, *Why* + *because*).

1 f	**2** c	**3** e	**4** b	**5** a	**6** d

◎ Ask Ss what Chanel No 5 is (a perfume) and if they have ever bought it or worn it. If they are familiar with it as a brand, ask them what image it has.

Ⓒ

◎ Tell Ss that the facts in the answers of Exercise B were all wrong and that they need to read the article to find the correct answers.

◎ Give them a few minutes to scan the article, then ask them to find the correct information. If necessary, tell Ss that the correct answers are similar to the incorrect ones in structure (e.g. that e) is still an amount of money, f) is still a year, etc.).

◎ Go through the answers with the class.

Sample answers
a) Because every target group is becoming more resistant to the traditional advertising methods.
b) It's a fairytale romance.
c) She is the international marketing director of Chanel fragrances.
d) She says it is a real piece of art.
e) Eighteen million pounds.
f) In 1921.

Ⓓ

◎ Ss work in pairs or small groups to discuss these questions. For question 1, you may want to give a small selection of brands for Ss to choose from, as their answers may depend on what they are promoting. Circulate, monitor and assist if necessary.

◎ Question 2 may work better as a whole-class discussion; you may want to start by trying to define what 'art' is.

◎ Praise strong language points and work on half a dozen points that need improving, getting Ss to say the correct forms.

Language review: Questions

Ss look at how questions are formed in the context of a consumer questionnaire.

◎ Remind Ss about how to form questions with *do*, *does* and *did*. Write the examples on the board:

I like the marketing plan. ➜ *Do you like the marketing plan?*

➜ *Does he/she like the marketing plan?*

◎ Remind them about forming questions with parts of the verb *to be*, by inverting the order of the subject and the verb.

The price is competitive. ➜ *Is the price competitive?*

◎ Remind them about forming questions in the present perfect with *has* or *had* and also by inverting the order of the subject and the auxiliary verb.

They have agreed to the credit terms. ➜ *Have they agreed to the credit terms?*

◎ Point out how you put the question word in front of the verb to form questions with words like *what*, *why*, *where*, *when* and *how*. Explain the steps like this:

The price is going up next year. ➜ *Is the price going up next year?*
➜ *When is the price going up?*

They are planning to launch. ➜ *Are they planning to launch?*
➜ *When are they planning to launch?*

Ⓐ

◎ Ask Ss in pairs to correct the grammatical mistakes and then go through them with the whole class, relating the examples to the above explanations.

1	What does *market niche* mean?
2	How much does it cost?
3	Why don't you sell it?
4	When must it be finished?
5	Did you go to the fair last week?
6	Is your boss coming tomorrow?

Ⓑ

◎ Do the first couple of questions with the whole class as examples, and then get pairs to work on the questions. (Tell your Ss not to ask each other the questions at this stage.)

◎ Circulate, monitor and assist if necessary.

◎ Ask pairs for their answers and clarify any difficulties relating to the structures and vocabulary.

1 Which group do you belong to?

2 How old are you?

3 Which wines do you prefer?

4 How often do you drink wine?

5 How much do you usually spend on a bottle of wine?

6 Do you have a personal wine cellar at home?

7 How many bottles of wine have you selected during the last year?

8 Which wine growing areas do you know?

9 When selecting wine, do you take the various growing areas into account?

10 Which taste do you prefer?

(C)

◎ Get Ss in pairs to ask each other the questions, and note the answers. Circulate, monitor and assist if necessary, especially with the question forms. If pairs are not discussing wine, check the questions they are asking.

◎ With the whole class, clarify points that are causing general difficulty. Get individual Ss to say the correct forms.

(D)

◎ With the whole class, give your Ss an example of a product and the questions they could ask about it, for example:

Flowers
– How often do you buy flowers?
– Do you buy flowers for particular occasions or with no particular reason in mind?
– How much do you spend, on average, when you buy flowers?

◎ Divide the class into groups and get them to work on the questions for their surveys. Circulate, monitor and assist if necessary.

◎ Bring the class to order and work on question forms that are still causing difficulty.

◎ Then get the Ss to form new groups. The members of each group administer the survey to each other. Circulate, monitor and assist if necessary. Note down language points for praise and correction afterwards.

◎ Bring the class to order. Praise strong points and work on half a dozen or so points that still need improvement.

◎ Then ask some individual Ss to talk about a person they spoke to, being careful with the third person. For example: *Agneta buys flowers once a week for her house. She spends up to $10 each time.* etc.

Skills: Telephoning: exchanging information

Ss listen to calls and note down specific information relating to numbers, names, etc.

(A) 🎧 7.5

◎ Get your Ss to listen to the numbers. Point out the use of *double* and *O* (mainly in *BrE*): *two double-five two five two.* Americans would say *two five five two five two.*

◎ Also point out groupings within numbers, with falling intonation at the end of the last group to show that that is the end of the number.

◎ Then get individual Ss to repeat the numbers.

1	2 ✓	3 ✓	4

(B)

◎ Explain what your Ss have to do. Get them to exchange numbers in pairs. Circulate, monitor and assist if necessary, especially with groupings within numbers and falling intonation at the end.

◎ With the whole class, work on any remaining difficulties.

(C)–(D) 🎧 7.6

◎ With the whole class, get Ss to listen to the recording of the alphabet.

◎ Show how the alphabet can be usefully arranged in similar sound groups, like this:

a	h	j	k				
b	c	d	e	g	p	t	v
f	l	m	n	s	x		
i	y						
o							
q	u	w					
r	z						

◎ Point out letters that speakers from your Ss' language background(s) tend to confuse. For example, French speakers confuse *a* and *r*, *e* and *i*, *g* and *j*.

◎ Then get your Ss to dictate addresses to each other in pairs. (If they come from different language backgrounds, and your Ss' level requires something more challenging, get them to use addresses from their own countries – this can be quite difficult.) Circulate, monitor and assist if necessary.

◎ With the whole class, go through common confusions and difficulties.

E 🎧 7.7

◎ Explain the situation and ask your Ss to look at the four questions.

◎ Play the recording once or twice. Explain any difficulties, but don't give the answers to the questions.

◎ Ask for the answers.

---
1 Yes
2 It has increased by two percent
3 Over £1.2 million
4 £30,000

F 🎧 7.8

◎ Explain the situation and ask your Ss to look at the information they will have to complete.

◎ Play the recording once or twice. Explain any difficulties, but don't give the answers to the questions.

◎ Then play the recording again, stopping after each piece of information required by the Ss.

◎ Ask for the answers.

---
1 Young Joo Chan
2 Korean
3 82 2 0735 8879
4 Friday 18th

◎ Work on dates. Ask Ss about dates for the first three days of the month, as they may have a tendency to write 1th, 2th, 3th rather than 1st, 2nd, 3rd. (The same goes for 21st, 22nd and 23rd and 31st.) Point out that it is acceptable to write 1 December, as well as 1st December. Tell them that this way they won't make any mistakes!

G 🎧 7.7, 7.8

◎ Play the recordings once or twice more and ask Ss to tick the expressions that they hear in the Useful language box. You may also want to refer them to the Telephoning section of the Vocabulary file on page 160.

Checking information
Sorry, did you say ...? ✓
Sorry, I didn't catch that. ✓
Could you repeat that, please?
Let me read that back to you.

Asking for information
Could you give me a few details? ✓
What about the new range? ✓
Did she say when she'd like to meet? ✓

Finishing a conversation
OK, that's it.
Thanks very much. That was very helpful.
I must go now.
I think that's everything. ✓

◎ Check the answers with the whole class. Work on the intonation of the expressions by getting individual Ss to repeat them after you.

H

◎ Give Ss the background to the role-play and allocate the roles. Tell them that during the role-play they should use the language from the Useful language box.

◎ Get Ss to prepare their roles. Circulate, monitor and assist if necessary.

◎ When they are ready, start the role-play. Use telephone equipment if available. Otherwise get pairs to sit back to back.

◎ Circulate and monitor. Note language points for praise and correction afterwards, especially in relation to language used whilst telephoning.

◎ Bring the class to order. Praise strong language points you heard, and bring Ss' attention to points that need improving, getting individual Ss to say the correct forms.

Case study

Kristal Water

Ss analyse the reasons for the failure of a new bottled water and propose corrective action.

Stage 1: Background and listening 🎧 7.9

◎ Give your Ss some very general information about the case study: a spring water has been launched but has failed to sell in the quantities that were expected. Tell them that they will have to make decisions about how to relaunch it.

◎ Before they read the background, ask your Ss to look at the information in the graph and the chart, and make statements about it, for example
– *Kristal costs $3 a bottle.*
– *Welbeck is cheaper than Kristal.*
– *Kristal and Fontainbleau are sold in health-food shops and delicatessens, but not in supermarkets or convenience stores.*

◎ Ask your Ss to read the background and information about the launch. Meanwhile, write the headings on the left of the table below on the board. Then elicit information to complete the column on the right.

Made by	US company HFDP
Source	Alaska
Advertised as	Purest water in the world
Targeted at	People who want a healthy lifestyle
Sales	60% below target / forecast
Consumer awareness (teach this term if necessary)	Low

◎ Play the recording, stopping after each consumer and ask your Ss to suggest notes that summarise the views of each consumer, like the ones given below.

Consumer 1	Nothing special. Expensive.
Consumer 2	Not worth extra cost. Fresh taste. Could be healthier but not persuaded.
Consumer 3	Difficult to find.
Consumer 4	Expensive. Hasn't tried it.
Consumer 5	Never heard of it. Asks where to buy it.

Stage 2: Task

◎ Divide the class into small groups. Explain that they should use the questions in the box as an agenda for their meeting.

◎ Circulate, monitor and assist if necessary. Note down language points for praise and correction afterwards, especially ones relating to marketing.

◎ Bring the class to order. Praise strong language points and work on half a dozen points that need improving, getting Ss to say the correct forms.

◎ Get a spokesperson for each group to present the group's ideas to the other groups. Encourage discussion with the whole class. (If the class is very big, this can be two parallel discussions.)

◎ Again, note down language points for praise and correction afterwards, especially ones relating to marketing.

◎ Praise strong language points and work on half a dozen points that need improving, getting Ss to say the correct forms.

◎ Ask one student (or one from each group) to say what the final conclusion was or to summarise the differing views.

---

1 to 1

This case study can be done as a discussion between teacher and student and then as a basis for a presentation by the student. Don't forget to note language points for praise and correction afterwards. Also point out some of the key language you chose to use.

Stage 3: Writing

◎ Make sure that your Ss understand what they have to do: write a sales leaflet for a campaign to relaunch Kristal. Tell them it can be written on the basis of the ideas for the relaunch that they had in their group or, if they prefer, on their own ideas for the relaunch. This can be done for homework.

 Writing file page 134

UNIT 8 | Planning

At a glance

	Classwork – Course Book	Further work
Lesson 1 *Each lesson (excluding case studies) is about 45–60 minutes. This does not include administration and time spent going through homework.*	**<u>Starting up</u>** Ss look at the different factors in planning various things, from a holiday to a career. **Vocabulary: Ways to plan** Ss look at various nouns and the verbs that typically precede them. **Listening: The secret of good planning** A UK government adviser talks about the secret of good planning.	*Practice File* Vocabulary (page 32)
Lesson 2	**Reading: Planning for economic development** How a Russian city is planning to boost its economy. **Language review: Talking about future plans** Ss look at the use of the present continuous and of *going to* for future plans, and of verbs such as *plan, hope, expect, would like* and *want*.	**Text bank** (pages 128 and 129) *Practice File* Language review (page 32) ***Business Grammar and Usage***
Lesson 3	**<u>Skills: Meetings: interrupting and clarifying</u>** Ss listen to a meeting, identify expressions for interrupting and clarifying and use them in a role-play.	**Resource bank** (page 153)
Lesson 4 *Each case study is about 1 to 1½ hours.*	**<u>Case study: The voice of business</u>** After analysing market research, Ss plan the first programme for a new business radio station.	*Practice File* Writing (page 34)

For a fast route through the unit focusing mainly on speaking skills, just use the underlined sections.

For 1-to-1 situations, most parts of the unit lend themselves, with minimal adaptation, to use with individual students. Where this is not the case, alternative procedures are given.

At a glance

Business brief

Planning is about **resource allocation**, the way that individuals and organisations deploy their (by definition) **limited resources** such as **time**, **money** and **expertise**.

In the case of individuals, you could say that there is a worldwide planning industry, with its calendars, diaries, electronic personal organisers and **time management** training. These (often very expensive) courses tend to hand out some fairly obvious advice.

- Make lists of things you have to do. Classify them in terms of urgency and priority.

- Pursue tasks single-mindedly. Do not allow yourself to waste time through distractions and interruptions.

- Delegate. Do not try to do everything yourself.

- Do not try to be a perfectionist in everything. Do each task so that it is 'good enough' for the circumstances.

But all these things are easier said than done.

For complex projects involving many people and tasks, the **Gantt chart** is the tool of choice. This is a diagram that shows the different stages of a project, indicating the tasks that can be done at the same time as others, and those that must wait until other tasks are completed. Originally conceived about 100 years ago, Gantt charts are now produced using computer software. Other computer-based **project management tools** have been developed by particular companies or are available commercially.

Companies also have to plan for events that they do not want, such as disasters. **Contingency planning** is designed to prepare for the worst, with specific plans of action for **disaster recovery**, including handling of the media and protecting, as far as possible, the company's reputation.

Organisational planning in its grandest form is one element of **strategy**, where companies make long-term plans about the future development of their activities. Here, they have to anticipate competitors' activities as well as trends in the general economic and political **environment**. Very large organisations have teams of **scenario planners** trying to predict how this environment may change and how they might prepare for and perhaps influence this change.

Read on

Rita Emmett: *The Procrastinator's Handbook: Mastering the Art of Doing It Now*, Walker, 2000

Iain Maitland: *Managing Your Time*, Chartered Institute of Personnel and Development, 1999

James Lewis: *Project Planning, Scheduling and Control*, McGraw Hill, 2000

Lesson notes

Warmer

- Write the word *planning* in big letters on the board.
- Ask Ss for words that they think of when they see the word. They will hopefully come up with things like *plan*, *proposal*, *forecast*, *intention*, *objective*, *goal*, *aim*. If they have trouble coming up with words, put hints on the board, for example for *plan*, you could write *pl _ _* , for *proposal*, write *propos _ _* . Give definitions of the words you are looking for, for example 'This is what you call something you think will happen, like a particular level of sales.' Answer: *forecast*.
- Write these words on the board and explain any unfamiliar ones.

Overview

- Ask Ss to look at the Overview section on page 70. Tell them a little about the things you will be doing, using the table on page 68 of this book as a guide. Tell them which sections you will be covering in this lesson and which in later lessons.

Quotation

- Write the quotation on the board and ask Ss to discuss it briefly in pairs.
- With the whole class, ask pairs what they understand by the quote. (The last part can be read in several ways: it can mean that you will be pleasantly surprised by the effectiveness of expecting the best and planning for the worst; or it can mean that preparing to be surprised (i.e. expect the unexpected) is the third thing Denis Waitley advises.)
- The photo shows a Formula 1 team working on a car during a race. Ask Ss why they think planning is important in this situation.

Starting up

Ss look at the different factors in planning various things, from a holiday to a career.

- To make the activity concrete, get Ss in pairs to make a complete list of stages for one of the four 'events', as in the example below. Allocate an event to each pair.

> **Holiday**
> Consult those going about the destination and dates.
> Phone or go to travel agent to obtain brochures.
> Look at prices and special offers.
> Check availability.
> etc.

- Circulate, monitor and assist if necessary.
- With the whole class, ask the pairs for their findings and compare different approaches to the same 'event' by different pairs.

- Do this as a quick-fire activity with the whole class. Compare the approaches of different people.

- Get your Ss in pairs to discuss the statements. Circulate, monitor and assist if necessary.
- With the whole class, compare the pairs' findings.

Vocabulary: Ways to plan

Ss look at various nouns and the verbs that typically precede them (operating verbs).

Ⓐ–Ⓑ

◎ Ask your Ss to match the verbs and nouns in pairs, using a bilingual or monolingual dictionary. Circulate, monitor and assist if necessary.
◎ With the whole class, ask for the matchings.

Exercise A
1 estimate costs
2 forecast sales
3 do research
4 collect information
5 consider options

Exercise B
The most likely combinations are:
1 write a schedule, a plan, a report
2 rearrange a deadline, a meeting
3 meet a deadline
4 arrange a deadline, a schedule, a meeting
5 prepare a schedule, a budget, a plan, a report
6 keep within a deadline, a schedule, a budget
7 implement a schedule, a budget, a plan, a report

Ⓒ

◎ Go through the nouns from Exercises A and B and check that the Ss understand and can pronounce them all.
◎ Tell Ss the subject of the text in Exercise C and ask them to complete it in pairs with nouns from Exercises A and B. Circulate, monitor and assist if necessary.

1 meeting
2 budget
3 information
4 options
5 research
6 report
7 costs
8 budget
9 schedule
10 deadline
11 sales

Ⓓ 🎧 8.1

◎ Play the recording and get Ss to check their answers as they listen.
◎ Check answers with the whole class and clarify any difficulties.

Ⓔ

◎ Tell Ss they have to plan a particular type of event. Divide the class into pairs and allocate a particular task to each pair.
◎ Circulate, monitor and assist if necessary, for example with vocabulary relating to their event.
◎ With the whole class, ask some of the pairs to give details of their plans. Try to persuade them to use some of the word combinations from this section in describing their plans.

Lesson notes

Listening: The secret of good planning

Teresa Graham OBE is an adviser to many businesses and to the UK government. Ss listen to her talking about what is important when planning and why it is important to revise plans regularly.

Ⓐ 🎧 8.2

- Ask Ss to read the rubric and ask if they know what 'OBE' stands for (Order of the British Empire; it is an honour given to people in the UK for services to the country).

- Ask Ss to read the five notes on 'Keys to good planning' and to guess what the missing words might be. If they struggle with this, ask them to identify what parts of speech are missing (e.g. 1 noun phrase; 2 verb phrase; etc.).

- Play the recording several times for Ss to complete the notes. Remind them that each gap may have up to three words.

- Go through the answers, playing the recording again if necessary and clarifying any difficulties.

> **Sample answers**
> **1** your business goal **2** Choose the structure
> **3** all the activities **4** talking to real **5** refine your plan

Ⓑ

- Write the expression *to reinvent the wheel* on the board and ask Ss what they think it means. (To waste time trying to solve a problem that has already been solved in a simple, effective way.) If necessary, help them by asking whether they think the wheel is a simple invention, or a complex one that can be improved on.

- Ask Ss if they have a similar expression in their language(s).

Ⓒ 🎧 8.3

- Tell Ss to read the two questions. Go through the vocabulary to explain any difficult terms (e.g. *template, funder, equity partner, leasing*) and ask Ss to predict what they think the answers will be.

- Play the recording. You may want to play it twice, and ask Ss to focus on one question each time.

- Go through the answers with the class and replay the recording, pausing after each answer.

> **1** a, c, d   **2** a, d, f

Ⓓ 🎧 8.4

- Explain that in the third part of the interview, Teresa gives an example of good planning.

- Ask Ss to read the five statements and ensure they understand them. You may want to explain that *SME* stands for *small or medium enterprise* and that Cadbury's is a major UK chocolate manufacturer.

- Play the recording and give Ss a few minutes to note their answers.

- Go through the answers, playing the recording again if necessary to focus on the correct information.

> **1** F   **2** T   **3** F   **4** F   **5** T

Ⓔ

- Ask Ss to work in pairs to discuss things that they planned well and badly. Ideally these should be in a business context, but if your Ss don't have much business experience, they can describe events from their lives.

- Remind them that the events don't have to be major ones – they could be a presentation or a family party.

- Invite one or two Ss to describe their partner's experiences.

- If appropriate, you could invite the rest of the class to give advice on how things could have been done better (although this would require a certain amount of tact!).

- Give feedback on good use of language and go over any errors.

Reading: Planning for economic development

How a Russian city is planning to improve its economy.

A

- These are fairly 'heavy' questions, so you may prefer to ask Ss to look at them in advance for homework, to give them a chance to do some research on the topic.
- Ask Ss to contribute facts and make a list on the board.
- Then have them work in pairs to discuss question 2, then choose two or three pairs to feed back to the class.
- Ensure they keep their lists of threat/opportunities for comparison in Exercise B.

B

- Ask Ss if they have heard of Nizhny Novgorod and if they know where it is (in western Russia, about an hour's flight to the east of Moscow).
- Give them five minutes to scan the article and find out whether any of their ideas from Exercise A are mentioned.

C

- Ask Ss to read the seven statements and explain any vocabulary they do not understand (e.g. *bureaucracy, assets*).
- Give Ss time to read the article again in more detail and to note whether the statements are true or false.
- Go over the answers, explaining any difficulties.

> **1** F **2** T **3** T **4** T **5** F **6** T **7** T

D

- Tell Ss to complete the sentences with phrases from the article. Each gap needs between two and four words.
- Go through the answers with the class.

> **1** intend to use **2** 're/are hoping to create **3** is planning to invest **4** will focus

- This exercise leads into the Language review, so you may want to ask Ss to note the expressions used to talk about planning for the future. You can also point out the different structures used with each verb (*intend to* + infinitive, *hope to* + infinitive, *plan to* + infinitive, *focus on* + –*ing* form) and the use of the present continuous.

E

- This discussion requires Ss to have some knowledge of their city's plans for the future, so it may be necessary to ask them to do some research in advance. They can, of course, choose any city for this; the point of the discussion is to draw a comparison with Nizhny Novgorod.
- Circulate, monitor and assist as they discuss, encouraging them to use phrases for describing planning and the language of comparison.
- Praise strong use of language and pick out two or three weak points for further practice.

Language review: Talking about future plans

The use of the present continuous and of *going to* for future plans, and of verbs such as *plan, hope, expect, would like* and *want*.

◎ Go through the examples and the explanations, dealing with any difficulties. Point out that *going to* and the present continuous are often interchangeable in talking about the future.

Ⓐ

◎ Go through the text with the whole class, getting Ss to underline the plans mentioned by the speaker.

'Well, I think you all know by now that <u>we're hoping to expand in China</u> and <u>we are going to move our headquarters from Hong Kong to Shanghai</u>. <u>We're planning to manage an executive complex in Dalian</u> and <u>we're also hoping to open a 240-room hotel next year in Zhongshan</u>. <u>We're expecting to make a profit within 5 years</u> although <u>we'd like to break even a bit earlier if possible</u>. Within 10 years <u>we want to become the major international hotel group in South-east Asia</u>.'

◎ Point out the contraction of *we would* if necessary.

Ⓑ–Ⓒ

◎ Do these exercises as quick-fire activities with the whole class. In Exercise C, get Ss to read through the whole text so as to avoid jumping to conclusions.

Exercise B
1 c 2 a 3 b

Exercise C
1 hoping
2 expecting
3 planning

Ⓓ

◎ With one student, have some of the exchanges suggested at the beginning of the exercise, to give other Ss the idea.

◎ Then get your Ss to do the exercise in pairs. Circulate, monitor and assist if necessary. Note language points for praise and correction afterwards, especially in relation to the verbs in this section.

◎ Bring the class to order. Praise some of the good uses of the verbs that you heard and work on others that require it.

◎ Then get one or two pairs to give examples of their exchanges.

Skills: Meetings: interrupting and clarifying

Ss listen to a meeting, identify expressions for interrupting and clarifying and use them in a role-play.

Ⓐ 🎧 8.5

◎ Tell Ss the subject of what they are about to hear: a planning meeting at a company that is about to move. Get them to look at the different points they will hear discussed.

◎ Play the recording once or twice and elicit the answers to the questions.

a 6 b 1 c 5 d 4 e 2 f 3

Ⓑ

◎ Ask your Ss, in pairs, to read the utterances aloud and class them as interrupting or clarifying. Circulate, monitor and assist if necessary.

1 clarifying
2 interrupting
3 clarifying
4 interrupting
5 clarifying

Ⓒ

◎ Get your Ss to look at the Useful language box. Ask them to repeat the expressions, concentrating on good intonation.

◎ Then explain the situation to your Ss and divide the class into groups of three or four. Get each group to quickly appoint a chair, who uses the six points as an agenda.

◎ Circulate, monitor and assist if necessary. Note language points for praise and correction afterwards, especially in relation to the language of interrupting, dealing with interruptions and clarifying from the Useful language box.

◎ Bring the class to order. Praise some of the good language that you heard and work on other points that require it.

◎ Ask one or two groups for an outline of the party they have planned.

Case study

The voice of business

After analysing market research, Ss plan the first programme for a new business radio station.

Stage 1: Background and listening 🎧 8.6

◎ Get Ss to read the background, explain any difficulties, and then check their understanding by getting one or two Ss to summarise it as a series of key points.

> Business programme on radio planned by EBA
> To be broadcast in Europe
> Language: English
> Duration: 30 minutes
> Audience: working people
> Frequency: three times a week

◎ Ask your Ss to analyse the results of the questionnaire in pairs. Suggest that they find what people most want to hear in the programme by adding the figures for 'Very interesting' and 'Quite interesting'. Circulate, monitor and assist if necessary.

◎ With the whole class, find what listeners most want to hear and least want to hear.

> They most want to hear:
> – business update (91% said 'Very interesting' or 'Quite interesting')
> – job vacancies (88%)
> – traffic and weather reports (87%)
>
> They least want to hear:
> – the future of business (57% said 'Not interesting')
> – profiles of business people (43%)
> – book reviews (43%)

◎ With the whole class, get individual Ss to summarise in a few words each of the four most common opinions expressed by the focus groups, for example:

> 1 up-to-date news
> 2 experienced presenter
> 3 investment advice
> 4 weather and traffic reports

◎ Then play the recording once or twice, stopping after each speaker, and get individual Ss to continue the list of things that people want to hear on the programme.

> 5 interesting report on an important business topic
> 6 two presenters – one man, one woman
> 7 something light and funny
> 8 lively phone-in
> 9 interviews with important people

◎ Get a student to recap these key points, write them on the board and keep them there while Ss are doing the task.

Stage 2: Task

◎ Explain the task and divide the class into groups of three or four. Each group should quickly appoint a chair, who should use points 1 to 3 and the list of key questions as an agenda.

◎ Tell the groups to start their discussions. Then circulate and monitor. Note language points for praise and correction afterwards, especially in relation to the language of planning.

◎ When the groups have come to their conclusions, bring the class to order.

◎ Praise some of the good language that you heard and work on half a dozen other points that require it.

◎ Then ask different groups to present their plans for the first programme.

> **1 to 1**
> This case study can be done as a discussion between teacher and student and then as a basis for a presentation by the student. Don't forget to note language points for praise and correction afterwards. Also point out some of the key language you chose to use.

Stage 3: Writing

◎ Tell your Ss about the writing task, pointing out especially the form it should take: a letter to a famous business person asking for an interview. This can be done as homework.

 Writing file page 130

9 Managing people

At a glance

	Classwork – Course Book	Further work
Lesson 1 *Each lesson (excluding case studies) is about 45–60 minutes. This does not include administration and time spent going through homework.*	**Starting up** Ss discuss the qualities and skills needed by good managers. **Listening: Good managers** A professor talks about what it takes to be a good manager. **Vocabulary: Verbs and prepositions** Ss work on the prepositions that follow certain verbs.	*Practice File* Vocabulary (page 36)
Lesson 2	**Reading: Young managers** Ss read an article giving advice to young managers on getting ahead. **Language review: Reported speech** Ss look at the structures used when reporting what other people have said.	*Text bank* (pages 130 and 131) *Practice File* Language review (page 37) ***Business Grammar and Usage***
Lesson 3	**Skills: Socialising and entertaining** Ss look at punctuality, dress, gifts, small talk, invitations and other cross-cultural issues when people from different cultures meet.	*Resource bank* (page 154)
Lesson 4 *Each case study is about 1 to 1¹/₂ hours.*	**Case study: The way we do things** Ss analyse the difficulties following a merger between two companies whose sales teams have different ways of working, and propose solutions.	*Practice File* Writing (page 38)

For a fast route through the unit focusing mainly on speaking skills, just use the underlined sections.

For 1-to-1 situations, most parts of the unit lend themselves, with minimal adaptation, to use with individual students. Where this is not the case, alternative procedures are given.

Business brief

In the 1960s, Douglas McGregor, one of the key thinkers in this area, formulated the now-famous **Theory X** and **Theory Y**. Theory X is the idea that people instinctively dislike work and will do anything to avoid it. Theory Y is the more enlightened view that everybody has the potential to find satisfaction in work. (Others have suggested Theory W (for 'whiplash'), the idea that most work since the beginning of human society has been done under conditions of total coercion, i.e. slavery.)

In any case, despite so much evidence to the contrary, many managers still subscribe to Theory X, believing, for example, that their **subordinates** need constant **supervision** if they are to work effectively, or that decisions must be **imposed** from above without **consultation**. This, of course, makes for **authoritarian** managers.

Different cultures have different ways of managing people. Some cultures are well known for the consultative nature of decision-making – all members of the department or work group are asked to contribute to this process. This is management by **consensus**. Many western companies have tried to imitate what they see as more **consensual** Asian ways of doing things. Some commentators say that women will become more effective managers than men because they have the power to build consensus and common goals in a way that traditional male managers cannot.

A recent trend has been to encourage employees to use their own **initiative**, to make decisions on their own without asking managers first. This **empowerment** has been part of the trend towards **downsizing**: reducing the number of management layers in companies. After **delayering** in this way, a company may be left with just a top level of senior managers and **front-line** managers and employees with direct contact with the public. Empowerment takes the idea of **delegation** much further than has traditionally been the case. Empowerment and delegation mean new forms of **management control** to ensure that the overall business plan is being followed and to ensure that operations become more profitable under the new organisation, rather than less.

Another trend is **off-site** or **virtual management**, where teams of people linked by e-mail and the Internet work on projects from their own premises. Project managers judge the performance of the team members in terms of what they produce and contribute to projects rather than the amount of time they spend on them.

Read on

Jane Weightman: *Managing People*, Chartered Institute of Personnel and Development, 1999

Peter Honey: *Improving Your People Skills*, Chartered Institute of Personnel and Development, 2001

Warren Bennis: *Douglas McGregor Revisited – The Human Side of Enterprise,* Wiley, 2001

Lesson notes

Warmer

◎ Write the word *managing* on the left of the board. On the right put the word *people*. Add lines underneath *people* and, if you think your Ss need more help, add initial letters as clues.

	people
managing	_____
	_____
	_____

◎ Ask Ss for other things that managers have to manage, apart from people. The board might end up looking like this.

	people
	schedules
managing	resources
	budgets
	conflict

Overview

◎ Ask Ss to look at the Overview section on page 78. Tell them a little about the things you will be doing, using the table on page 76 of this book as a guide. Tell them which sections you will be doing in this lesson and which in later lessons.

Quotation

◎ Write the quotation on the board. Ask Ss to discuss it in pairs and see if they can think of management tasks that do not involve motivating other people.

◎ With the whole class, ask pairs for their opinions.

> Here, they might mention financial management, project management and resource management; you can then discuss how far these involve motivating people.

Starting up

Ss discuss the qualities and skills needed by good managers.

(A)

◎ With the whole class, look through the list of qualities required by managers. Ask Ss in pairs to choose the six most important. Circulate, monitor and assist if necessary.

◎ Ask pairs about their selections. You could get pairs to 'vote' for six qualities and write up the scores on the board. Above all, encourage discussion by getting Ss to say why they have chosen particular qualities.

(B)

◎ Do this exercise as a class discussion. Again, ask *why* these qualities are needed.

> You could suggest patience, language ability, flexibility, sense of humour, curiosity, optimism, tolerance, awareness of your own cultural assumptions and expectations. Explain them if necessary.

Listening: Good managers

A professor at the London Business School talks about what it takes to be a good manager.

(A) 9.1

◎ Ask SS what they think a professor of organisational behaviour might study (how people behave in organisations).

◎ Tell them to read the notes and predict what words might fill the gaps, reminding them that up to three words each time are missing.

◎ Play the recording and allow Ss a minute to complete the notes.

◎ Check their answers, playing the recording again if necessary for clarification.

> **Sample answers**
> **1** motivate everyone   **2** unique and different
> **3** through the eyes   **4** listening to people

(B) 9.2

◎ Tell Ss to read the four statements and remind them that these are summaries, i.e. that they will not hear the exact words in the recording.

◎ Play the recording twice, giving Ss a minute in between to reread the summaries.

◎ Elicit the answer from the class.

> Statement 3

Lesson notes

(C) 🎧 9.3

◎ Ask Ss to read the four statements and clarify any problems with vocabulary (e.g. *superficial*) and pronunciation (e.g. *unique*).

◎ Play the recording, then give Ss a few minutes to note whether they think the statements are true or false.

◎ Go through the answers with the class, playing the recording again for clarification if necessary.

1 F   2 T   3 F   4 T

(D)

◎ Divide the class into pairs or small groups for the discussion. Encourage Ss to think about the points raised by Professor Nicholson, as well as contributing their own ideas.

◎ You may prefer to divide the class into two and allocate each pair/group just one of the questions, then ask a few Ss to present their conclusions to the others.

◎ Circulate, monitor and assist where necessary. Note good uses of language, and also weak points that need further practice, and feed back on these at the end of the discussion.

Vocabulary: Verbs and prepositions

Ss work on the prepositions that follow certain verbs.

(A)–(B)

◎ Get Ss to focus on the subject of this section, prepositions that follow certain verbs, by writing on the board:

respond to employees' concerns promptly

◎ With the whole class, explain any vocabulary difficulties and ask for the matches.

1 c 2 g 3 e 4 a 5 b 6 d 7 f

◎ Then, with the whole class, get Ss to say which the most important qualities are. Encourage discussion.

(C)–(D)

◎ Write up the two example sentences on the board and point out the different prepositions that can follow *report*, depending on its meaning.

◎ Explain to your Ss what they have to do and then ask them to work on the exercises in pairs. Circulate, monitor and assist if necessary.

Exercise C			
	Someone	Something	Both
1 a) report to	✓		
b) report on			✓
2 a) apologise for			✓
b) apologise to	✓		
3 a) talk to	✓		
b) talk about			✓
4 a) agree with	✓		
b) agree on		✓	
5 a) argue about		✓	
b) argue with	✓		

◎ Underline that you say *to agree with someone, to agree on something*. Try to eliminate any tendency for Ss to say *I am agree with you*.

Exercise D
1 with
2 to
3 about
4 for
5 about
6 with
7 to
8 on

◎ Ask for the answers with the whole class. Clarify any problems.

(E)

◎ Write an example or two on the board to show your Ss the sort of thing that you want: questions using these verbs and prepositions. For example:

When you make a mistake, do you apologise for it?

Do you argue with your colleagues a lot?

◎ Get Ss in pairs to write their own questions and to ask them to each other. Circulate, monitor and assist if necessary.

◎ With the whole class, get some of the pairs to ask and answer the questions they wrote.

◎ Deal with any persistent problems in this area, getting Ss to say the correct forms.

Reading: Young managers

Ss read an article giving advice to young managers on getting ahead.

Ⓐ

◎ Divide the class into pairs or small groups for the discussion. If your Ss are from different countries, you may want to ensure they are working in mixed groups to make the most of any contrasts raised in question 1.

◎ Circulate, monitor and assist where necessary.

Ⓑ

◎ Ask Ss to read the first part of the article (down to line 45) and answer the questions.

◎ Go through the answers, clarifying any difficulties.

> 1 Building credibility with key people is a way for young managers of showing everyone that they are capable of doing their job.
>
> 2 Young managers should first recognise their weaknesses, and then look for a mentor to get support and advice.

Ⓒ

◎ Tell Ss to read the second part of the article (the bullet points of advice).

◎ Read the first definition with the class and ask Ss to locate the answer (favouritism) in the text (line 51).

◎ Ask Ss to find words for the remaining definitions.

◎ Go through the answers with the class.

> 1 favouritism   2 a clique   3 a coalition   4 to crack
> 5 arrogance   6 to over-deliver   7 rousing

Ⓓ

◎ Ss work in pairs to decide which three of the seven pieces of advice given in the article are the most important. Circulate, monitor and assist if necessary.

◎ Ask each pair to announce their choices; keep a note on the board so that you can see which piece of advice gets the most votes.

◎ If a pair mentions a piece of advice that no one else has chosen, ask them to justify their choice.

Language review: Reported speech

Ss look at the structures used when reporting what other people have said.

◎ Parts of this are difficult, so take it easy. Go through the explanations and the examples slowly. Write the examples on the board to draw Ss' attention to their features.

Say, tell and ask can in themselves be difficult, but concentrate here on the reported speech aspect.

Point out how the verb in reported speech goes one tense back, except where things are very recent or generally true.

Ⓐ

◎ Do this activity with the whole class. Work on the process of finding the right answer, rather than just asking for the answer and moving on to the next question.

> 1 said
> 2 told
> 3 told
> 4 said
> 5 told
> 6 said

Ⓑ

◎ Ask your Ss to read the dialogue in pairs.

◎ Then divide the class into fours – groups containing Ss A, B, C, and D.

◎ Get Ss A and B in each group to read the dialogue again for the whole class, stopping at the end of each utterance. Then get Ss C and D to put what has just been said into reported speech, like this:

> Student A: I want to motivate our managers more.
> Student C: *Philip said (that) he wanted to motivate their managers more.*
> *OR Philip told Amanda (that) he wanted to motivate their managers more.*
> Student B: Are you delegating the less important decisions?
> Student D: *Amanda asked Philip/him if he was delegating the less important decisions.*
> Student A: I think so. And I'm making more time to listen to their suggestions.
> Student C: *Philip said (that) he thought so. He also said that he was making more time to listen to their suggestions.*
> Student B: That's good. Responding to their ideas is really important.
> Student D: *Amanda said (that) it was good and that responding to their ideas was really important.*
> Student A: Is the department investing enough in training?
> Student C: *Philip asked if the department was investing enough in training.*
> Student B: Yes, it is. This year's budget is bigger than last year's.
> Student D: *Amanda said that it was and that this year's budget was bigger than last year's.*

◎ Get one group of four to do this for the whole class to give other Ss the idea. Then get all the groups of four to do it simultaneously. Circulate, monitor and assist if necessary.

◎ Bring the class to order and go through any difficulties.

© 9.4

◎ Explain the context to your Ss and play the recording once or twice, stopping after each message. Use the example to show Ss what you are after. Clarify any difficulties.

◎ Elicit the answers and write them on the board.

> **2** Jason phoned about the management training course. He said he wanted to confirm his place on the course and he asked who was leading it.
>
> **3** Carol rang about next Friday's meeting. She asked how many people would be at the meeting and what time it would finish.
>
> **4** Maria phoned about the budget. She wanted to know how much you (had) spent on the Tokyo trip. She said she needed to fill in the expenses claim by Friday.

◎ Explain any remaining difficulties.

Skills: Socialising and entertaining

Ss look at punctuality, dress, gifts, small talk, invitations and other cross-cultural issues when people from different cultures meet, and the language needed in these situations.

◎ Talk about the importance of socialising and ask your Ss to do the exercise in pairs. If possible, form pairs with members from different countries, who then explain the situation in their countries to each other.

◎ Circulate, monitor and assist if necessary.

◎ With the whole class, go through the various points, inviting comments and encouraging discussion.

> **1** What counts as 'being on time'? How late do you have to be before you're considered 'late'? Discuss this in relation to different business and social situations, such as meetings and dinner parties. Is the answer the same in all cases?
>
> **2** Again, refer to different situations. Teach the expression smart–casual: dressing smartly but in casual clothes, perhaps with 'designer' names. Does the concept of smart–casual exist in your Ss' countries? Do dress-down Fridays exist, where companies allow their employees to dress less formally than on other days? (A phenomenon of the dot-com boom era, this trend may be disappearing – ask your Ss about this if you think they will be aware of it.)
>
> **3** You could also talk about how to introduce yourself. Do you say (the equivalent of) John Smith – Smith, John Smith or just Smith or just John? Does this vary depending on the degree of conservatism of the organisation?
>
> **4** When do you give gifts? What should you give? Does the recipient unwrap them immediately or wait till later? Teach the expression That's very kind of you.
>
> **5** How often do people shake hands? Every day on meeting, as in France, or less often? When is kissing or hugging appropriate, if at all? Should Westerners in Asia bow (practise the pronunciation of this word) or just use the universal gesture of shaking hands?

B–© 9.5

◎ Ask Ss to look at the two questions in Exercise B and play the recording. Explain any difficulties, but don't give the answers to the questions.

◎ Elicit the answers to Exercise B.

> **Exercise B**
> 1 Alexandra invites Rachel to have dinner at a restaurant with colleagues.
> 2 Rachel refuses politely.

◎ Ask your Ss to look at the exchanges in Exercise C. Play the recording again once or twice and get Ss to complete the exchanges.

> **Exercise C**
> 1 kind of you
> 2 if you
> 3 mind
> 4 another time

◎ Ask your Ss to read this part of the conversation in pairs. Point out the usefulness of the expressions used.

D 9.6

◎ Explain the situation and play the recording once or twice. Help with any difficulties, but don't give the answers to the exercise.

◎ Elicit the questions to which the answers are given.

> **1** What do people here like doing in their spare time?
> **2** What about you, Sven, what do you usually do after work? In the evenings?
> **3** How about you, Marta?

E 9.7

◎ Play the recording once or twice. It doesn't matter if Ss don't understand every word. The idea is for them to get the gist in order to answer the question.

> Sven showed Marta round Stockholm and took her for a meal.

F 9.7

◎ Play the recording again once or twice and get Ss to listen for the order of the utterances.

> **a** 4 **b** 6 **c** 5 **d** 3 **e** 1 **f** 2

◎ Clarify any difficulties.

G

◎ Explain the first situation. Refer Ss to the Useful language box and recap all the expressions there.

◎ Get your Ss to enact the role-play in pairs. Circulate and monitor.

◎ Clarify any difficulties. Then get one or two confident pairs to do their role-plays for the whole class.

◎ Give the background to the second situation and go

through the different things Ss have to find out. Remind them that one of the aims of the role-play is to use as many of the expressions from the Useful language box as possible.

- Then get Ss to do the role-play in pairs. Circulate and monitor. Note down language points for praise and correction afterwards, especially in relation to language used whilst socialising and entertaining.

- Bring the class to order. Praise strong language points and work on half a dozen points that need improving, getting Ss to say the correct forms.

- Get one of the pairs to do their role-play again for the whole class.

Case study

The way we do things

Ss analyse the difficulties following a merger between two companies whose sales teams have different ways of working, and propose solutions.

Stage 1: Background

- Point out to Ss that the title of the case study is a reference to one standard definition of culture: 'The way we do things round here': the 'here' in question can be a country, a region, a company or other organisation, or a social class, and the 'way we do things' refers to accepted values and ways of behaving. As your Ss will see, the case study is about two very different ways of doing things.

- Go through the background information and elicit key points from Ss.

- MPM formed by merger of two different companies, Muller and Peterson.
- The sales team is led by Muller's Sales Manager. Peterson's Sales Manager is his deputy.
- One year later – the two sales teams have very different aims and methods.

- Split the class into two halves. Ask one half to look at the information about Muller's sales reps and the other half, at that about Peterson's reps. Tell them they have to reduce these ideas to some key points in note form. Circulate and monitor to check they have got the idea.

Meanwhile, write up a table on the board with the headings on the left. Then, from each group, elicit key points to complete the table along the lines shown below.

	Muller	Peterson
General approach	Mainly interested in money ➜ maximise profit	Co-operative, work together ➜ profitability by keeping customers happy
Delivery	Promise early, unrealistic dates ➜ customers complain	Do not promise early delivery – company should always stick to dates
Sales reports and confirmation of orders	Not good at writing – late, incomplete reports and no written confirmation of orders	Good at writing – detailed reports, on time and written confirmation of orders
Payment system	Happy with low basic salary, high commissions	Would like higher basic salary and bonus for team
Information about customers	Don't share it – very competitive	Share it
Sales techniques	Aggressive, with expensive gifts ➜ build loyalty	Based on trust ➜ build loyalty. No pressure. Inexpensive gifts only

Stage 2: Task

◎ Explain the purpose of the first meeting – to prepare for the main meeting that will come later, in which they discuss ideas to get the sales reps to work together more effectively. In the first meeting, four different types of people meet separately. Divide the class into groups of three or four and allocate roles A, B, C and D. If the class is very large, you could have two group As, two group Bs, etc.

◎ Get each group to read the appropriate role. Circulate and monitor to check they are looking at the correct page. Make sure each group has a chair, who will use the six points on the agenda to structure the meeting. The aim is to establish what new norms and rules should be decided for the merged company in the next meeting.

◎ When the discussions are under way, circulate and monitor. Note down language points for praise and correction afterwards.

◎ When the groups have come to some sort of conclusion, bring the class to order.

◎ Praise strong language points and work on half a dozen points that need improving, getting Ss to say the correct forms.

◎ Don't ask what conclusions each group came to. These will emerge in the next meeting.

◎ Then form new groups, each with at least one representative from each group A above. The chair in each group is the Sales Manager (i.e. someone from group A in the previous activity). The chair again uses the six points on the agenda as the basis for the meeting. The aim is to establish new norms and rules for the merged company, hopefully a compromise between the norms and rules of Muller and those of Peterson.

◎ When the discussions are under way, circulate and monitor. Note down language points for praise and correction afterwards.

◎ When the groups have come to some sort of conclusion, bring the class to order.

◎ Praise strong language points and work on half a dozen points that need improving, getting Ss to say the correct forms.

◎ Ask what conclusions the different groups came to.

---

1 to 1

This case study can be done as a discussion between teacher and student and then as a basis for a presentation by the student. Don't forget to note language points for praise and correction afterwards. Also point out some of the key language you chose to use.

Stage 3: Writing

◎ Tell your Ss that they have to write the Recommendations section of a report to the CEO of MPM, as if they were the company's Sales Manager, summarising the actions decided on in the meeting. Tell them to use the beginning of the report shown in the Course Book to start them off. This can be done as homework.

 Writing file page 135

Revision

This unit revises and reinforces some of the key language points from Units 7–9, and links with those units are clearly shown. Point out these links to your Ss – in some cases, they will need information from the original activities to do the exercises here.

These exercises can be done in class individually or collaboratively, or for homework.

For more speaking practice, see the Resource bank section of this book beginning on page 141.

7 Marketing

Vocabulary (A) – (B)

- ◎ These exercises revise the compounds from page 63.
- ◎ Ss should try to complete the missing words in each group without looking back at the unit if possible.
- ◎ Check they have the answers correct before they go on to complete the sentences in Exercise B.

> **Exercise A**
> **1** product   **2** market   **3** advertising   **4** consumer   **5** sales
> **Exercise B**
> **1** advertising budget   **2** product range   **3** sales targets   **4** consumer goods
> **5** market segment

Questions

- ◎ Ask Ss to review the ways of forming questions on page 66.
- ◎ Ss unjumble the questions, then use them to complete a dialogue. Check that their questions are correct before they proceed to the dialogue completion.

> **a)** Has our market share increased?
> **b)** What time does it start?
> **c)** Have you finished your sales report?
> **d)** Isn't that fantastic?
> **e)** What about our new range of furniture?
> **f)** What are they like?
> **g)** Could you tell Marco?
> **h)** How are things going?
> **i)** Does Susan know the good news?
>
> **1** h   **2** c   **3** f   **4** a   **5** d   **6** i   **7** b   **8** g   **9** e

8 Planning

Vocabulary

- ◎ This tests the collocations from page 71.
- ◎ Ensure Ss understand that in each case, two of the verbs *do* combine with the underlined noun; they have to cross out the one that does not.

> The following verbs should be crossed out.
> **1** estimate   **2** implement   **3** collect   **4** forecast   **5** done

Reading

- ◎ This exercise uses the context of good planning (page 72) to practise identifying markers to sequence sentences.
- ◎ Ask Ss to order the sentences, then go through the correct answer.

> c, a, e, b, d

◎ Ask Ss to identify the clues that enabled them to order the sentences: time adverbials (*then, once*), sequence adjectives (*next*), pronouns requiring antecedents (*them, that*).

(B)

◎ This revises language for future planning (page 74), but also, once complete, provides a model letter of invitation.

◎ Tell Ss to do the matching exercise, then check answers, clarifying any difficulties. Ensure all Ss have the correct answers before doing the Writing activity that follows.

> 1 i 2 f 3 h 4 g 5 a 6 d 7 e 8 c 9 b

Writing

◎ This follows directly on from Exercise B in Reading above and could be used for homework. Ss would probably find it helpful to write out the original letter of invitation in full.

9 Managing people

Vocabulary

◎ This tests the verb/preposition combinations from page 80.

◎ Ss need to use the prepositions following each gap, as well as the contextual meaning, to decide which verb to use.

> 1 listen 2 communicate 3 respond 4 deal 5 believe 6 delegate 7 invest

Reported speech

(A)–(B)

◎ Both these exercises revise the Language review topic from page 82.

◎ Exercise A focuses on the use of *say* and *tell* in the past tense. Ss should reread point 1 from the box on page 82 if necessary.

> **Exercise A**
> 1 told 2 said 3 told 4 said; told 5 told; said 6 said; told

◎ Exercise B is trickier, as it requires Ss to use the correct reporting verb and make the necessary transformations. You may need to remind Ss that they have to watch out for changes to pronouns and time phrases as well as verb tenses.

> **Exercise B**
> **Sample answers**
> Rob told Sue (that) he had a problem at work.
> Sue asked Rob if he had missed another deadline.
> Rob said (that) the problem was not his work, but the new manager.
> Sue asked (Rob) what was wrong with her.
> Rob said (that) she couldn't communicate clearly and (that) she didn't listen to people's concerns.
> Sue asked (Rob) what he was concerned about.
> Rob said (that) he was not worried about anything personally.
> Sue asked (Rob) if he had tried talking to her.
> Rob said he had not. She was only starting work next / the following Monday.

Reading

◎ This article summarising the role of a manager requires Ss to use contextual clues to put the missing phrases in the correct places.

> 1 c 2 e 3 b 4 d 5 f 6 a

Conflict

At a glance

	Classwork – Course Book	Further work
Lesson 1 *Each lesson (excluding case studies) is about 45–60 minutes. This does not include administration and time spent going through homework.*	**Starting up** Ss do a quiz to find out how good they are at dealing with conflict. **Listening: Handling conflicts** An expert in handling business conflict talks about common causes of conflict in organisations. Ss then talk about their own experiences in this area.	
Lesson 2	**Reading: Conflict management** Ss read two parts of an article on conflict management, then compare what they have read. **Vocabulary: Word building** Ss look at related nouns and adjectives and their opposites.	**Text bank** (pages 132 and 133) *Practice File* Vocabulary (page 40)
Lesson 3	**Language review: Conditionals** Ss look at the first and second conditional, and their use in negotiating. **Skills: Negotiating: dealing with conflict** Ss look at ways of defusing conflict and the language to use in this situation.	*Practice File* Language review (page 41) *Business Grammar and Usage* **Resource bank** (page 155)
Lesson 4 *Each case study is about 1 to 1½ hours.*	**Case study: European Campers** Ss analyse a conflict between a manager and a salesman and propose a solution.	*Practice File* Writing (page 42)

For a fast route through the unit focusing mainly on speaking skills, just use the underlined sections.

For 1-to-1 situations, most parts of the unit lend themselves, with minimal adaptation, to use with individual students. Where this is not the case, alternative procedures are given.

Business brief

Conflict may well be productive in some cases. In any business situation, there are often a number of different ideas about the way to proceed. Usually only one way can be chosen, so conflict is inevitable. Ideally, airing the different ideas in discussion will lead to the best one being chosen. But the process may become political, with an idea being defended by the person or group putting it forward after it has become apparent that it is not the best way to go, and unwillingness to 'lose face' by abandoning a long-cherished idea. There may be conflict between different levels in an organisation's **hierarchy** or between different departments, with hostility to ideas from elsewhere – the **not-invented-here syndrome**.

Examples of unproductive conflict include disputes between colleagues or between managers and subordinates that go beyond ideas and become personal. Companies can spend a lot of time and energy resolving these disputes. In countries with high levels of **employee protection**, dismissing troublesome employees can lead to a long process of consultation with the authorities and even litigation, for example where an employee sues their company for **unfair dismissal**. Defending an action like this is of course costly and a distraction from a company's normal business.

Labour–management conflict in the form of tactics such as **strikes** and **go-slows** can also be very expensive and time-consuming. The goodwill of a company's customers, built up over years, can be lost very quickly when they are hurt by such a dispute. But there are sometimes cases where the public sympathise with the employees and don't mind the disruption. Both sides may put a lot of effort into presenting their case and gaining public sympathy with the use of advertising, public-relations firms, and so on. Many countries have legislation with compulsory **cooling-off periods** before strikes can begin, official procedures for **arbitration** between the two sides, and so on.

In dealings between companies, **supplier–customer relationships** can degenerate into conflict. Conflict seems to be endemic in some industries, for example construction, where contractors are often in dispute about whether the work has been performed properly or whose responsibility a particular problem is. This can lead to protracted legal proceedings.

More and more companies in the US are specifying in contracts that any disputes should be settled using **alternative dispute resolution (ADR)**, avoiding expensive legal wrangling. Specialised organisations have been set up to facilitate this.

Read on

Harvard Business Review on Negotiation and Conflict Resolution, Harvard Business School Press, 2000

Daniel Dana: *Conflict Resolution*, McGraw Hill, 2001

John Macdonald: *Resolving Conflict*, Hodder, 2000

Lesson notes

Warmer

- Write the word *conflict* in big letters on the board.
- Ask Ss for the things that they think of when they see the word. They will probably come up with things like *disagree, disagreement, dispute, argue, argument, war*, etc.

Overview

- Ask Ss to look at the Overview section on page 90. Tell them a little about the things you will be doing, using the table on page 86 of this book as a guide. Tell them which sections you will be doing in this lesson and which in later lessons.

Quotation

- Write the quotation on the board and ask Ss to discuss it briefly in pairs.
- With the whole class, ask pairs what they think it means (that people do not learn to be good at their jobs if things always go well; a certain amount of difficulty or conflict can be a positive thing).
- Ask Ss if they agree with this view, and whether it applies to all areas of life.
- Point out the spelling of *skilful*.

Starting up

Ss do a quiz to find out how good they are at dealing with conflict.

- Tell your Ss to do the quiz in pairs. Each member of the pair asks the other member the questions. Both then work out their individual scores. Circulate and monitor to check they have understood the procedure and to help with any vocabulary or pronunciation problems, such as the pronunciation of *criticise*.
- Bring the class to order and go round the pairs asking them to talk about each person's answer for a particular question, for example, 'I'm in a meeting and people cannot agree. I suggest a ten-minute break. Paula proposes something new.' Then ask another pair about the next question and so on.
- Then ask the whole class to say with a show of hands which score they got and which profile they have. Discuss the results tactfully.

Listening: Handling conflicts

An expert in handling business conflict talks about common causes of conflict in organisations.

(A)

- Divide the class into pairs or small groups and give them five minutes to come up with possible causes of conflict. If they have experienced such conflict, ask them to analyse what the root cause was.
- Bring the class to order and make a list on the board.

(B) 10.1

- Tell Ss they are going to listen to someone who specialises in helping companies resolve conflicts.
- Play the recording, then, as a whole class, go through the list you made on the board in Exercise A and tick the causes that Eileen mentioned. As the causes you listed may not be expressed in the same way, you may need to make a judgement about whether they are the same or not.
- Play the recording again and add any other causes that Eileen mentioned to the list.

> The causes that Eileen mentions are: unrealistic expectations about what a contract can deliver; lack of flexibility; lack of communication; differences of opinion about how an arrangement is meant to work; changes in personnel or management structures; a machine component failing; a specification not being thought through.

(C) 10.1

- Ask Ss to read the five causes and see if they can guess what the missing words are.
- Play the recording for them to confirm their guesses/complete the gaps.
- Check their answers and address any difficulties.

> **1** unrealistic   **2** flexibility   **3** communicating   **4** personnel   **5** management

- The missing words are all multisyllabic – do a quick test by asking Ss which syllable is stressed in each one (*unrealistic, flexibility, communicating, personnel, management*).

(D) 10.2

- Check that Ss understand what a *mediator* is, and how to pronounce it, with the stress on the first syllable.
- Play the recording and ask Ss if they identified any of the key elements Eileen lists. Write any correct answers on the board.
- Play the recording until Ss have identified all three elements.

- creating focus (i.e. ensuring that there is a full and frank discussion with the parties in dispute about the issues as they understand them)
- creating the right atmosphere for difficult conversations to take place (in other words, creating an environment for the parties to discuss difficult issues thoroughly)
- making sure that the decision-makers are willing to get involved in the mediation process

E

- To give your Ss the idea, tell them (without naming names, of course) about conflicts you were involved in and how you tried to deal with them.
- Then ask your Ss tactfully about conflicts they were involved in and how they dealt with them. Get them to use correctly some of the vocabulary from this section.

Reading: Conflict management

Ss read two parts of an article on conflict management, then compare what they have read.

A

- This may be best done as a class discussion. Encourage Ss to make a list on the board of qualities, encouraging them to explain why they think a mediator needs each one. They will probably start with things such as *patience*, but encourage them to think of less obvious qualities, such as *determination* and *detachment*.
- Ask Ss how they think disagreement can be a positive thing. If they have trouble thinking about the abstract concept, encourage them to think of a specific example of disagreement, then discuss how it might have enabled the participants to see different aspects of the subject that they had not considered before.
- This can then be applied to the context of a business meeting.
- Encourage Ss to refer to the Vocabulary file on page 158 and to use the expressions listed there.

B

- Divide the class into pairs and nominate each pair as either A or B.
- Ask the pairs to look at the relevant article and do the related vocabulary matching task.
- Quickly check answers before asking pairs to read their article.

Article A: 1 d **2** c **3** a **4** b
Article B: 1 c **2** d **3** b **4** a

- Each article contains five pieces of advice. Ask the pairs to rank them from most useful (1) to least useful (5). Encourage Ss to list the advice in shortened note form for easy reference.

C

- Rearrange the class to work in pairs of A+B. Ss then explain their top two tips to their new partner, as agreed in Exercise B. Encourage them to use their own words as far as possible.
- They then describe any advice that they do not agree with.
- Circulate, monitor and assist if necessary.
- Bring the class to order and compare choices. Did all the A pairs/B pairs choose the same top two pieces of advice? Did they all disagree with the same items?
- Praise any good use of language that you heard and identify four or five errors that need further practice.

D

- This discussion will work best if you have a group of Ss from different cultures, or at least a group from a culture that is markedly different from your own, so that comparisons can be made.
- If Ss are not in work, focus on the first question.
- Invite different Ss to give examples of how conflict is dealt with, then invite comment from other Ss. Don't be too strict about mistakes at this point, as the focus is on fluency, but make a note of common errors and go over these at the end.

Vocabulary: Word building

Ss look at related nouns and adjectives and their opposites.

◎ If possible, ensure that your Ss have a good monolingual dictionary such as the *Longman Dictionary of Contemporary English* or a good bilingual dictionary for this exercise.

> As professional language trainers, we take word classes such as nouns and adjectives for granted, but be sure that your Ss understand the difference. One obvious advantage of using bilingual dictionaries is that Ss can see very clearly the equivalent words in their own language. If your Ss are all from one language background, you could get them to say what the translations are.

◎ Do the first item as an example for the whole class. Then get your Ss to fill in the first two columns of the chart in pairs. Circulate, monitor and assist if necessary.

◎ Bring the class to order and ask for the answers, clarifying any difficulties. Practise the pronunciation of nouns and adjectives.

◎ Then point out how the opposites are formed. (It's probably easier to tell your Ss to learn the opposites one by one rather than try to apply 'rules'.) Get your Ss to complete the third column in pairs.

Noun	Adjective	Opposite
1 patience	patient	impatient
2 calmness	calm	nervous
3 weakness	weak	strong
4 credibility	credible	not credible*
5 emotion	emotional	unemotional
6 consistency	consistent	inconsistent
7 sympathy	sympathetic**	unsympathetic
8 formality	formal	informal
9 enthusiasm	enthusiastic	unenthusiastic
10 creativity	creative	not creative

* Point out that the word *incredible* does exist, but that it means 'amazing' or 'large'.

** Point out the difference between *sympathetic* (= trying to understand someone's problems and give them help) and *nice* (= generally friendly).

◎ Go through the answers, explaining any difficulties. Practise the pronunciation of the opposites with the whole class.

◎ Do this as a quick-fire activity with the whole class.

1 impatient
2 creative
3 unemotional
4 weak
5 unsympathetic
6 informal

◎ Get Ss to work in pairs on this. Tell them to note down the things they agree and disagree about. Circulate, monitor and assist if necessary. Be sure to get your Ss to distinguish correctly between nouns and adjectives, for example *Patience is a very important quality* but *It's important to be patient.*

◎ Bring the class to order. Help with any general difficulties. Then get some of the pairs to summarise their views, for example:
Paula thinks that calmness is important, but I totally disagree with her. I think it's important to show emotions such as anger and impatience. But we agree that it's important to be strong and not to show weakness in negotiations.

Language review: Conditionals

Ss look at the first and second conditional, and their use in negotiating.

- Go through the explanations, writing the examples on the board and underlining the verbs.

Ⓐ

- Go through the sentences with the whole class, getting Ss to comment on them and correct them.

---

1   can be corrected in two ways:
   a) If you *give* us a 10% discount, *we'll* place our order today. or
   b) If you *gave* us a 10% discount, we *would/we'd* place our order today.
   In b) the speaker sounds less sure that a discount will be offered.
2   can also be corrected in two ways:
   a) If I *have* more money, *I'll* go on a cruise.
   b) If I *had* more money, *I would/I'd* go on a cruise.
   a) might occur with *one day, in the future*, etc, but is less likely to occur as real usage than b).
3   If I *go* to London next week, *I'll* visit their sales office.
4   can also be corrected in two ways:
   a) If I *work* from home, *I'll* have more time with my children.
   b) If I *worked* from home, I *would* have more time with my children.
   Working from home sounds more like a realistic possibility in a) than it does in b).

Ⓑ

- With the whole class, explain any unfamiliar vocabulary (such as *signing-on bonus*). Explain the idea of the exercise, using the example as an illustration. Write it on the board in order to focus Ss' attention on it. Also point out that *If you pay in euros* could be followed by b, c, e, f, as well as g.
- Get your Ss to do the rest of the exercise in pairs, thinking about the context of each exchange. Circulate, monitor and assist if necessary.
- Bring the class to order and clarify any general difficulties. Ask Ss for their answers.

Tell Ss that all the combinations are grammatically possible if the verb tenses are correct, but that these are the most probable from the point of view of meaning.
1   b, c, e, f, g – Seller in a commercial negotiation talking to the buyer
2   b, c, e, f, g – Seller talking to buyer
3   h – Employer talking to an employee
4   e – Buyer talking to seller
5   e – Buyer talking to seller
6   a, h – Employer talking to salesperson
7   a, b, c, e, f – Someone in a company working on a distribution agreement talking to a possible distributor
8   a, d – Employer talking in a recruitment interview with a salesperson or
   b, c, e, f, g – Seller talking to buyer

Ⓒ

- Go through the example with the whole class, explaining any difficulties. Work on the pronunciation of *wouldn't*.
- Ask your Ss to work on the activity in pairs. Circulate, monitor and assist if necessary.
- Bring the class to order and ask Ss for their answers. Write one answer for each question on the board as a model.
- If there is time, make a link back to the quiz in the Starting up activity at the beginning of the unit. This time, Ss could answer the questions with conditionals, for example: 'In a meeting, if two people cannot agree, Paula would intervene and propose something new, but I would say nothing.' Go through some of the questions and answers with the whole class.

Skills: Negotiating: dealing with conflict

Ss look at ways of defusing conflict and the language to use
in this situation.

(A)

◎ Go through the first two or three points with the whole
class, without being prescriptive. Good ways of defusing
conflict in some places may be considered bad in others,
and vice versa – see what your Ss think about this. Deal
with any vocabulary difficulties in the remaining points.

◎ Then ask your Ss to discuss the remaining points in pairs.
Circulate, monitor and assist if necessary.

◎ Bring the class to order and discuss the points with the
whole class.

---

1 There is more eye contact in some cultures than others.
Where there is little eye contact to begin with, there
may be even less when there is conflict, but it's hard to
imagine a situation where no eye contact at all would
help. At the other end of the scale, staring at one's
counterpart across the table wouldn't be helpful either.

2 Some places may consider this conciliatory, others
provocative. If in doubt, don't smile too much.

3 Again, this may be considered provocative. Discuss with
your Ss if it is possible to have a facial expression and
body language that are 'neutral' in all cultures.

4 It depends – if the conflict is about a major issue, there
might be no point in discussing anything else until it is
resolved.

5 In some cultures, silence is a sign of respect, a sign that
you are thinking carefully about what has been said.
But there must always be a point at which it becomes
uncomfortable.

6 Some cultures might find this strange – the implied idea
being that, if you saw what the other person meant, you
wouldn't be in conflict with them. Tell Ss not to use this
expression too often.

7 Information gathering is always useful, but persistent
questioning about points that have already been
covered and that are perfectly clear will cause irritation
and may cause further conflict.

8 Easier said than done. A good idea in principle, but
ideas are often inextricably bound up with the person
expressing them.

9 Humour is appropriate in some cultures and not in
others. It could help to defuse a situation of conflict in
some places, but in others it might aggravate it.

10 Good idea, but don't overdo it. It could sound
patronising.

(B) 🎧 10.3

◎ Give the background to the situation. Play the recording
once or twice and clarify any difficulties.

◎ Elicit the answers.

---

1 To have five reserved parking spaces for staff on a 'first
come, first served' basis. Explain this expression.

2 She says it's not a solution – staff need somewhere
to park.

3 The idea that the company will pay 30 percent of the
cost of parking in the public car park.

(C) 🎧 10.3

◎ Play the recording again and get Ss to complete the
utterances.

---

1 understand, saying
2 how about, What if
3 possibility
4 could, might

(D)

◎ Go through the expressions in the Useful language box,
working on intonation.

◎ Discuss the extracts in Exercise C with your Ss and get
them to classify them.

---

1 Calming people down
2 Creating solutions
3 Creating solutions
4 Creating solutions

(E)

◎ Tell Ss that they should try to use the expressions from the
Useful language box in the role-play.

◎ Give the background information and explain any
difficulties, for example *subsidise*.

◎ Divide the class into pairs, allocate roles and get your Ss to
prepare them. Circulate, monitor and assist if necessary.

◎ When Ss are ready, get them to start the role-play. Circulate
and monitor. Note language points for praise and
correction afterwards, especially in relation to the language
in the Useful language box.

◎ When the pairs have finished, bring the class to order.
Praise strong language points that you heard and go
through half a dozen that need improvement, getting
individual Ss to say the correct forms.

◎ With the whole class, ask some of the pairs what happened
in their negotiations and encourage general discussion
about the outcomes.

Case study

European Campers

Ss analyse a conflict between a manager and a salesman and propose a solution.

Stage 1: Background

◎ Tell your Ss to silently read the first two sections. Meanwhile, write the headings on the left of the table below on the board.

◎ Ask Ss for key points to complete the column on the right of the table. Encourage them to suggest notes similar to the ones here, rather than longer sentences.

Company	European Campers
Products	Camping and outdoor equipment
Based in	Bordeaux, France
Profits	Dramatic rise in last two years
Chief Executive	Charles Holden
Marketing Manager	Todd Foster – American with MBA
Top salesman	Olivier Moyon
Olivier's results	Excellent – 24% of company sales
Problem with Olivier	Difficult to manage
Examples of unacceptable behaviour	– Dangerous driving and/or possible drink problem – Overspends on gifts to clients – Blocks access to clients by Todd – Uncommunicative (e.g. doesn't reply to messages, misses meetings) – Lack of sales reports

Stage 2: Listening 🎧 10.4

◎ Get your Ss to silently read the rest of the information. Meanwhile, write the headings on the left of the table below on the board.

◎ Ask Ss for key points to complete the column on the right of the table.

Origin of conflict	Order from department store chain to be delivered by end of month
Production Manager Jacques Picard's view and reason for this	Couldn't be produced on time – order from good customer had priority
Olivier's reaction	Anger, rudeness to Jacques
Result	Jacques complained to Todd – 'Olivier is rude and cares only about himself.'

◎ Then play the recording once or twice. Explain any difficulties, such as *let someone down*, and get Ss to summarise the conversation, for example as below.

Olivier Moyon	Todd Foster
Jacques Picard has let him down – no order = no commission, no bonus	Busy time – Jacques under pressure
Jacques makes no effort. Not happy with Todd either – too much control	Need for discipline
Says he will resign – no other solution	

Stage 3: Task

◎ Explain what will happen in the role-play. Ask your Ss to work in pairs and allocate roles. Circulate, monitor and assist if necessary.

◎ When the pairs are ready, tell them to start the role-play. Circulate and monitor. Note down language points for praise and correction afterwards, especially in relation to the language of conflict.

◎ When the pairs have come to a conclusion, bring the class to order. Praise strong language points and work on half a dozen points that need improving, getting Ss to say the correct forms.

◎ Ask some of the pairs what happened in their role-plays. Compare and contrast the different outcomes and encourage discussion.

> **1 to 1**
> This case study can be done as a discussion between teacher and student and then as a basis for a presentation by the student. Don't forget to note language points for praise and correction afterwards. Also point out some of the key language you chose to use.

Stage 4: Writing

◎ Make sure that your Ss understand what they have to do: write a letter to Olivier Moyon as if from the Head of Personnel at European Campers, telling him the outcome of the meeting. This can be done for homework.

 Writing file page 130

New business

At a glance

	Classwork – Course Book	Further work
Lesson 1 *Each lesson (excluding case studies) is about 45–60 minutes. This does not include administration and time spent going through homework.*	**Starting up** Ss discuss some ideas to encourage people to start new businesses and give examples of companies in different sectors. **Vocabulary: Economic terms** Ss look at words used to describe an economy and put them into practice. **Listening: Starting new businesses** Ss listen to a professor describing the main problems facing new businesses.	*Practice File* Vocabulary (page 44)
Lesson 2	**Reading: The human touch** Ss read an article about putting together the best team to run a new business. **Language review: Time clauses** Ss look at clauses with *when, while, before, after, until* and *as soon as.*	**Text bank** (pages 134 and 135) *Practice File* Language review (page 45) ***Business Grammar and Usage***
Lesson 3	**Skills: Dealing with numbers** Ss practise using numbers, fractions, decimals and amounts of money.	**Resource bank** (page 156)
Lesson 4 *Each case study is about 1 to 1½ hours.*	**Case study: Marcia Lee Jeans** A US clothing company wants to build a factory overseas. Ss analyse the economies of four countries and propose the best place to build the factory.	*Practice File* Writing (page 46)

For a fast route through the unit focusing mainly on speaking skills, just use the underlined sections.

For 1-to-1 situations, most parts of the unit lend themselves, with minimal adaptation, to use with individual students. Where this is not the case, alternative procedures are given.

Business brief

A recent TV ad for an airline shows an executive receiving an e-mailed presentation from a potential supplier and then quickly forgetting about it when another potential partner walks into the room and gives his presentation in person. The ad is trying to persuade businesspeople of the merits of **face-to-face contact** in drumming up new business. Flying to meetings is still the preferred way of doing things: companies worldwide spend $3 billion on video-conferencing equipment every year, but US companies alone spend $410 billion a year on business travel. **Road warriors** (even if they often travel by plane) will probably be necessary to gain new business for some time to come.

Clients and suppliers refer to each other as partners to underline the fact that they are in a **relationship** with mutual benefits: the supplier is making money out of helping the client to make money by providing products or services to customers. Some cultures give great importance to getting to know potential partners before working with them. There is some truth in the idea that Americans walk into a room expecting to reach a deal immediately; Asians, to build a relationship that may later lead to a deal. (See also the Business brief for Unit 6.)

In the past, companies often worked with large numbers of suppliers. Car manufacturers, for example, worked with numerous component suppliers, perhaps playing them off against each other to demand lower and lower prices. The tendency now is to work more closely with fewer suppliers. This is a necessary part of **just-in-time (JIT) delivery** and **total quality management (TQM)**. It is much easier to make improvements in these areas when dealing with fewer organisations. This means that it is difficult for new suppliers to break into the privileged circle and get new business.

Another form of new business is **start-ups**. At one end of the scale, there are one-person operations, often started by people who have gained expertise as salaried employees in organisations and then struck out (or been forced to strike out) on their own. At the other end, there are **serial entrepreneurs**, who are gifted at transforming ideas into businesses, and who found a number of start-ups, moving on when each business becomes viable. Their talent lies in combining ideas with people and finance, and they may be less interested in the more mundane activity of running established operations.

Breaking into new markets is another form of new business. A company may try to break into **e-commerce** and may often spend large amounts of money before making any. (See Unit 2.) Likewise, a company trying to establish itself in a country where it has not been present before can make large losses before seeing any **return on investment**. It may be necessary to have local partners who are already familiar with the market and are willing to invest in a **joint venture**.

Read on

Bob Reiss et al.: *Low Risk, High Reward: Starting and Growing Your Business with Minimal Risk,* Free Press, 2001

Charles and Elizabeth Handy: *The New Alchemists,* Hutchinson, 1999

Stuart Crainer, Des Dearlove: *Generation Entrepreneur,* FT.com books, 2000

David Ford et al.: *Managing Business Relationships,* Wiley, 1997

Lesson notes

Warmer

◎ Write the words *new business* in big letters on the board.

◎ Ask Ss for types of new business.

> The most obvious type of new business is when there is a new *start-up*, but get Ss to think also about *existing companies*.
> With their existing products, companies can
> – get new customers similar to the ones they have already
> – find different types of new customers
> – sell in new areas or countries
> Companies can also develop new products for
> – existing customers
> – existing sales areas or countries
> – new customers
> – new sales areas or countries

Overview

◎ Ask the Ss to look at the Overview section on page 98. Tell them a little about the things you will be doing, using the table on page 94 of this book as a guide. Tell them which sections you will be doing in this lesson and which in later lessons.

Quotation

◎ Write the quotation on the board and ask Ss to discuss it briefly in pairs.

◎ With the whole class, ask pairs for their opinions.

> This quotation plays on the phrases *to have your heart in something* and *to have something in your heart*. The former means to really put a lot of effort into something to make sure it succeeds, and the latter means that something is very important to you. In other words, for a business to succeed, you must care about it and put all your effort into it.

Starting up

Ss discuss some ideas to encourage people to start new businesses and give examples of companies in different sectors.

◎ Go through the list of conditions, explaining any difficulties. Tell your Ss to work in pairs. Make the activity concrete for the Ss by asking them which conditions would be most important if they were starting a company.

◎ Bring the class to order and ask the pairs what conclusions they came to. Ask them what sorts of businesses they had in mind when discussing the points. Encourage general discussion.

> **Low taxes:** Ss may talk about a **flexible labour market**, where there are not only low taxes on companies but also low **social costs** (low payments from companies and employees for benefits such as health care and unemployment benefit), where it is easy to fire people when activity decreases, and where people quickly find new jobs when activity increases again.
> **Skilled staff:** Ss might also mention the requirement for a good national education system and good company training of employees.
> **Low interest rates** mean that it is cheap to borrow money to develop new business activities.
> **Cheap rents** for office and factory space are of course more attractive than expensive ones, but having your office in the right place at a higher rent may be more attractive than having it in the wrong place at a lower one.
> A **stable economy** is beneficial because business people are able to plan better when there is less uncertainty about future inflation, taxes, etc.
> **Good transport links** are important for your employees to get to work and for salespeople to get to customers, but also for distribution of goods if your business does this.
> **Training courses** provided or funded by the government can be helpful in developing the skills of budding entrepreneurs.
> **High unemployment** may mean that the wages you can pay are lower, but you may not be able to find the people with the skills you want if you set up your business in an area with a high level of joblessness.
> In manufacturing, a **strong currency** means that imported raw materials are cheaper but that your exports will be more expensive than those from some competing countries. But if your products offer more benefits, they may justify a higher price.
> **Government grants** may be used to try to persuade companies to set up in areas with high unemployment but, if the area is unsuitable for other reasons (such as unskilled staff, distance from markets, etc.), these grants will not be enough.
> **Other conditions:** Ss may talk about the importance of language in setting up abroad. For example, countries such as India, where English is widely spoken in business, may be attractive for this reason – see, for example, the growth of India's software businesses.

B–C

◎ Work on the language, for example companies that were *publicly owned* or *state-owned*, that have now been *sold off*, *privatised* or *denationalised*.

◎ With the whole class, get Ss to talk about the companies they know, probably ones in their own country/countries.

◎ You could ask whether some industries such as rail will or should always be publicly owned because of their national importance, safety issues, uncertain return on investment for investors, etc. (Some Ss might refer to the unhappy UK experience in this area.) However, avoid getting into ideological debates about the relative merits of public and private ownership.

Vocabulary: Economic terms

Ss look at words used to describe an economy and put them into practice.

A

◎ Go through the pronunciation of the economic terms without explaining their meanings. Then ask your Ss to work on the matching exercise in pairs. Circulate, monitor and assist if necessary.

◎ With the whole class, go through the matches, explaining and recapping pronunciation where necessary.

> 1 c 2 d 3 b 4 f 5 g 6 i 7 a 8 e 9 h 10 j

B–C 11.1

◎ Ask your Ss to do the exercise in pairs. Circulate and assist if necessary.

> 1 inflation rate
> 2 interest rate
> 3 exchange rate
> 4 GDP
> 5 balance of trade
> 6 unemployment rate
> 7 foreign investment
> 8 tax incentives
> 9 government bureaucracy
> 10 labour force

◎ Play the recording and ask pairs to check their answers.

◎ Clarify any difficulties.

D

◎ Get your Ss to work in pairs again. Circulate, monitor and assist if necessary.

◎ Alternatively, this activity could be done as homework, to give your Ss a chance to gather the necessary information.

◎ You could advise Ss to consult the information for particular economies in *Financial Times World Desk Reference* published by Dorling Kindersley. There is also a regularly updated website: www.dk.com/world-desk-reference

Listening: Starting new businesses

Ss listen to a professor describing the main problems facing new businesses.

A 11.2

◎ Ask Ss what they think an 'Enterprise Centre' might be (somewhere that liaises with businesses in order to help them set up or expand).

◎ Play the recording and ask Ss what Professor Mumby-Croft sees as the main problems.

> A lack of business and management skills (e.g. not enough knowledge of finance and book-keeping, of marketing, of human resource issues).

◎ Play the recording again, or encourage Ss to read the transcript to check.

B 11.3

◎ Explain to Ss that they are going to hear Professor Mumby-Croft answering a question, and they have to identify the question from the options given.

◎ Have them read the four options, then play the recording once.

◎ Give them a minute to reread the options, then play the recording again for them to check that their chosen question makes sense.

◎ Check their answers.

> Question 3

C 11.4

◎ Allow Ss a minute to read the six statements, then play the recording.

◎ Ss note whether they think each statement is true or false.

◎ Play the recording again for them to check, then go through their answers, correcting the false ones.

> 1 T 2 F 3 F 4 T 5 F 6 T

Reading: The human touch

Ss read an article about putting together the best team to run a new business.

(A)

◎ Divide the class into small groups to work on the first question. Encourage them to use the frameworks given.

◎ Bring the class together and ask each group to contribute their ideas. Praise them for correct use of the structures.

◎ Ask Ss to vote on which ingredient they think is most important.

(B)

◎ Ask Ss to scan the article on page 101 quickly to identify the four elements.

◎ List them on the board.

> **1** the ability to sell   **2** the ability to count   **3** experience
> **4** contacts, relationships, a network

(C)

◎ Ss now read the article again, more closely this time, and decide if the statements are true or false.

◎ Go through the answers together, asking Ss to correct the false statements.

> **1** F *No one person has all the skills, experience, contacts or reputation that are required to get a business up and running. So, in order to succeed, you will have to form a core team of people.* (lines 7–15)
> **2** T It may be hard to make that decision, but it may be the right thing to do, as great innovators are not necessarily good at managing people.
> **3** T *The business is managed by managing the flow of cash.* (lines 35–37)
> **4** T An effective team will have customer experience, product experience and start-up experience.
> **5** T *Succeeding with an innovation-based company takes everything* (lines 75–77)
> **6** F There is no magic formula. But getting the right team together is the most important piece of the puzzle.

(D)

◎ The mix of individuals in each group for this activity will obviously greatly influence the discussion, so you may want to choose which Ss work with which.

◎ If Ss do not have much experience, encourage them to focus on hobbies or areas of interest for their company.

◎ Control the progress of discussions by allowing a limited time for each stage; this will ensure that Ss cover each element of the discussion and not spend all the time on one stage.

◎ Circulate, monitor and assist if necessary.

◎ At the end, ask each group to give a brief presentation, describing their business, presenting their team and summarising their strengths and weaknesses in a mini-SWOT analysis.

Language review: Time clauses

Ss look at clauses with *when, while, before, after, until* and *as soon as.*

◎ Go through the examples, pointing out the verb tenses used. Ask Ss if the tenses would be the same in their own language(s).

> Many Latin-based languages are different in their treatment of this – for example *When I'll be on the plane, I'll read all the contracts* could be the French 'translation' for future uses.
> In 3, point out that *As soon as they have signed the contract, we'll announce the deal* is also possible.

(A)–(B)

◎ Ask your Ss to do the exercises in pairs. Point out that they should look at overall sense in Exercise A before deciding on the matches. Circulate, monitor and assist if necessary.

◎ With the whole class, ask for the answers.

> **Exercise A**
> **1** g **2** e **3** f **4** d **5** a **6** b **7** h **8** c
>
> **Exercise B**
> **1** before / until
> **2** when / as soon as
> **3** when / before / after / as soon as
> **4** when / before / after / as soon as
> **5** when / while

(C)–(D) 🎧 11.5

◎ Do this as a quick-fire activity with the whole class, discussing the process of finding the right answer.

> **1** before   **5** When
> **2** as soon as   **6** when
> **3** before   **7** when
> **4** While

◎ Play the recording once or twice and get Ss to check their answers.

(E)

◎ Ss work in pairs to describe their routine, either at work or for studying. Remind them that they should use time clauses to describe the sequence of events.

◎ Circulate, monitor and assist if necessary, paying particular attention to the use of tenses in the time clauses. Praise correct usage and note the most common mistakes.

◎ When Ss have finished, recap on the rules that caused the most difficulty and ask Ss to produce correct examples.

Skills: Dealing with numbers

Ss practise using numbers, fractions, decimals and amounts
of money.

(A) 🎧 11.6

◎ Go round the class and ask individual Ss to say a number
   each. Then play the recording.

Refer your Ss to the Useful language box.
1 For **b), c)** and **e)–g)**, point out the difference
   between *BrE* (*Three hundred and sixty-two, Thirty-six
   thousand five hundred and three*) and *AmE*
   (*Three hundred sixty-two, Thirty-six thousand five
   hundred three*).
2 With decimals, tell your Ss that the figures after the
   decimal point are said individually, for example *Nine
   point eight seven five*.
3 Point out that you read ¾ as *three-quarters* in *BrE* and
   AmE, but that you can also say *three-fourths* in *AmE*.
   Work on the pronunciation of *-th* and *-ths* in *one-eighth*
   and *six-sevenths*.
4 Point out that you can write % as *percent* or *per cent*.
5 Work on the pronunciation of *euros*.

(B)

◎ Before getting your Ss to answer the questions, teach or
   remind them about the words *about* and *roughly*. (Tell
   them that, in spoken English, these words are better than
   approximately, which sounds rather formal.)

◎ Ask your Ss to ask and answer the questions in pairs. If
   they come from different organisations, pair Ss from
   different places. Circulate, monitor and assist if necessary.
   Note down language points for praise and correction later,
   especially in relation to figures.

◎ With the whole class, get some of the Ss to talk about the
   figures given to them by the person they spoke to.

◎ Praise strong language points and work on half a dozen
   points that need improving, getting Ss to say the correct
   forms.

(C) 🎧 11.7

◎ Tell Ss what they should do in the exercise and then play
   the recording once or twice, explaining any difficulties.

◎ With the whole class, go through the answers.

---

1 **a)** 1.2%
  b) 1,258,000
2 **a)** $1.8 billion
  b) 18%
3 **a)** ¹/3
  b) 5,000
4 **a)** 0.5%
  b) 2.8%

(D)

◎ Explain the idea behind the exercise to your Ss. Then divide
   the class into pairs, allocating the roles.

◎ Circulate and monitor. Note down language points for
   praise and correction afterwards, concentrating on the use
   of numbers.

◎ When the pairs have finished exchanging information, bring
   the class to order. Praise strong language points and work
   on half a dozen points that need improving, getting Ss to
   say the correct forms.

◎ Quickly ask Ss for the information and write it up on the
   board.

Biggest cities (population in millions)	
1 Tokyo	26.4
2 Mumbai (Bombay)	18.2
3 Mexico City	18.1
4 São Paulo	17.8
5 New York	16.6
6 Lagos	13.4

Computers per 100 people	
1 Luxembourg	73.2
2 Singapore	45.8
3 United States	45.5
4 Switzerland	42.1
5 Australia	14.1
6 Denmark	37.7

Oldest populations (% aged over 65)	
1 Italy	18.2
2 Greece	17.9
3 Sweden	17.4
4 Japan	17.1
5 Spain	17.0
6 Belgium	16.7

Cars per 1,000 people	
1 Lebanon	732
2= Brunei	576
2= Luxembourg	576
4 Italy	539
5 Iceland	510
6 Germany	506

◎ With the whole class, discuss which markets would be best
   for the launch of the new range of mobile phones. Discuss,
   for example, whether the fact that there are a lot of
   computers is a good indicator of technical sophistication
   and therefore willingness to buy mobiles, if the relative age
   or youth of the population is a factor, etc.

Lesson notes

Case study

Marcia Lee Jeans

A US clothing company wants to build a factory overseas. Ss analyse the economies of four countries and propose the best place to build it.

Stage 1: Background

◎ Get your Ss to silently read the background information. Meanwhile, write the headings on the left of the table below on the board.

◎ Ask Ss for key points to complete the column on the right of the table. Encourage them to suggest notes like the ones here, rather than longer sentences.

Company	Marcia Lee jeans
Based in	NY
Price range	Upper
Segment	Fashion conscious people aged 15–40
Factories	East Coast US, not owned by Marcia Lee
Costs	Kept low
Wants to expand into	Europe and South-east Asia
New factory – no. of workers	2,000
Source of denim	Imported from several countries
New factory – location	To be decided among countries A, B, C, D

Stage 2: Task 1: Pairwork

◎ Explain to your Ss that they should work in pairs to compare the benefits and disadvantages of each country. Suggest that they draw a chart with headings like those in the chart on page 101 of this book.

◎ With the whole class, complete the chart with notes about Country A to give Ss the idea. Point out that *high*, *average*, *low* are used in relation to the other three countries. Then get Ss individually to complete the rest of the chart. Circulate, monitor and assist if necessary.

Stage 3: Task 2: Small group discussion

◎ When pairs have completed their charts, divide the class into groups of three or four and get them to discuss the relative merits of each place for Marcia Lee's new factory.

◎ Circulate and monitor. Note down language points for praise and correction afterwards, especially in relation to numbers.

◎ When the groups have come to some sort of conclusion, bring the class to order. Praise strong language points and work on half a dozen points that need improving, getting Ss to say the correct forms.

Stage 4: Task 3: Large group discussion

◎ If the class is very large, the discussion can be run in two or more parallel groups. Appoint a chair for the group, or a chair for each group if there is more than one. Get each of the small groups from stage 3 to contribute to the decision on the most suitable location for the new factory.

◎ Circulate and monitor. Note down language points for praise and correction afterwards, especially in relation to numbers.

◎ When the group(s) has/have come to some sort of conclusion, bring the class to order. Praise strong language points and work on half a dozen points that need improving, getting Ss to say the correct forms.

◎ Ask the group(s) what conclusions were reached and how they made their choice.

◎ To prepare for the writing task, get Ss to write down key points from the discussion that led to the choice that they made.

> **1 to 1**
> This case study can be done as a discussion between teacher and student and then as a basis for a presentation by the student. Don't forget to note language points for praise and correction afterwards. Also point out some of the key language you chose to use.

Stage 5: Writing

◎ Make sure that your Ss understand what they have to do: write a letter to the head of the chamber of commerce in the country the group has chosen, asking for a meeting. You may want to ask your Ss to include in the letter some of the positive points about the country that led them to their choice. This can be done for homework.

 Writing file page 130

	Country A	Country B	Country C	Country D
Economy: general	lot of debt, trying to modernise	modern	unstable exchange rate	government encouraging privatisation
growth	low	low	high	average
inflation	average	very low	high	average
interest rates	high	high	average	high
unemployment	very high	low	high	high
Transport	good rail but poor roads and seaports, new airport	good road and rail, airport, no seaport	good near ports, good airport, bad roads	bad road and rail, but ten-year investment plan
Labour: skilled workforce	no	no	no	yes, but short hours
unionised	no	yes	yes	yes
wages	very low	high	low but rising	low
Other comments: business	good government grants	member of trading group, strict pollution laws, no tax incentives, high taxes	limit on profits to be taken out of country, not much paperwork, strong protest movement against foreign business	lot of paperwork, pollution problems, tax-free profits for first three years, part of profits into training fund
general	military government, bribery, political problems (independence for north)	stable government	first free elections last year	—

Products

At a glance

	Classwork – Course Book	Further work
Lesson 1 *Each lesson (excluding case studies) is about 45–60 minutes. This does not include administration and time spent going through homework.*	**Starting up** Ss talk about products that they like and their attitudes to companies that make products. **Vocabulary: Describing products** Ss look at some adjectives that can be used to describe products. **Listening: Best buys** Ss listen to six people talk about their best purchases.	*Practice File* Vocabulary (page 48)
Lesson 2	**Reading: Brand image** Ss read about a new brand of soft drink. **Language review: Passives** Ss look at passives in the context of where goods are made and produced.	*Text bank* (pages 136 and 137) *Practice File* Language review (page 49) ***Business Grammar and Usage***
Lesson 3	**Skills: Presenting a product** Ss listen to a sales manager presenting a product to buyers and then present a product themselves.	*Resource bank* (page 157)
Lesson 4 *Each case study is about 1 to 1½ hours.*	**Case study: Minerva A.G.** Ss present ideas for new products to a shop chain that specialises in innovative goods. The directors of the chain decide which are the best.	*Practice File* Writing (page 50)

For a fast route through the unit focusing mainly on speaking skills, just use the underlined sections.

For 1-to-1 situations, most parts of the unit lend themselves, with minimal adaptation, to use with individual students. Where this is not the case, alternative procedures are given.

Business brief

When we think of business, we usually think of **tangible products** that we can see and touch: computers on the desk or cars in the showroom. We may also think of **primary products** like coal or agricultural goods. But manufacturing forms a diminishing part of most advanced economies: only 17 per cent of the US economy, for example. What manufacturing there is is increasingly **lean**, with 'Japanese' techniques such as **just-in-time (JIT)** ordering of components and **total quality management (TQM)** becoming widespread.

There is an unresolved argument about whether economies need manufacturing at all to survive and flourish. In many people's minds, nevertheless, there is great regret when a factory closes in a 'traditional' industry: there is something more 'real' about work in a car plant than in a call centre. (The call centre may be selling **intangible products** such as mortgages: more and more services are described in product terms.) But the car plant may provide more work indirectly, for example at the component manufacturers that supply it.

We define ourselves partly by the products we own and use, wherever they are made. Economies in different parts of the world are at different stages of development in the way products are bought and perceived. In newly industrialised countries, such as some of those in Asia, more and more people are now able to afford **consumer durables** like washing machines for the first time, and companies that sell these types of goods can make large amounts of money. In the West, the market for televisions or washing machines is basically one of **replacement**. In a situation like this, **design**, **brand** and **image** become more important. Previously prestigious products, like certain makes of luxury car, become increasingly affordable, and manufacturers have to be careful to stay ahead of the game to avoid their brands being perceived as 'ordinary'.

The cars, televisions and washing machines of the 1950s may have had more style, but modern products are technically far better now than they were then. Consumers may complain about **designed-in obsolescence** and unnecessary **sophistication** of products with too many features that are never used, and manufacturers may have started to take this into account, simplifying the ways they are used. Consumers are also able to obtain and compare information about different products more and more easily. **Consumerism** is a force that manufacturers increasingly have to reckon with.

Read on

William M Feld: *Lean Manufacturing,* St Lucie Press, 2000

David Lewis, Darren Bridger: *The Soul of the New Consumer: Authenticity – What We Buy and Why in the New Economy,* Nicholas Brealey, 2000

Paul Postma, Philip Kotler: *The New Marketing Era,* McGraw Hill, 1998

Lesson notes

Lesson notes

Warmer

◎ Write the words *a product* in big letters on the right of the board.

◎ Ask Ss for verbs that come in front of the word. The board could end up looking like this:

invent develop make distribute market sell buy improve	**a product**

◎ Tell Ss they will see more verbs like this in the Vocabulary section of the unit.

Overview

◎ Ask Ss to look at the Overview section on page 106. Tell them a little about the things you will be doing, using the table on page 102 of this book as a guide. Tell them which sections you will be doing in this lesson and which in later lessons.

Quotation

◎ Write the quotation on the board and ask Ss to discuss it briefly in pairs.

◎ With the whole class, ask pairs for their opinions. (They may point out that this may not be true if the product has a fundamental flaw.)

Starting up

Ss talk about products that they like and their attitudes to companies that make products.

Ⓐ – Ⓑ

◎ Talk about a product that you like and what it says about you to give your Ss the idea. Then ask some of them what products they like, why, and what they say about them; also ask what types of cars, clothes, music or food they prefer, and what items they could not live without.

◎ Then get your Ss to talk about their dream products. Encourage them to refer to the Vocabulary file on page 158.

Ⓒ

◎ Get your Ss to look at the statements and then discuss them in pairs. Circulate, monitor and assist if necessary.

◎ Bring the class to order and ask the pairs for their opinions. Encourage discussion.

1 Attitudes to animal testing vary widely between cultures. Do not be surprised if your Ss see nothing wrong with it.

2 This is one of the key issues in the globalisation debate. Pro-globalisers say that this is a good way of getting countries onto the development ladder: after assembling multinationals' products, countries with the right business and political leadership will move on to developing and manufacturing their own. Anti-globalisers say that multinationals take advantage of low wage costs and then move on somewhere else if they rise too high.

3 Some Ss may complain about high marketing and advertising costs that add to the 'real' cost of goods. Others may say that competition depends on good communication and marketing, and that this competition drives down the cost of products in the long run. See what they think.

Vocabulary: Describing products

Ss look at some adjectives that can be used to describe products.

◎ Go through the words and check their meanings and pronunciations (especially stress) with your Ss.

> Ensure especially that your Ss understand the difference between *economical* and *economic*. *Economic* is the adjective related to *economy*: for example *economic issues*. Give Ss an example with *economical*, which means getting good value for money, for example *Buying in bulk is economical.*

◎ Get your Ss to work in pairs and to think of specific products that match the adjectives. Get them to develop a context for the example, as in the box that follows. Show them one or two before they start, to give them the idea. Circulate, monitor and assist if necessary.

> I think French clothes are so *attractive* – I really like this year's summer collection in the Redoute catalogue.
>
> The new Mini is very *economical* – it does 100 kilometres on six litres of petrol.
>
> Rolex watches are *expensive* – but they're worth the money.
>
> Flared jeans are very *fashionable* at the moment – Levi's new range is very good.
>
> Japanese cars are famous for being *reliable* – I've had a Toyota for ten years and it has never broken down.
>
> The main thing about Nike trainers is that they are *comfortable* – I can't wear ordinary shoes any more.
>
> The furniture at Ikea is *practical* – you take it home and put it together yourself, so you don't have to wait for it to be delivered.
>
> If you want an example of a *popular* newspaper, look at *The Sun* in the UK – it sells over 3 million copies a day and is read by more than 5 million people.

◎ With the whole class, gather ideas from the different pairs.

Ⓑ

◎ Do this as a quick-fire activity with the whole class. Write the words in the table on the board.

◎ Get Ss to practise saying them with the correct stress.

un-	in-	im-
unattractive uneconomical unfashionable unreliable uncomfortable unpopular	inexpensive	impractical

Ⓒ–Ⓓ

◎ Again go through the words and check their meanings and pronunciations (especially stress) with your Ss.

◎ Get Ss to work on the exercise in pairs and then go round the class asking for the answers.

Exercise C
1 high-tech
2 hard-wearing
3 high-quality
4 best-selling
5 long-lasting
6 well-made

◎ Get your Ss in pairs to think of specific companies and products that match the adjectives. Circulate, monitor and assist if necessary. (After the activity in Exercise A, they should have the idea.)

Exercise D: Possible answers
1 Siemens makes *high-tech* healthcare equipment among many other products.
2 Gore-Tex produces *hard-wearing* materials for outdoor clothes.
3 Habitat sells *high-quality* furniture.
4 Dell assembles the world's *best-selling* PCs.
5 Cummins makes *long-lasting* diesel engines.
6 Gucci shoes are *well-made* and fashionable .

◎ With the whole class, ask pairs for their ideas.

Ⓔ

◎ Do the matching as a quick-fire activity with the whole class.

◎ Then get Ss to call out the correct order. Some Ss may point out that it is possible to have other orders, for example when a product is promoted after it is launched or is modified after it is launched.

1 c 2 e 3 g 4 b 5 d 6 a 7 f 8 h
Order: 7, 2, 5, 4, 3, 1, 8, 6

Listening: Best buys

Ss listen to six people talk about their best purchases.

Ⓐ 12.1

◎ Tell Ss that they will hear six people talking about the best things they have bought (not a product in every case). Play the recording once or twice and ask Ss to match the speakers to the objects.

1 b 2 f 3 a 4 c 5 d 6 e

Ⓑ 12.1

◎ Ask your Ss to look at the questions. Then play the recording again, stopping after each speaker and explaining any difficulties.

◎ Ask Ss for the answers.

1 Mark
2 Marina
3 Sharon and Clare
4 Nada and Fiona

Ⓒ

◎ Ask Ss to work in pairs and read the transcripts on page 156. Give them a minute to decide which one they like best, then ask them to write three questions to ask that person. Circulate, monitor and assist if necessary.

◎ When all the pairs have written their questions, ask Ss to swap them with another pair.

◎ Encourage Ss to correct any mistakes they find, then to invent answers to the questions.

Lesson notes

Reading: Brand image

Ss read about a new brand of soft drink.

 A

- If your Ss are all from the same country, this is probably best handled as a class discussion. Otherwise, Ss should work on groups from the same country (or as near as possible), although you need to monitor them closely to ensure they are using English for their discussion.
- Ask Ss to think of global brands, such as Coca-Cola®, as well as locally produced drinks.
- Bring the class together and discuss one or two global brands plus a few of their local ones and compare the brand images.
- Ask Ss whether they like these drinks and how effective they think the advertising campaigns are.

 B

- Ss scan the article to find the information. You could do this as a competition to see who can find each piece of information first.
- Go through the answers quickly with the class.

1	Guaraná Antarctica
2	Coca-Cola, Pepsi, Cadbury Schweppes
3	Red Bull
4	180 million

C

- Tell Ss to read the article again more closely.
- Then explain that they have to find the correct heading for each paragraph. There are eight choices and only four paragraphs, so they need to consider which headings are the most appropriate.
- Give Ss a reasonable amount of time to do this, then go through the answers.

1 d	**2** a	**3** f	**4** b

- If Ss had different answers, ensure that they understand why they were not appropriate.

D

- The first question could be done as a quick class survey; the second question requires more discussion and could be set for homework or a mini-project.

Language review: Passives

Ss look at passives in the context of where goods are made and produced.

◎ Go through the examples and explanations. Remind Ss that the past participle is the third form that they see in verb tables, for example *make, made, made*. (The other three verbs in the examples are regular: *use, used, used; dominate, dominated, dominated; grind, ground, ground*.)

A

◎ Go through the products on the left of the table, explaining meanings and practising pronunciations where necessary.

◎ Ask your Ss to work on the exercise in pairs. Circulate, monitor and assist if necessary.

◎ When the pairs are ready, ask them for the correct answers.

> The following answers are not complete. Ask your Ss about other places where things are produced. Ensure they use the correct verbs.
> Diamonds are mined in South Africa.
> Microchips are produced/manufactured/made in The United States.
> Semiconductors are produced/manufactured/made in Malaysia.
> Electronic goods are produced/manufactured/made in Japan.
> Coffee is produced/grown in Brazil.
> Leather goods are produced/manufactured/made in Spain.
> Oil is produced/refined in Kuwait.
> Rice is produced/grown in China.
> Watches are produced/manufactured/made in Switzerland.
> Coal is mined in Poland.
> Copper is mined in Zambia.
> Mobile phones are produced/manufactured/made in Finland.

B

◎ Do this as a quick-fire activity with the whole class.

> 1 The gold variety of the kiwifruit is planted worldwide.
> 2 These Renault cars are made in France.
> 3 This rice is grown in India.
> 4 The staff were asked for their opinions.
> 5 My car is being repaired at the moment.
> 6 The missing file has been found.
> 7 This toy was made in Japan.

C

◎ Explain what is required, for example, by completing the first two gaps with the whole class. Then ask your Ss to work on the exercise in pairs.

◎ With the whole class, ask pairs for the answers.

> 1 are developed
> 2 is modelled
> 3 is planned
> 4 are used
> 5 are arranged
> 6 are manufactured
> 7 is exported
> 8 are shipped
> 9 are packaged
> 10 are maintained
> 11 are respected
> 12 are not exploited

Lesson notes

Lesson notes

Skills: Presenting a product

Ss listen to a sales manager presenting a product to buyers and then present a product themselves.

(A) 🎧 12.2

◎ Tell Ss about what they are going to hear – a sales manager presenting a product to some buyers.

◎ Play the recording once or twice, explaining any difficulties, and get Ss to say which words they hear.

attractive ✓	fashionable	stylish✓	robust ✓
elegant ✓	user-friendly ✓	high-quality ✓	well-designed✓
reliable	flexible ✓	popular	practical ✓

◎ Practise the stress and intonation of these words with your Ss.

(B) 🎧 12.2

◎ Play the recording again, this time getting Ss to concentrate on the missing words and phrases in items 1 to 10.

1 attractive; stylish
2 is made
3 tell you
4 comes
5 selling price
6 ideal
7 special features
8 Another advantage
9 robust; elegant
10 meet the needs

◎ With the whole class, ask for the answers. Work on any remaining difficulties.

(C)

◎ Tell your Ss that they will be presenting a product themselves. Go through the language in the Useful language box, explaining any difficulties and working on stress and intonation.

◎ Get your Ss to work in groups of three or four. Get each group to select one of the products (or allocate them yourself if this will save time) and prepare a presentation about it. (Tell your Ss to invent any missing information.)

◎ Circulate, monitor and assist if necessary. Note down language points for praise and correction afterwards, especially language used for product presentations.

◎ When the groups are ready, bring the class to order. Praise strong language points and work on half a dozen points that need improving, getting Ss to say the correct forms.

◎ Then get your Ss to form new groups, ideally with members who worked on different products. Each student should give a product presentation to the new group they are in. If possible they should stand up and pretend to show the actual product or even draw it on a sheet of cardboard which they stick to the wall. Again, note down language points for praise and correction afterwards.

◎ Bring the class to order and again praise strong language points and work on half a dozen points that need improving, getting Ss to say the correct forms.

---

1 to 1

This presentation can of course be done by an individual student. Don't forget to note language points for praise and correction afterwards. Also point out some of the key language you chose to use.

Case study

Minerva A.G.

Ss present ideas for new products to a shop chain that specialises in innovative goods. The directors of the chain decide which are the best.

Stage 1: Background

- Give your Ss some general background on the case – a chain of stores sells unusual, innovative (teach this word if necessary) products. Get your Ss to read the background. Meanwhile, write the headings on the left of the table on the board. When the Ss have finished reading, elicit information to complete the table.

Company	Minerva A.G.
Based in	Munich, Germany
Product range	Products based on new technology, but also everything from furniture to clothes to household goods
Reputation	Original designs, high quality
Slogan	Creativity, Imagination, Style, Novelty, Originality

Stage 2: New products

- Go through the extract about the survey with the whole class, clarifying any difficulties.

- Then get Ss to work in pairs and look at the products being offered to Minerva A.G. Allocate each pair to a particular product. Circulate, monitor and assist if necessary, clarifying any difficulties.

- Bring the class to order and ask one of the pairs to talk about each product, using complete sentences, for example:

  Company B is offering a Personal Satellite Navigation System. It fits in your pocket and you can download maps of any city in the world, so you won't need to carry paper maps again. The maps include tourist information. The product is slim and lightweight and is available in silver or black. It costs €320.

Stage 3: Task

- Explain that the Minerva board has asked several innovative companies to present their new products.

- Get your Ss to work in groups of three or four. Ask each group to select one of the products (or think of an alternative product) and prepare a presentation about it. One group member will present to the Minerva board, and each group should decide at this point who their presenter will be. The presenter can draw and label the product on a sheet of cardboard.

- Circulate, monitor and assist if necessary. Note down language points for praise and correction afterwards, especially language used in product presentations.

- When the groups are ready, bring the class to order. Praise strong language points and work on half a dozen points that need improving, getting Ss to say the correct forms.

- Then ask the product presenters from the old groups to stand to one side for the moment. Get the remaining Ss in the class to form new groups of three or four. Explain that these groups are Minerva directors.

- Each group of directors will get a presentation about each of the four innovative products in turn. Tell the presenters that they should present the product in such a convincing way that Minerva will buy as many as possible. The Minerva directors should ask questions about the products after each presentation.

- Presenting Ss go round the class to different groups of directors. Each presentation should last ten minutes, including questions. When each presentation is over, bring the class to order and send the presenters round to a new group of directors.

- Again, during the presentations note down language points for praise and correction afterwards.

- Bring the class to order and again praise strong language points and work on half a dozen points that need improving, getting Ss to say the correct forms.

- Then ask each group of Minerva directors to discuss the products they have seen and then say which product most impressed them, and why.

> **1 to 1**
> This case study can be done as a discussion between teacher and student and then as a basis for a presentation by the student. Don't forget to note language points for praise and correction afterwards. Also point out some of the key language you chose to use.

Stage 4: Writing

- Make sure your Ss understand what they have to do: as a director of Minerva A.G., write a short report on one of the products and recommend whether the company should order a large quantity or not. This can be done as homework.

 Writing file page 135

D

Revision

This unit revises and reinforces some of the key language points from Units 10–12, and links with those units are clearly shown. Point out these links to your Ss – in some cases, they will need information from the original activities to do the exercises here.

These exercises can be done in class individually or collaboratively, or for homework.

For more speaking practice, see the Resource bank section of this book beginning on page 141.

10 Conflict

Vocabulary

◎ This exercise practises the vocabulary that was the focus of the word-building section on page 93.

◎ Ensure Ss understand why the distractors are wrong in each case.

> **1** c **2** c **3** a **4** b **5** a **6** b **7** c

Reading

◎ This e-mail picks up the function of complaining about colleagues which came up in the case study on pages 96–97.

◎ There are no distractors in this task, but Ss should read the surrounding text carefully to ensure that the phrases make sense in context.

> **1** e **2** b **3** d **4** a **5** c

Writing

◎ This follows on from the previous task. Refer Ss to the Writing file on page 133 for guidance on writing e-mails.

◎ Tell Ss to make sure they include all five points mentioned.

11 New business

Economic terms

◎ This crossword puzzles reviews the vocabulary from page 99. Encourage Ss to do as much as they can without referring back to the unit.

> **Across: 1** sector **5** unemployment **6** Exports **8** incentives **9** interest
> **Down: 1** skilled **2** team **3** domestic **4** inflation **7** rate

Time clauses

◎ This matching exercise practises the language from page 102. If necessary, ask Ss to reread the Language review box on that page first.

> **1** c **2** g **3** d **4** f **5** b **6** h **7** a **8** e

12 Products

Vocabulary

◎ This is a revision of the terms from the Vocabulary section on pages 106–107.

> **1** manufacture **2** best-selling **3** unreliable **4** launch **5** distribute **6** inexpensive
> **Hidden word**: fashionable

Passives

◎ Before completing this text, Ss should look again at the Language review box on page 110.

> **1** have been sold **2** was launched **3** be bought **4** has (recently) been extended
> **5** will be set up **6** will be imported **7** are tested **8** have been approved

Writing

◎ In this final writing task, Ss can choose to give positive, negative or mixed feedback. Refer them to the Writing file (page 133) and the Vocabulary file (page 158) if necessary.

Text bank

Teacher's notes

Introduction

The Text bank contains articles relating to the units in the Course Book. These articles extend and develop the themes in those units. You can choose the articles that are of most interest to your Ss. They can be done in class or as homework. You have permission to make photocopies of these articles for your Ss.

Before you read

Before each article, there is an exercise to use as a warmer that allows Ss to focus on the vocabulary of the article and prepares them for it. This can be done in pairs or small groups, with each group reporting its answers to the whole class.

Reading

If using the articles in class, it is a good idea to treat different sections in different ways, for example reading the first paragraph with the whole class, then getting Ss to work in pairs on the following paragraphs. If you're short of time, get different pairs to read different sections of the article simultaneously. You can circulate, monitor and give help where necessary. Ss then report back to the whole group with a succinct summary and/or their answers to the questions for that section. A full answer key follows the articles (starting on page 138).

Discussion

In the Over to you section following the exercises, there are discussion points. These can be dealt with by the whole class, or the class can be divided, with different groups discussing different points. During discussion, circulate, monitor and give help where necessary. Ss then report back to the whole class. Praise good language production and work on areas for improvement in the usual way.

Writing

The discussion points can also form the basis for short pieces of written work. Ss will find this easier if they have already discussed the points in class, but you can ask Ss to read the article and write about the discussion points as homework.

A career in retail banking

Level of difficulty: ● ● ○

Text bank

Before you read

Can you name some of the major retail banks in your country? What special skills do you think you need to work in a bank?

Reading

Read the article from the *Financial Times* and answer the questions.

Retail banking: Appeal of the softer side of the business

Clare Gascoigne

Retail banking used to be an aspirational career. But as the banks have changed, so has the attraction. 'Graduates have to be
5 led into thinking about retail banking,' says Terry Jones of the Association of Graduate Career Advisory Services. 'They think first about the investment banks
10 or accountancy – they think retail is not as interesting as working on mergers and acquisitions or trading.'

He may be right. High-street bank
15 managers are no longer as respected as they used to be. Staff are much more concerned with selling products and financial services, and much of the
20 customer contact has moved to big call centres or the Internet. 'The work feels relatively low status,' says Mr Jones.

However, the banks don't feel the
25 same way. 'We are looking for people who are customer driven, who can form good working relationships and lead sales teams,' says John Morewood,
30 senior manager for graduate recruiting at HSBC. 'We look for graduates who have had experience of working with customers.'

35 HSBC is typical of the high-street banks in running two main graduate schemes. The executive management scheme is a two-year development programme that
40 aims to put graduates into a leadership role. It takes between 25 and 30 every year. 'These people have the potential to go very high,' says Mr Morewood. 'We are
45 looking for strategic thinkers.'

The second scheme, which is more concerned with retail and commercial banking, takes between 120 and 150 people a year
50 and gives graduates responsibility much earlier.

FINANCIAL TIMES

1 Choose the correct meaning for the word in *italics*.
   a) 'Banking used to be an *aspirational* career' (line 2) means people
      i) wanted to work in that sector because it was highly respected.
      ii) knew they would get excellent training in that sector.
   b) A *call centre* (line 21) is where customers can
      i) meet employees.
      ii) speak to staff on the phone.
   c) 'The work feel relatively *low status*' (line 22) means
      i) it is not considered to be very important.
      ii) the job is easy to do.
   d) 'We are looking for *strategic thinkers*' (line 45) means people who
      i) can make decisions quickly.
      ii) are able to make top-level decisions.

2 True or false?
   a) Retail banking is not as attractive as it used to be.
   b) Graduates prefer to work in other financial areas.
   c) Retail banking staff have to sell products and financial services.
   d) Banks are not interested in recruits with customer experience.
   e) The executive management scheme lasts three years.
   f) This scheme is training people for high-level positions.
   g) More people are recruited on HSBC's second scheme.

Over to you

Do you think that working in a bank is a high- or low-status kind of job? Is it important for bank managers have a degree from a good university?

UNIT 1   Careers

Training on the job

Level of difficulty: ● ● ○

Before you read

Do have apprenticeship schemes in your country? What are the advantages of working your way up through a company? What benefits do you think there are for the employee of doing an apprenticeship?

Reading

Read the article from the *Financial Times* and answer the questions.

Cost-effective route to create future managers

Andrew Taylor

Mike Turner, chief executive of BAE Systems, Europe's biggest defence company, and a member of the Apprenticeships Task Force, is a prime example of how starting at the bottom of the corporate ladder can lead to a top job. 'I began my working life as an apprentice,' said Mr Turner, who argues that apprenticeships remain one of the most cost-effective ways of filling skill shortages, as well as developing managers of the future.

According to the task force's report, published today, BAE expects to save up to £1m a year by training apprentices rather than hiring and retraining outside workers, 'as apprenticeships cost 25 per cent less than training non-apprentices'.

It is 'much more attractive to recruit young people as apprentices, as recruitment costs are lower, staff turnover is lower and apprentices quickly identified with company values', according to the task force. BT, the telecommunications group, for example, had 'calculated a benefit of over £1,300 per apprentice per annum when compared to non-apprentice recruitment'.

Companies, even in industries such as construction and engineering, where training costs were high, found that young people in the later years of their apprenticeships were making 'a high contribution relative to their wage costs', said the task force.

Honda had reported that it took two years to retrain someone trained by another car manufacturer. Apprentices by contrast 'quickly understood their [Honda] company values and practices'.

Apprenticeships were also a 'cost-effective way of replacing an ageing workforce and ensuring the effective transfer of knowledge', Xerox, the office equipment group, told the task force.

FINANCIAL TIMES

1 Match the words to form expressions from the article.

1	prime	a)	life
2	corporate	b)	shortages
3	working	c)	values
4	skill	d)	ladder
5	staff	e)	turnover
6	company	f)	example

2 Answer these questions.
a) Who is Mike Turner?
b) How much does BAE expect to save by training apprentices?
c) What three major advantages of recruiting apprentices are mentioned in the task-force report?
d) How much did BT save?
e) When do apprentices make a productive contribution to a company?
f) Why does Honda like apprentices?
g) What are the two main benefits of apprenticeships, according to Xerox?

Over to you

Do you think experience on the job is more important than qualifications?

UNIT 2   Selling online

Film deals online

Level of difficulty: ●●○

Before you read

Have you ever visited the Amazon website? Have you bought anything from Amazon? Why do you think the company has been so successful?

Reading

Read this article from the *Financial Times* and answer the questions.

Amazon goes to Hollywood with film deal

Joshua Chaffin and Jonathan Birchall

Amazon, the largest online retailer, is going to Hollywood after striking its first deal for the film rights to a best-selling novel.

5 It is expected to team up with a Hollywood studio and producer after it acquired the screen rights to *The Stolen Child*, a fantasy tale by first-time author Keith
10 Donohue. As part of the agreement, Amazon pledged that it would market the film and its subsequent DVD on its website.

The deal comes during
15 speculation that Amazon is poised to broaden its film ambitions by introducing a new video download service in conjunction with major Hollywood studios.
20 Amazon said it did not intend to co-finance the film, but that the company's brand, retail expertise, and customers around the world could make it 'an extremely
25 valuable partner in the marketing and distribution of this film'.

Amazon has this year increased its involvement in video programming on its site,
30 launching a weekly interview programme with artists and authors. In 2004, the company also produced five short live-action films on its website, featuring
35 famous actors, which it used to promote its credit card and the range of goods available on its US site.

Another asset Amazon could
40 bring to the film-making process is the consumer research compiled by its website. Based on its sales data, for example, Amazon would be well positioned to target the
45 film at customers who have read the book and others like it, or bought similar DVDs from the site.

The deal also reflects the growing presence of non-
50 traditional producers in Hollywood.

FINANCIAL TIMES

---

1 Match the words and expressions (1–9) with their meanings (a–i).

1	striking	a)	collected
2	acquired	b)	ready
3	pledged	c)	bought
4	subsequent	d)	following
5	poised	e)	extend, widen
6	broaden	f)	promised
7	in conjunction with	g)	using, including
8	featuring	h)	making, signing
9	compiled	i)	together with

2 True or false?

a) Amazon has bought screen rights to *The Stolen Child*.
b) The author has written several other books.
c) Amazon may provide a new video service.
d) Amazon will invest a large amount in the film.
e) Famous actors have been used to advertise Amazon products.
f) Amazon will be able to target potential customers easily.

3 Complete the different forms of these words from the article. The first has been done for you.

NOUN	VERB
expectation	*expect*
a) agreement	
b)	feature
c)	grow
d)	intend
e)	launch
f) speculation	
g) involvement	
h)	promote

Over to you

Have you ever downloaded a film onto your computer? Do you think eventually people will stop going to the cinema? Why (not)?

UNIT 2   Selling online

Online advertising

Level of difficulty: ● ● ●

Before you read

Do you pay attention to the advertisements online? Do you like them or do they annoy you? Do you think they are more effective than traditional advertising media?

Reading

Read the article from the *Financial Times* and answer the questions.

Online advertising

The volatility of Internet stocks says a lot about what is expected from them. It says rather less about the true health of the online advertising market.

Carat, the media buying group, expects Internet advertising worldwide to grow by 25 per cent this year. In developed markets, growth rates are even faster. US first-quarter online advertising growth, for example, was 38 per cent, and there remains plenty of room for further rapid expansion. Credit Suisse expects US online spending to grow at an annual rate of 22 per cent over five years, but that still leaves it with a total market share of about one-tenth.

Demand from advertisers, however, is strengthened because people believe that online advertising generates a high return on investment. Measurement is never easy, but based on survey data from TNS Media Intelligence, online currently enjoys a return on investment of 26 per cent, compared with 17 per cent for magazines, the next closest category.

Online offers the opportunity for manufacturers to reach a larger number of consumers. A recent study found that US food companies are increasingly using the Internet to target children with interactive games and commercials, which is a concern for anti-obesity campaigners, but an example of the potential of 'rich media'.

With expected overall advertising market growth of only 4 to 5 per cent this year, traditional media continue to lose share. In the UK, for example, print media advertising shrank 5 per cent last year, while online grew by almost two-thirds. Share prices of Internet stocks will continue to fluctuate greatly, but it is traditional print media companies that face the toughest future.

FINANCIAL TIMES

1 True or false?
  a) This year, Internet advertising is expected to increase by a quarter.
  b) In some markets, the increase will be lower.
  c) Credit Suisse predicts spending in the US to fall below 22%.
  d) Online advertising in the US enjoys approximately 10% of the market share.
  e) The return on investment of online advertising is higher than for other media.
  f) Experts say that traditional media continue to lose market share.
  g) In the UK, online advertising has grown by 5%.
  h) Internet stocks should become more stable in the future.

2 Choose the alternative that best explains the words in *italics*.
  a) the *volatility* of Internet stocks (line 1)
    i) amount
    ii) unpredictability
    iii) attraction

  b) online advertising generates a high *return on investment* (lines 23–24)
    i) amount of money earned from the investment
    ii) amount of money budgeted for the investment
    iii) amount of money spent on the investment
  c) *Anti-obesity campaigners* (line 40) are people who are
    i) fighting against weight loss.
    ii) always going on diets.
    iii) trying to reduce the number of overweight people.
  d) 'Stocks will continue to *fluctuate*' (line 51) means they will continue to
    i) remain stable
    ii) go up
    iii) go up and down

Over to you

Do you think there are any products which should not be advertised or sold online?

If you produce or want to sell a product, would you advertise it on the Internet? Why (not)?

UNIT 3   Companies

Computer company success

Level of difficulty: ●○○

Before you read

What do you know about Hewlett-Packard? Have you ever used or bought any HP products? How competitive do you think the computer technology market is?

Reading

Read the article from the *Financial Times* and answer the questions.

HP beats forecasts and raises outlook

Kevin Allison

Hewlett-Packard, the world's second-biggest computer maker, continued to benefit from its $1.9bn cost-cutting drive, after it
5 reported higher profits for the third quarter and raised its outlook for the year. HP reported net earnings of 48 cents a share – sharply higher than the 3 cents a
10 share reported one year ago.

Mark Hurd, who launched the company's $1.9bn restructuring after he became chief executive last year, said: 'We remain focused
15 on growth and continue to perform well in the market.' He said HP was on track to close its latest cost-cutting round by the end of the year, although he added
20 that the company would 'always be looking for ways to optimise' costs.

Sales grew 6 per cent to $21.9bn as HP expanded in growing Asian
25 markets and saw renewed activity in its core US market. HP shares rose 1.3 per cent to $34.43 ahead of the announcement.

Mr Hurd said that the company's
30 personal computer division saw margins of 4 per cent – the highest since HP bought Compaq, a rival personal computer maker, for $21bn in 2002. 'We continue to see a competitive environment [in PCs],
35 but I would not call it an extraordinarily difficult [environment],' he said.

HP, which makes products
40 ranging from laptop computers to printers and servers that power corporate data networks, said revenues in the Americas grew 8 per cent year on year to $9.7bn.
45 Asia also experienced strong growth, with revenue up 7 per cent. Sales in Europe, the Middle East and Africa were behind, however, with revenues up just 2
50 per cent.

FINANCIAL TIMES

1 Match the numbers (1–11) with what they refer to (a–k).

1 $1.9bn	a) revenue increase in Asia
2 48 cents	b) sales turnover in past year
3 3 cents	c) cost of buying Compaq
4 6%	d) current share value
5 $21.9bn	e) share price rise before announcement
6 1.3%	f) percentage increase in sales
7 $34.43	g) margins on computer sales
8 4%	h) amount saved by HP in its cost-cutting drive
9 $21bn	i) current net earnings per share
10 7%	j) revenue increase in Europe, the Middle East and Africa
11 2%	k) last year's net earnings per share

2 Complete the sentences below with a preposition from the box.

for	from	on	of

a) The company benefitted .... increased investment in R&D.
b) The outlook .... the next year looks very bright.
c) Our strategy focuses .... bringing the customer the best quality for the least money.
d) We are always looking .... ways to improve our products.
e) We work hard to stay ahead .... the competition.
f) They bought the company .... $21bn last year.
g) Prices of our products range .... $5 to $5,000.

Over to you

Why do you think sales were slower outside the USA?
What is important to you when buying a computer?

UNIT 3 Companies

Change for success

Level of difficulty: ●●○

Before you read

Do you think that company structures (business models) need to change frequently? Why (not)? Do you think companies have to operate internationally to grow?

Reading

Read the article from the *Financial Times* and answer the questions.

A foreign way to avoid dying at home

Jonathan Moules

Tony Jones has made his money by fixing things, including changing his business model to cope with a 'dying' UK manufacturing industry.

He created Advanced Total Services (ATS) in the 1990s, a business that repaired the electronics on industrial machinery. He sold ATS for £4m in 1998, but soon started a new company, Lektronix, operating in the same market as ATS, but which aimed to expand faster by modifying the business model.

ATS had eight offices across the UK so local people were near factories. However, Lektronix only had three, focusing on the larger manufacturers. Consequently, Lektronix generated the same sales volume as ATS with a third of the number of customers and significantly lower operating costs.

Lektronix faced two big challenges. Firstly, it had created its own competition, ATS, and secondly it was dealing with a smaller market as British manufacturers either closed or moved abroad. Overseas expansion was attractive, because in many markets there was no competition. The main problem was Mr Jones's lack of experience in international expansion.

His first target market was the Czech Republic. He decided to test the market by visiting potential customers. He spent three days visiting 20 companies, and his first local recruit was one of his cab drivers who had a background in sales. The rest of the Czech team was found through a local employment agency run by a Briton who spoke Czech.

The most difficult part was taking the first step, according to Mr Jones. 'Once you commit to doing it, you will meet people who know people who can help.'

FINANCIAL TIMES

1 Use the correct form of words from the article to complete these sentences.
   a) If a machine breaks down, you have to r _ _ _ _ r it.
   b) An industry which is disappearing is said to be d_ _ _ g.
   c) If you c_ _ _ _e a company, you start or set one up.
   d) When sales are falling, we say your market share is d _ _ _ _ _ _ g.
   e) We m _ _ _ _ y a plan or system when the situation changes.
   f) A difficult situation can be called a c _ _ _ _ _ _ _ e.
   g) A company needs to r _ _ _ _ _ t good staff if it wants to succeed.
   h) People who might be your customers are known as p _ _ _ _ _ _ _ l customers.

2 True or false?
   a) ATS is owned by Tony Jones.
   b) Lektronix provides a similar service to ATS.
   c) Mr Jones set up Lektronix in exactly the same way as ATS.
   d) Lektronix has far more customers than ATS.
   e) Lektronix's operating costs are not as high as those of ATS.
   f) Many manufacturers in the UK have closed down.
   g) The market in other countries is very competitive.
   h) Mr Jones went to the Czech Republic to see what he could set up.
   i) Mr Jones employed most of the staff there himself.

Over to you

What potential risks do you think companies face when they set up in another country for the first time?

UNIT 4   Great ideas

Ideas from consumers

Level of difficulty: ●●○

Before you read

Can you think of some recent innovative products which are on the market?

Reading

Read the article from the *Financial Times* and answer the questions.

How ordinary people generate great ideas

Simon London

Working out where great ideas come from is one of the big puzzles of modern management. Corporate research laboratories and in-house product development groups are only part of the answer. Innovative products and processes can come from start-ups, competitors, university campuses and ordinary employees.

Eric von Hippel, a professor of management of innovation at the Massachusetts Institute of Technology, has spent three decades studying the role played by customers in shaping new products. The results are nicely summarised in *Democratizing Innovation*, a useful book on what he calls 'user-centered innovation'.

For example, people who do extreme sports such as windsurfing or ice-climbing, play a significant role in the development of equipment which is then mass-produced by manufacturers. Surgical equipment companies are often led towards new products by surgeons who operate using the equipment.

Users are often the first to develop many, and perhaps most, new industrial and commercial products. For example, 3M, the industrial products group, has programmes in place to collect ideas generated by key users. Von Hippel found that these products at 3M were likely to be more innovative, enjoy higher market share, have greater potential to develop into an entire product line.

Mass-producing products developed by key users is only one possible approach. Alternatives include selling toolkits with which customers can build their own creations. For example, International Flavors & Fragrances supplies customers with the tools to design their own food flavours. Users themselves develop the products.

These examples revolutionise the traditional division of labour between producer and consumer. *Democratizing Innovation* shows that the flow of ideas and expertise is more complex.

FINANCIAL TIMES

1 True or false?
   a) Most new ideas come from in-house research.
   b) It took Eric von Hippel three years to write his book.
   c) People who go windsurfing have helped to create new products.
   d) Surgeons are unlikely to be involved in product development.
   e) 3M uses consumers' ideas to create new products.
   f) Von Hippel believes that user-led products are often better than those developed inside a company.
   g) Some companies use toolkits to design their products.
   h) The division of labour between product and consumer has changed.

2 Choose the correct alternative for the word in *italics*.
   a) A *puzzle* (line 2) is something which is
      i) difficult to understand.
      ii) very interesting.
   b) A *decade* (line 15) is a period of
      i) five years.
      ii) ten years.

   c) A *key user* (line 44) is
      i) an important consumer.
      ii) the market leader.
   d) If you *revolutionise* something (line 54), you
      i) modify it a little.
      ii) change it completely.
   e) If something is *complex* (line 59), it is quite
      i) complicated.
      ii) big.

Over to you

Work in small groups and think of a product you would like to improve.

Discuss how you can improve it, explaining:

- why you think it needs changing
- what idea(s) you have
- what benefits the change(s) will bring.

UNIT 4 Great ideas

Ideas from R&D departments

Level of difficulty: ● ● ●

Before you read

How important do you think it is for big companies to invest in Research and Development? What do you know about General Electric (GE) and its products?

Reading

Read the article from the *Financial Times* and answer the questions.

GE keeps innovation under control

Francesco Guerrera

General Electric's Global Research Centre covers 550 acres, employs 1,000 PhDs, and has $500m a year in funding. GE's scientists have to
5 develop new products for one of the world's largest companies, with interests ranging from jet engines and nuclear power stations to microwave ovens and
10 wind turbines.

The research centre's past achievements remind companies they need to keep innovating in order to keep growing. The light
15 bulb, lasers and special glass for optical lenses were all historical breakthroughs when GE researchers developed them.

Today, consumers and producers
20 take them for granted.

With globalisation and the emergence of low-cost manufacturing in Asia and elsewhere, companies around the
25 world have discovered that growth only comes from selling better, more advanced products.

Thomas Edison, one of GE's forefathers, would have been
30 proud: a GE research project for jet fighters resulted in an invention which revolutionised the way doctors recognise illnesses.

35 During the 1980s, scientists at GE's global research centre were looking at ways to improve aircraft controls used by aircraft pilots.

Years later, one scientist, who had
40 also worked in a related medical programme, suggested applying the technology to X-rays. By the mid-1990s, GE was studying 'digital X-rays', which give a more
45 accurate view of organs and bones than was previously possible. In 2000, the company began marketing the first digital X-ray machine. The technology is
50 currently used in less than 10 per cent of the one million radiology procedures done every day, but GE believes that it will eventually replace traditional equipment.
55 GE believes more of its inventions will find uses outside their intended sectors.

FINANCIAL TIMES

1 Match the words and expressions (1–8) to their meanings (a–h).

   1 microwave oven
   2 wind turbine
   3 achievement
   4 remind
   5 breakthrough
   6 take for granted
   7 emergence
   8 forefather

   a) important new discovery
   b) a machine to cook food quickly
   c) someone who started the company a long time ago
   d) success
   e) not recognise the value of something
   f) machine which uses wind to make energy
   g) the appearance or arrival of something
   h) help remember

2 Answer these questions.
   a) How big is GE's Global Research Centre?
   b) What kind of products does GE produce?
   c) Which three products pioneered by GE are mentioned?
   d) Who was Thomas Edison?
   e) Give two examples of how research in one field lead to innovation in another.

Over to you

How difficult do you think it is to invent something completely new today? Should companies around the world work together to develop new ideas?

UNIT 5   Stress

Investing in stress-free companies

Level of difficulty: ● ● ○

Before you read

How big a problem is stress in the workplace? What are some of the main causes of stress?

Reading

Read the article from the *Financial Times* and answer the questions.

Investors are turning up the heat on stress

Alison Maitland

Workplace stress is attracting shareholders' attention. In a report, Henderson Global Investors, which manages £66.5bn ($117bn) of assets for individuals and institutions, asks companies to do more to deal with the causes of stress and reveal its costs.

A survey of 22 leading UK companies finds that most companies recognise stress as a potential risk to workers' health, but more than one-quarter have no system to assess this risk. Stress has become the biggest cause of sickness absence in Britain. It accounted for 36 per cent of days lost in 2004/05.

Jane Goodland, author of the report, says Henderson wants to understand how companies in which they invest are tackling this issue. She believes that preventive approaches to stress management can lead to business benefits.

To highlight the potential costs to individual companies, Henderson created two models – one for the transport and communications sector and another for the retail sector. It calculates the cost of stress-related absence in the transport and communications sector at £18m to £24m a year for a company with 100,000 employees. A retail company of the same size can expect annual costs of £5m to £6m. Previous research shows that larger workplaces appear to experience more stress-related absence per employee than smaller ones.

The BT group has recognised the seriousness of the problem. BT reports that 40 per cent of its work-related ill health is due to stress and mental illness. It has reduced sickness absence and saved costs in three ways: by reducing the sources of stress; identifying early signs; and helping individuals who are suffering or recovering from stress.

FINANCIAL TIMES

---

1 True or false?
- a) *Assets* (line 5) are things of value which belong to a company.
- b) If you *reveal* something (line 8), you hide it from someone.
- c) When you *assess* something (line 14), you calculate the value of it.
- d) *Absence* (line 16) means sickness.
- e) If you are *tackling* a problem (line 22), you are dealing with it.
- f) When you want to stop something from happening, you take *preventive* (line 23) action.
- g) If you *highlight* something (line 26), you draw attention to it.
- h) The *source* (line 51) of a problem is the result of the problem.

2 Number the paragraph headings in the correct order.
- a) One company's method of decreasing absence and costs ☐
- b) Majority of companies are aware of the problem ☐
- c) Examples of savings which could be made ☐
- d) Companies should tell investors the cost of stress ☐
- e) Companies who deal with stress will have advantages ☐

Over to you

Do you think it is the responsibility of companies to reduce stress? How would you deal with stress in the workplace?

UNIT 5 | Stress

Technology – helpful or stressful?

Level of difficulty: ●●●

Before you read

Do you think technological developments always make life easier?

Reading

Read the article from the *Financial Times* and answer the questions.

Freedom or slavery?

Alan Cane

Early morning in California, and Elizabeth Safran, a public relations consultant, is dealing with a huge number of e-mails. Everybody in the small company works from home and relies on e-mail and instant messaging to stay in touch. Elizabeth worries about her work–life balance and thinks that technology 'makes us more productive, but everybody is working all the time – weekends, evenings. It's too much.'

Five o'clock Friday afternoon in the UK, Paul Renucci, managing director of a systems integration company, switches off his computer. He now works at home and is off to pick up his children. In the past, it would take him two hours to get home from the office.

Ms Safran and Mr Renucci represent different sides of a modern problem: the capabilities of the latest communications technologies, such as e-mail, text, instant messaging and videoconferencing, make it difficult to draw the line between work and leisure and raise important questions about the nature of 'flexible working' – where employees can work where and when they choose.

There are three issues here. First, does the rise of portable, networked devices such as the Blackberry and Palm Treo really damage an individual's work and life? Second, what is the effect of these devices on traditional workplace relationships? And third, how do individuals manage them?

A Microsoft survey found that where flexibility had increased, so had productivity and employee morale, together with lowered stress levels and staff turnover.

However, individuals can suffer technology-related stress as work moves into their free time and from the complexity of the gadgets they must use, such as mobile phones where manufacturers try to persuade customers to upgrade more frequently.

FINANCIAL TIMES

1 True or false?
a) The staff in Elizabeth Safran's company all work in the head office.
b) Elizabeth is happy with the way she works.
c) It takes Paul Renucci a long time to get to work.
d) It is sometimes hard to separate work and free time.
e) Technology means that people can work wherever they want.
f) A Microsoft survey reported that everyone benefits from flexible working.
g) Technology can be stressful for individuals.

2 Use the a word or expression from the article to complete these sentences.
a) If a company depends on someone, it r _ _ _ _ _ on that person.
b) When you ask someone to stay in t _ _ _ _ , it means you want to see or speak to them again.
c) The c _ _ _ _ _ _ _ _ of a machine is what kind of things it is able to do.
d) F _ _ _ _ _ _ _ w _ _ _ _ _ describes when you can work where and when you want.
e) If you can carry a piece of equipment, it is described as p _ _ _ _ _ _ _ .
f) A d _ _ _ _ _ is a small machine which helps you do something.
g) Everyone needs to do more work – the company wants to improve p _ _ _ _ _ _ _ _ _ _ _ .
h) The way staff feel about the company and their work is described as staff m _ _ _ _ _ .

Over to you

Do you think that the use of modern technology can cause stress? Why (not)?

UNIT 6   Entertaining

Entertain in style

Level of difficulty: ● ● ○

Before you read

How important do you think entertaining clients is?
Should companies also reward staff in a similar way?

Reading

Read the article from the *Financial Times* and answer the
questions.

Yachts: Business and the ultimate pleasure

Jill James

In a world where corporate hospitality and staff incentives are big business, yachts are chartered by many companies.
5 Miriam Cain of Camper & Nicholsons, a company which hires and sells yachts, says companies use them because they offer high levels of security and
10 privacy.

They are like six-star, self-contained private resorts, complete with business and conference facilities and entertainment and
15 relaxation amenities. Their controlled environment is a key selling point, but at €90,000 a day they may seem too expensive for

most companies.
20 It is important to get professional advice when chartering a yacht. Edmiston is one of the best-known names in the yachting world, with offices in
25 London, Monte Carlo, Los Angeles, Golfe Juan and Mexico. Their expertise and specialist knowledge of large yachts has led to partnerships with such companies
30 as Netjets, Boeing Business Jets and Premier Automotive Group, owners of Aston Martin, Land Rover and Jaguar.

Attention to Detail is the brand
35 name of the company that manages corporate charters for Edmiston's. They will not say who individual clients are, except that a

lot of Attention's business comes
40 from the telecommunications and motors sectors. The company can arrange anything the client wants, including celebrities, guest speakers, music and
45 entertainment.

Yacht company Moody does a lot of business for conferences in Cannes, especially during the film festival. Companies use the yachts
50 for accommodation, meetings and presentations. They also specialise in charters for the Monaco Grand Prix. These are mostly for companies wanting to entertain or
55 impress clients and reward successful employees.

FINANCIAL TIMES

1 Match the words to make expressions from the article.

1	corporate	a)	facilities
2	staff	b)	advice
3	conference	c)	knowledge
4	professional	d)	hospitality
5	specialist	e)	incentives

2 True or false?
- **a)** People like using yachts because they are more secure than other venues.
- **b)** Some yachts can cost up to €90,000 a week.
- **c)** Edmiston charters are managed by a company called Attention to Detail.
- **d)** Their clients are mainly famous musicians.
- **e)** Moody organises the Cannes Film Festival.

3 Use the correct form of the words from the article to complete these definitions.
- **a)** If you want to encourage someone to do something, you may offer them an i _ _ _ _ _ _ e.
- **b)** When you want to hire a plane or boat for your own use, you c _ _ _ _ _ r it.

- **c)** It's important to have good s _ _ _ _ _ _ y so that no one gets into a building without permission.
- **d)** A town, usually near the sea, where people go for holidays is known as a r _ _ _ _ t.
- **e)** A _ _ _ _ _ _ _ s are the facilities which are offered by a hotel, for example.
- **f)** When someone has a lot of knowledge and experience, we say they have e _ _ _ _ _ _ e.
- **g)** If you make a p _ _ _ _ _ _ _ _ _ n, you give a talk to people about a specific subject.
- **h)** When someone does a job well, it is nice to r _ _ _ _ d them with a gift or bonus.

Over to you

Would you enjoy a company event on a yacht? Why (not)?

Work in groups to plan a company event to reward staff.
Discuss
- which staff should be invited
- where you would hold the event
- what kind of entertainment you would provide.

Photocopiable

UNIT 6 Entertaining

Golf sponsorship

Level of difficulty: ●●○

Before you read

Why do some big companies sponsor major sporting events? Can you think of any examples?

Reading

Read the article from the *Financial Times* and answer the questions.

How golf appeals to blue-chip sponsors

Jill James

The current popularity of golf is matched by the number of companies who want to sponsor the game. Banks and motor manufacturers are two big business sectors that have invested billions of dollars in sponsorship.

Honda, Ford, Chrysler, Buick, Nissan and Mercedes all sponsor PGA tournaments. BMW and Volvo feature on the European Tour. Elsewhere, HSBC, Barclays and RBS (Royal Bank of Scotland) have all built on their initial involvement and sponsor either Asian or European tour events.

Even smaller companies are getting involved. OKI Printing Solutions, sponsors of Portsmouth Football Club, decided to enhance its profile in the golf market by announcing a sponsorship of the OKI Castellón Open de España Senior on this season's European Seniors Tour.

Buick created one of the biggest splashes in sponsorship history in 1999 when it signed Tiger Woods for a reported $20m to $25m for five years. And that was mainly to have its company name on his golf bag. The company says it was definitely worth the money and is sponsoring his current contract.

Businesses sponsor golf competitions for publicity and to attract certain client groups to their products. Golf is still a game played by relatively wealthy people. And that is the main commercial attraction for most companies.

RBS says: 'Research has shown golf to be the closest to our key target audience of executive-level business people in our geographic priorities of the US and the Europe/UK, and more recently the Asia Pacific countries. Golf was chosen as the only "global" sport that, cost effectively, targets this audience on both sides of the Atlantic.'

FINANCIAL TIMES

1 Match the words (1–6) with their definitions (a–f).

1	popularity	a)	a way to attract public attention
2	initial		
3	enhance	b)	most important things
4	profile	c)	first
5	publicity	d)	big interest
6	priorities	e)	improve
		f)	image

2 Complete these sentences with the correct word from the article.

a) Several British banks are involved with .... and .... golf tournaments.

b) Smaller companies can improve their .... by sponsoring golf.

c) Buick felt that sponsoring Tiger Woods was .... doing.

d) People who play golf are usually quite .... , which attracts companies.

e) RBS chose to sponsor golf because it .... clients in both the USA and Europe.

Over to you

Imagine your company wants to sponsor a sporting event. In small groups, discuss:

- which sport would be best for your company
- which event you should sponsor
- who you should invite to the event.

Text bank

UNIT 7   Marketing

Luxury brands

Level of difficulty: ● ○ ○

Before you read

What do you consider to be luxury products? Does luxury always mean better quality?

Reading

Read the article from the *Financial Times* and answer the questions.

Advertising: Tried and tested or tired formula?

Claire Adler

If you studied the advertisements in any glossy magazine with the logos and company names covered up, how easily could you identify the brands?

In reality, advertisements for most luxury brands are depressingly similar. According to Mark Tungate, author of *Fashion Brands: Branding Armani to Zara*, many brands are owned by huge corporations with demanding shareholders, so they can't afford to take risks.

Luxury brands are expert at creating word-of-mouth advertising through fashion weeks, events and PR. Milton Pedraza, chief executive of New York's Luxury Institute, however, believes selling reputation and tradition is not enough. He says luxury brands should train their marketers to focus on customer needs through research and testing, as Procter & Gamble does.

Recently, brands have started using specialist luxury advertising agencies. Dawn Coulter, managing director of McCann Erickson's Luxury Box, whose clients include Gucci, says a new approach is being driven by the restructuring of many luxury organisations. Furthermore, there is a greater interest in luxury goods from consumers who mix and match luxury with cheaper products.

In luxury advertising, LVMH is the biggest player. 'The advertising spend of LVMH alone – €2bn this year – represents more than half the luxury industry's spend,' says Antoine Colonna at Merrill Lynch. He predicts a move towards more frequent campaigns, to prevent losing share of this difficult market. According to Simon Sylvester, the main differences between advertising luxury goods and consumer goods is 'in the luxury market, the benefits and features of a product are not as important as making sure who has them and who doesn't.'

FINANCIAL TIMES

---

1 Who says what? Match the following statements (a–f) with the person (1–5) who made them.

a) Luxury brand companies will advertise more often.

b) Several luxury brand companies are changing their organisation structure.

c) Companies owning luxury brands are reluctant to use innovative advertising.

d) The advertising focus on luxury brands is on the customer, not the product.

e) More ordinary consumers are buying luxury products.

f) Luxury-brand marketing people need to concentrate more on what the customer wants.

1 Mark Tungate
2 Milton Pedraza
3 Dawn Coulter
4 Antoine Colonna
5 Simon Sylvester

2 Match the words (1–8) with their meanings (a– h).

1	glossy	a)	status or position
2	depressingly	b)	concentrate
3	demanding	c)	method
4	reputation	d)	looks shiny and expensive
5	focus	e)	miserably, sadly
6	approach	f)	stop or avoid
7	predict	g)	difficult, tough
8	prevent	h)	forecast

Over to you

Do you think that luxury-brand advertisements are all the same?

Find some advertisements in glossy magazines and compare them.

If you wanted to sell a luxury product, how would you advertise it?

UNIT 7 | Marketing

Food and drink companies

Level of difficulty: ●●○

Before you read

Does the way a soft drinks company advertise its products encourage you to buy them? Do you think people prefer to buy 'healthy' drinks these days? Why (not)?

Reading

Read the article from the *Financial Times* and answer the questions.

Marketing: Investors adapt to consumer trends

Jenny Wiggins

When the world's biggest soft drink company starts changing its marketing tactics, investors should ask why. Coca-Cola, which
5 has traditionally promoted itself via the Coke brand, using slogans such as 'Coke is it', now wants to inform consumers that Coke is not the only drink it sells. Its most
10 recent campaign, called 'Make every drop count', says: 'You've always known us as Coca-Cola, the soft drink. Now it's time you knew us as Coca-Cola the company.'
15 The television, print and Internet advertisements in the UK come at a time when consumers

are ditching foods and drinks that are perceived as unhealthy (such
20 as sugary fizzy drinks and salty crisps) for products that appear to offer some kind of health benefit.

Coke is using the new campaign to impress upon consumers the
25 fact that it sells all kinds of drinks, including bottled water, juices and teas. The campaign is important for the company, because it risks losing money if it does not sell the
30 kinds of drinks consumers now want to buy.

Analysts say that growing demand for healthier kinds of foods and drinks is not a fashion,
35 but a long-term trend that increasingly affects corporate

profits. Companies which benefit are those that already produce the kinds of products consumers
40 want, or companies that are taking steps to adapt existing products. These include Danone, the French company, as well as Swiss food company Nestlé, which
45 has made nutritional foods a core strategic focus.

Companies that do not meet consumer needs are suffering. In March, Asda took the juice drink
50 Sunny D (previously known as Sunny Delight) off its shelves after finding its customers did not want to buy it.

FINANCIAL TIMES

Text bank

1 Number the paragraph summaries in the correct order. Two of the summaries are not used.

a) Companies need to change, as healthy foods are here to stay. ☐

b) Coke needs to inform customers about its whole product range. ☐

c) Unfortunately, if companies do not change, they will find it very difficult to survive. ☐

d) If customers fail to recognise Coke's whole range of products, the company will face financial problems. ☐

e) Advertisements for healthy products are very popular. ☐

f) The campaign is well timed, as people want more healthy products.? ☐

g) Many companies are benefiting from a bigger market share. ☐

2 Match the words and expressions (1–8) with their meanings (a–h).

1	tactics	**a)**	seen or believed to be
2	slogan	**b)**	make someone understand something
3	ditching	**c)**	change or modify something
4	perceived as		
5	impress upon	**d)**	the centre or heart of something
6	adapt		
7	core	**e)**	a saying to catch your attention in an ad
8	suffering	**f)**	doing badly, failing
		g)	approach
		h)	dropping or rejecting

Over to you

Do you think that advertisements are enough to change people's ideas about a product range? Do you always believe everything you see and hear in advertisements? Why (not)?

UNIT 8 Planning

Expansion plans ?

Level of difficulty: ● ● ○

Text bank

Before you read

Do you prefer shopping in a supermarket or small shops? Why? How easy or difficult do you think it is for supermarkets to move into other countries?

Reading

Read the article from the *Financial Times* and answer the questions.

Tesco plans to open Las Vegas supermarkets

Jonathan Birchall and Elizabeth Rigby

Tesco's unusually low-profile US expansion strategy is about to take it to Las Vegas, one of the fastest growing cities in the US, in addition to its plans to open stores in the Los Angeles and Phoenix areas next year.

Tesco is the UK's biggest supermarket chain, and retail analysts predict it will become Britain's biggest non-food retailer by the end of the year, overtaking Argos Retail Group.

The US push is part of Tesco's plan to expand in its domestic market and abroad. Tesco is looking for sites in Las Vegas for its planned Fresh & Easy range of mini-supermarkets.

Tesco announced its US plans in March, after conducting comprehensive market research that included a trial store in a warehouse in Los Angeles that looked like a film set. Tesco has not said how many stores it plans to open in the US and declined to comment on its strategy for Las Vegas.

The company said in March it would invest £250m ($476m) a year to fund its US expansion, a budget that should enable it to open as many as 200 stores a year. Las Vegas, with 1.7m people, is in Nevada, the fastest-growing state in the US. There is intense competition there for new customers between its existing traditional supermarkets – dominated by Kroger and Safeway – and Wal-Mart, the largest US retailer, which now has about 20 per cent of the overall US grocery market.

Tesco's strategy is based on creating a range of small stores on sites of about 14,000 sq ft similar to its Tesco Express concept in Europe.

FINANCIAL TIMES

1 Match the words (1–8) to their meanings (a–h) as they are used in the article.

1	predict	**a)**	doing or carrying out
2	conducting	**b)**	idea or design
3	trial	**c)**	expect or forecast
4	declined	**d)**	test
5	witnessing	**e)**	experiencing or seeing
6	intense	**f)**	controlled
7	dominated	**g)**	refused
8	concept	**h)**	strong

2 True or false?
 a) This year, Tesco plans to open a store in Phoenix.
 b) Tesco is already UK's largest non-food retailer.
 c) Tesco has plans to expand both in UK and abroad.
 d) Tesco is planning to make films in the USA.
 e) Tesco will open up to 200 stores in America.
 f) Wal-Mart has more of the US grocery market than Safeway.
 g) Tesco's strategy is to have large food stores in America.

Over to you

Do you have any foreign supermarkets in your country? If so, have they been successful? Why (not)?

UNIT 8   Planning

Survival plans

Level of difficulty: ● ● ●

Before you read

How important is planning for a company? How often should companies revise their plans?

Reading

Read the article from the *Financial Times* and answer the questions.

Ford restructuring plan shifts up a gear

Doug Cameron

Ford will unveil its accelerated restructuring plan at the end of next month as the US car-maker tries to halt losses and adapt to a
5 huge change in domestic demand. Mark Fields, president of Ford Americas, yesterday said it would speed up the 'Way Forward' plan announced in January in response
10 to the changes in buying habits caused by high fuel prices and market trends.

    Ford suffered from the fall in demand for large pick-up trucks
15 and utility vehicles, once its most profitable segment, in the face of $3-a-gallon petrol prices. It has also been hit by the poor performance of its luxury car segment and has
20 hired advisers to explore a potential sale of non-core assets.

    Mr Fields outlined a range of future product launches, including an addition to the luxury Lincoln
25 brand. 'I can confirm that our plans do include more new products and quicker and deeper cost-cutting,' he said. They may have to add to the 14 plant closures and 12,000 job cuts
30 outlined in January. 'Acceleration doesn't mean a new plan. It means a new timetable.'

    Mr Fields said Ford's own new product line-up had seen it gain
35 market share in the light-truck sector and maintain the steady share in the car segment, despite being overtaken in July sales by Toyota, the first time the Japanese
40 auto-maker has claimed the second spot in the US market behind GM.

    Ford is also considering plans to invest $1bn at its plants in
45 Michigan to improve flexibility and boost research and development to keep up with changing consumer tastes.

FINANCIAL TIMES

---

1 Which of these are part of Ford's plans?
  a) increasing exports
  b) building new factories
  c) launching new product in Lincoln brand
  d) further cost-cutting
  e) restructuring
  f) laying off staff
  g) investing in existing factory
  h) producing new truck designs

2 Choose the correct definition of the word in *italics*.
  a) If you *unveil* a plan (line 1), you
    i) show it to people.
    ii) keep it secret.
  b) When a company *adapts to* something (line 4), it
    i) agrees to do something.
    ii) it makes necessary changes.
  c) We *speed up* (line 8) when we need to go
    i) faster.
    ii) more slowly.

  d) *Non-core* (line 21) assets of a company are ones which are
    i) the most important.
    ii) the least important.
  e) 'He *outlined* (line 22) a range of future plans' means he
    i) showed diagrams of the plans.
    ii) described them briefly.
  f) If something *boosts* sales (line 46), it means that sales are
    i) up.
    ii) down.
  g) If a company *keeps up with* (line 47) changing consumer tastes, it
    i) makes changes according to consumer tastes.
    ii) is always changing product designs.

Over to you

What would you advise Ford to do next?

Text bank

UNIT 9 Managing people

Giving staff more freedom

Level of difficulty: ● ● ○

Before you read

What kind of manager do you think you are / would be? Do you think it's better to work for a manager with strong opinions or one who asks staff for their ideas?

Reading

Read the article from the *Financial Times* and answer the questions.

Secrets of the maverick cobbler

James Wilson

Fifteen years ago, Mr Timpson bought out his partners in the shoe-repair business that bears his family name. In 1995, he bought
5 Automagic, the shoe-repair and key-cutting chain. Since then Timpson has turned to key cutting, watch and jewellery repairs and engraving, acquired
10 two big high-street rivals and broken through £100m in annual sales. Still only Mr Timpson owns shares.

'We are committed to being
15 independent. I'm not interested in a deal that involves equity being given to anybody,' says Mr Timpson, who is company chairman, while his son James is
20 managing director. To some, the company style might seem rather old-fashioned, with holiday homes for staff, training schemes and newsletters with personal input
25 from Mr Timpson.

Tight control of the business ensures the company's commitment to what Mr Timpson calls 'upside-down management':
30 giving power to those a long way from head office in Manchester. Mr Timpson believes that the most important staff are those who cut customers' keys and reheel their
35 shoes. Everyone else, from area managers to the boardroom, is there to serve the shop staff, who are given plenty of freedom as long as they prioritise customers'
40 needs.

'I think it would be difficult for some professional manager to come in and do it our way. I don't expect other people to come up
45 with the ideas. That is my job or James's job. But I can't then tell them what is going to happen. I have got to persuade them. My form of management is a lot of
50 communication. It won't work unless they approve of it,' says Mr Timpson.

FINANCIAL TIMES

1 True or false?
   a) Timpson's repairs watches and jewellery.
   b) There are several family shareholders.
   c) Employees can use holiday homes owned by the company.
   d) Mr Timpson believes that only people in head office can make decisions.
   e) People who work in his shops are very important.
   f) The most important thing is to look after customers.
   g) Management's job is to support staff in the shops.
   h) Mr Timpson encourages staff to come up with ideas.
   i) Communication is a key factor in Mr Timpson's management style.

2 Choose the alternative that best explains the words in *italics*,
   a) A *cobbler* (headline) is someone who makes
      i) keys ii) shoes iii) jewellery
   b) In business, a *rival* (line 10) is a
      i) competitor
      ii) supplier
      iii) sub-contractor

   c) If a company is *committed* (line 14) to doing something, it means it has
      i) negotiated to do it
      ii) promised to do it
      iii) refused to do it
   d) If you *persuade* (line 48) someone to do something, you
      i) stop them from doing it.
      ii) make them believe it is a good idea to do it.
      iii) keep telling them to do it.

3 Complete these sentences with the correct preposition.
   a) The company is committed ...... listening to what customers say.
   b) Mr Timpson is not interested...... selling any of his shares.
   c) It can be difficult ...... some people to take responsibility.
   d) Mr Timpson does not expect his staff to come up ...... new ideas.

Over to you

Would you like to work for a boss like Mr Timpson? Why (not)? What do you think is the most important quality or skill a manager should have?

UNIT 9   Managing people

Improving the work environment

Level of difficulty: ●●○

Before you read

Do you think that companies should have social events to bring everyone together? If so, what sort of events do you think work best?

Reading

Read the article from the *Financial Times* and answer the questions.

Bonds that keep workers happy

Alison Maitland

Many people would laugh at the idea that the workplace can be a relaxing place. With their mobiles, laptops and BlackBerries, they
5 would be more likely to complain about the way their work takes over their private lives.

The employees of Europe's best workplaces take a very different
10 view, however. One noticeable theme to emerge from this year's survey is the strong attraction that many employees feel to their work and the personal bonds they
15 have with their colleagues and managers.

At Confinimmo, a small Belgian property investment company in
20 this year's European top 10, employees go on a paid team-building trip each time a new person joins their department. Celebrations and informal lunches are another way of bringing
25 employees and managers together. 'Although the company has seen strong growth, it keeps its feeling of a small, familiar team,' says one employee.
30 At Boehringer Ingelheim, a family-owned Danish drug company that has been in the top 100 since the survey began four years ago, there are social events
35 and celebrations all year, often attended by employees' children.

Champagne and chocolate are brought out to mark achievements. 'Our managing
40 director knows everyone by his first name,' says one member of the 132-strong workforce.

It is, of course, easier to create a family feeling in a small business.
45 But bonding is also a feature of the smaller European offices of Microsoft, which is in this year's top 10. The employees of the software giant in Norway, for
50 example, go mountain-hiking together and recently climbed seven of the highest mountains in southern Norway to symbolise their seven business goals.

FINANCIAL TIMES

1 Match the words and expressions (1–5) with their meanings (a–e).

1 bonds — a) represent
2 theme — b) come out of
3 emerge — c) links, connections
4 giant — d) topic
5 symbolise — e) huge company

2 True or false?
a) Employees of Europe's best workplaces think the workplace can be like home.
b) At Confinimmo, every new person has to pay for a team-building trip.
c) Confinimmo feels like a smaller firm than it is.
d) This is the first time the Danish company has been in the top 100 companies.
e) Employees' children are welcome at the social events.
f) The MD knows the first name of all his employees.
g) Bonding is easier in a small company.
h) Microsoft has failed to rank in the top ten this year.

Over to you

What can companies do to make the workplace a more enjoyable place to be in? What is important to you when choosing a company to work for?

UNIT 10 Conflict

Better leadership

Level of difficulty: ●●●

Before you read

What do you think can cause conflict in the workplace? Do you think that managers should be trained to deal with conflict?

Reading

Read the article from the *Financial Times* and answer the questions.

Understand your team and the rest is easy

Richard Donkin

Mark Gerzon, author of *Leading Through Conflict: How Successful Leaders Transform Differences into Opportunities,* has noticed that
5 most things in life involve conflict.
Some of these conflicts emerge when people come together from different backgrounds where views, cultures and beliefs may
10 not be shared by their colleagues. Today some 63,000 companies are operating internationally, employing 90 million people and responsible for a quarter of the
15 world's gross national product.
'We simply cannot manage a whole company, a whole community, and certainly not a whole planet, with leaders who
20 identify with only one part,' he writes. He therefore believes that future corporate leaders will need to be experts in mediation rather than the controlling style of
25 leaders which was apparent during the 20th century.
These controlling leaders always blamed someone else for failures and achieved success only because
30 employees were frightened of losing their jobs. Sadly such methods still exist in some companies.
Similarly, people who question
35 management in companies where employee morale is very low are seen as trouble makers and are often dismissed by the company.
But suppose they have a point?
40 Trouble makers are likely to respect a leader with good mediation skills because they feel that someone is listening to their complaints.
45 One problem with mediation in leadership is that it takes time, something this highly competitive world has little of. That is why the most competitive teams need
50 individuals who are all capable of leadership. People need to talk all the time about their various tasks and work towards the same objective, and any conflicts should
55 be managed in a way that does not disrupt the harmony of the team.

FINANCIAL TIMES

---

1 True or false?
a) Mark Gerzon believes that conflict exists in nearly every part of life.
b) Conflict can occur when people work together.
c) Leaders need to understand only one part of the company.
d) Twentieth-century leaders rarely accepted responsibility for their mistakes.
e) People who disagree with management feared they will lose their jobs.
f) Good mediators are likely to be respected by staff.
g) Using mediation to resolve conflict takes time.
h) A competitive team needs one good leader.

2 Choose the correct alternatives.
a) If a manager is good at *mediation* (line 23), she/he
  i) makes good decisions.
  ii) is able to resolve conflict.
b) To *blame* someone (line 28) is to
  i) say they are responsible for a mistake
  ii) apologise to them for a mistake
c) If employee *morale* (line 36) is low, staff are
  i) motivated.
  ii) unhappy.
d) A *trouble maker* (line 37) is someone who
  i) solves problems.
  ii) causes problems.

Over to you

What sort of mix of people do you need to make a good team? What different types of leader do you think there are?

UNIT 10 Conflict

Outsourcing conflict

Level of difficulty: ● ● ●

Before you read

Why do companies outsource? What kind of problems might there be with outsourcing?

Reading

Read the article from the *Financial Times* and answer the questions.

Misunderstanding and mistrust bedevil contracts

Andrew Baxter

A catalogue of mistakes and misunderstandings is revealed today in a global study of IT outsourcing deals which helps to
5 explain why there is much mistrust and tension between clients and suppliers. The study, by PA Consulting Group, includes the views of all parties in an
10 outsourcing relationship – clients, suppliers and the lawyers who mediate between them.

The problems it reveals are both surprising and disappointing,
15 because over the past 15 years, many North American and European companies have benefited hugely from moving large parts of their IT operations
20 to external service suppliers, either 'onshore' or in countries such as India.

In this mature market, says PA, outsourcing deals should not go
25 wrong. But deals do fail because buyers and suppliers of outsourcing do not have a clear idea of each other's objectives.

Poor communication of
30 objectives results in big differences between what clients want and what suppliers think they want. Meanwhile, clients are not putting sufficient time and
35 effort into planning the outsourcing process.

The study says misunderstandings are created when the relationship between
40 clients, suppliers and lawyers is built on undeclared assumptions which creates a climate of mistrust.

For example, only a fifth of the suppliers questioned felt clients
45 effectively communicated their objectives, and two-thirds of clients thought they should have verified their suppliers' ability to deliver.
50 Poor investment in three key areas is preventing the evolution of IT outsourcing as a way to transform an organisation: the sourcing strategy is ill-conceived,
55 creating a gap between client and supplier; the programme is not tailored to the needs of the organisation; and the internal team for managing the
60 relationship with the supplier is inadequate.

FINANCIAL TIMES

1 Which of these things are mentioned as causes of conflict?
   a) The involvement of lawyers
   b) Poor language skills
   c) Weak management teams
   d) The failure of parties to understand each other
   e) Lack of planning
   f) Failure to check suppliers ability to do the job
   g) Lack of investment in suppliers

2 Use the correct form of words from the article to complete these statements.
   a) The car company will r _ _ _ _ l its new model at the motor show.
   b) A well-developed market is called a m _ _ _ _ e market.
   c) The aims of a company are called its o _ _ _ _ _ _ _ _ s.
   d) When you think something is true, but do not have all the facts, you make an a _ _ _ _ _ _ _ n.
   e) If you have to check that a deal is good, you need to v _ _ _ _ y the details.
   f) Another word for development is e _ _ _ _ _ _ n.
   g) If you have a product or service just for you, it is t _ _ _ _ _ _ d to your specifications.
   h) If something is lacking, you can say it is i _ _ _ _ _ _ _ e.

Over to you

Is outsourcing always a good idea? What sort of jobs do you think can be outsourced successfully?

UNIT 11　New business

Need for fast expansion

Level of difficulty: ●●○

Before you read

Would you like to set up your own business? Why (not)? What sort of problems do you think new businesses face in today's business world?

Reading

Read the article from the *Financial Times* and answer the questions.

Hippychick completes first steps and prepares for growth

Jonathan Moules

Julia and Jeremy Minchin, entrepreneurs, are learning that small businesses grow fast. Julia founded Hippychick, an upmarket parenting products business, in 1999. She had already worked in a start-up as marketing head at Cobra Beer and was keen to start a business of her own.

Hippychick's launch product was the Hipseat, a baby carrier which is strapped to the user's waist. The company now sells a range of items, from baby boots to mattress protectors, many of which are distributed under licence through Mothercare, Early Learning Centre, Boots, John Lewis and about 500 independent toy shops. 'We are not inventors, but we are very good suppliers,' Julia says. They also export successfully to 45 countries. The Hippychick workforce consists of just eight people, but the Minchins are under pressure to expand as the business hits a period of high growth.

Turnover for the past financial year was £1.2m and is expected to hit £2m during the current 12 months of trading. In three years, the Minchins expect turnover to be £5m.

Getting the right product mix is crucial, and Julia, who oversees marketing in the business, would like to have more Hippychick-branded products. However, she is reluctant to expand into some areas, such as clothing, because it is such a difficult market.

Operations have moved to a 6,000 sq ft warehouse, and they are now considering taking a 3,500 sq ft space next door. Renting the additional space would cost another £15,000 a year, but Jeremy believes that doing nothing is not an option.

FINANCIAL TIMES

1　Match the numbers (1–10) to what they refer to (a–j).

1	1999	a)	size of potential warehouse
2	500	b)	the past year's turnover
3	45	c)	the year the company was founded
4	8	d)	predicted turnover in three years
5	£1.2 million	e)	cost of renting additional space
6	£2 million	f)	expected turnover for current year
7	£5 million	g)	number of countries exported to
8	6,000	h)	current number of employees
9	£15,000	i)	size of current warehouse
10	3,500	j)	toy shops distributing Hippychick products

2　Choose the best answer to complete each sentence.

a) Julia has a background in
　i) baby products.
　ii) marketing.
　iii) farming.

b) Some of Hippychick's products are
　i) produced by Mothercare.
　ii) sold in Hippychick's own shops.
　iii) distributed through toy shops.

c) According to Julia, she and her partner
　i) are very good at supplying products.
　ii) come up with brilliant ideas.
　iii) are trying to invent new products.

d) The turnover of the company
　i) doubled last year.
　ii) should be £2m this year.
　iii) will increase by £5m next year.

e) What does Julia say about product mix?
　i) She wants to sell more brands.
　ii) She will start selling clothing brands.
　iii) She wants more Hippychick brands.

f) What are the company's options for the future?
　i) to rent a 6,000 sq ft warehouse
　ii) to spend £15,000 on more warehouse space
　iii) to do absolutely nothing

Over to you

Can you think of any new products which have come onto the market recently? Why do you think they are successful or not? Is it easy to set up a new business in your country?

UNIT 11　New business

Problems of success

Level of difficulty: ● ● ●

Before you read

How difficult do you think it is to spot a gap in a market?
Have you ever thought of a product/service which you'd like
to see on the market, but which doesn't exist at the moment?

Reading

Read the article from the *Financial Times* and answer the
questions.

The gains from growing pains

Alicia Clegg

The best start-up ideas are often
the simplest. But entrepreneurs
often need to experiment with
business models as their ventures
5 grow. For young retail companies,
one of the biggest challenges is
getting the right mix of outlets as
they perfect their products.
Christian Rucker, founder of The
10 White Company, which made pre-
tax profits of £2.2m the year before
last, is a classic example.
    While working as an editor at
fashion magazine *Harper's*, Ms
15 Rucker spotted a gap in the market
for stylish white bed linen and
accessories priced midway between

designer labels and mass-market
lines. After finding £20,000 from a
20 local government grant and shares
inherited from her grandmother,
she launched her business in 1994,
initially through mail order. Last
year, The White Company made
25 sales of £49.5m, up by almost £10m
on the previous year.
    'Offering choice is part of great
customer service,' says Ms Rucker,
whose company owns 14 shops,
30 plus space in department stores
and franchises in Dubai. 'One
channel feeds another. Someone
might see something in a store then
place an order online. Customers
35 will spend more because you are
making it easy for them.'

Having survived the early days,
the entrepreneur must find ways
of sustaining growth in future,
40 without sacrificing the
individuality that attracted their
customers in the first place.
    Ms Rucker, who aims for sales of
£110m by 2011, believes the
45 solution is to improve quality.
'There comes a point when it's
easy to drop the quality a little and
take a higher profit margin. But,
as the quantity goes up, you can
50 actually afford to buy slightly
better materials but keep the price
[for customers] the same.'

FINANCIAL TIMES

1 Complete this summary with the correct figures from
the article.
Ms Rucker started her business in **a)** …… with just **b)** ……. .
The year before last, her profit before tax was **c)** ……. . And
last year, turnover increased by **d)** …… to reach **e)** ……. . She
has set a sales target of **f)** …… by 2011.

2 True or false?
a) Young retail companies have problems finding the right
place to sell their products.
b) Ms Rucker works for a fashion magazine.
c) She used a bank loan to set up her company.
d) She believes that customers like choice.
e) It is important to keep a product's unique features
when a company expands.
f) Ms Rucker says that quality can only be improved when
a product is profitable.

3 Match the words (1–8) with their meanings (a–h).
1	experiment	a)	at first
2	venture	b)	giving up, losing
3	outlet	c)	shop
4	classic	d)	try new things
5	midway between	e)	activity
6	initially	f)	keeping
7	sustaining	g)	typical
8	sacrificing	h)	in the middle of

Over to you

How important is the quality of something you are buying?
Are you prepared to pay more for good-quality products and
services?

UNIT 12 Products

Launching several new products

Level of difficulty: ● ● ○

Before you read

In what ways can technology help to save lives?

Reading

Read the article from the *Financial Times* and answer the questions.

Raymarine to launch 12 new products

David Blackwell

Raymarine, the marine electronics group, is to launch 12 new products this year, including a device that uses the satellite
5 positioning system to pinpoint anyone falling overboard.

The company also expects continuing strong sales of the E-series of navigation products,
10 launched a year ago. These products use one screen to display information such as navigation charts, fish-finding equipment and engine performance.
15 Last year, the company moved most of its production from Portsmouth to Hungary, where all its printed circuit boards are now made. It expects to complete the
20 transfer of all production facilities to Hungary by the end of this year.

The restructuring led to charges of £10.9m for the year to December 31, leaving pre-tax profit at £8.1m,
25 compared with £5.3m for the previous year. However, adjusted operating profits rose 38 per cent to £19.4m (£14.1m) after a rise in sales from £106.3m to £121.9m.

30 **FT Comment**

* This is both a restructuring story and one of the few successful consumer electronics stories. The fact that the company was still
35 manufacturing anything in the UK shows how old-fashioned it was, and the outsourcing to Hungary should add at least £5m to profits next year and £10m the following
40 year. It should also enable the company to lift its market share in a market that is expanding as more people retire and have money to spend on leisure. In the
45 US, for example, many of those who move to Florida and take up boating love spending their money on such equipment. Profits this year are expected to be about
50 £21m, rising to £28.5m next year.

FINANCIAL TIMES

1 Match the words (1–8) with their meanings (a–h).

1	marine	a)	stop working
2	pinpoint	b)	relocation
3	overboard	c)	free time
4	navigation	d)	make a slight change
5	transfer (n)	e)	locate
6	adjust	f)	connected to the sea
7	retire	g)	into the sea (from a boat)
8	leisure	h)	finding the direction

2 Choose the correct word from the box to complete the summary.

abroad expanding launch manufacturing
operating outsourcing overboard
restructuring retire

Raymarine produces electronic devices for use on boats. One of its new products can signal when someone has gone **a)** .... The company is now moving its **b)** ...... to Hungary. The **c)** ...... has been expensive, but a lot of money should be saved by **d)** ...... to Hungary. The market is **e)** ...... because more people in the USA are buying boats when they **f)** ....

Over to you

Raymarine is going to launch 12 new products. What kind of strategy do you think a company needs when launching so many products in one year?

UNIT 12 Products

Following new trends

Level of difficulty: ●●●

Before you read
Do companies need to come up with new products all the time to be successful?

Reading
Read the article from the *Financial Times* and answer the questions.

Kraft gives products healthy makeover

Jeremy Grant

Ever since it was invented by Kraft Foods in 1937, packaged macaroni and cheese has been the ultimate American comfort food. In the past six months, Kraft has been re-inventing 'Supermac' with a version made with healthy ingredients.

Kraft believes that many of its famous products – like Ritz crackers, introduced in 1934, Kool-Aid powdered soft drinks and Jell-O instant pudding – must be brought up to date to take advantage of the 'health and wellness' trend in the food industry. Food companies typically charge customers more for 'healthy' products. And Kraft needs such customers more than most of its rivals.

Its products like 'Supermac', aimed at the middle-income consumer, are the most vulnerable to private-label competition. It has also struggled to maintain the right price gap between its brands and non-branded competition.

Kraft risks being left out as consumers buy more expensive products – a trend highlighted by Campbell Soup's success with more expensive soups sold in cartons and marketed as 'restaurant quality'.

Roger Deromedi, Kraft chief executive, admits Kraft could be doing better. However, Mr Deromedi says the launch of new products carrying premium prices – such as luxury Carte D'Or chocolate launched last quarter in the UK and Germany – has improved sales mix. Also, new product revenues jumped by 50 per cent in two years, driven by new items like DiGiorno microwaveable frozen pizzas.

Kraft also plans to target older consumers with higher spending and has been eliminating slower-selling product lines. 'It's re-inventing the brands within the categories that exist. That is the power of our company – the strength of our brands.'

FINANCIAL TIMES

---

1 True or false?
a) Packaged macaroni cheese was first sold in 1937.
b) Kraft is changing its products because of changes in the market.
c) Healthy products are cheaper than less healthy products.
d) One of Kraft's competitors is Campbells.
e) Sales of Campbell's restaurant-quality soups were poor.
f) Completely new products are doing less well than expected.
g) Kraft plans to improve the slower-selling products.

2 Choose the correct meaning for the words in *italics*.
a) If you give something a *makeover* (headline), you
   i) change its look or content.
   ii) promote the product in a different way.
b) 'The *ultimate … comfort food*' (lines 3–4) means
   i) the best food to make you feel happy.
   ii) the highest-quality food possible.

c) 'A *version* of something' (line 24) means
   i) an unusual design of something.
   ii) a different type of something.
d) If something is *vulnerable* (line 26), it is
   i) likely to be in danger.
   ii) dangerous to people.
e) If you *struggle* to do something (line 40), you
   i) find it hard to do it.
   ii) enjoy trying to do it.
f) *Premium* prices (line 51) means
   i) discounted prices.
   ii) more expensive prices.
g) If you *eliminate* something (line 00), you
   i) sell it cheaply.
   ii) remove it.

Over to you

Do you look for healthy products when you shop? Do you think that all food companies should change their products to more healthy ones?

Text bank

Text bank answer key

Unit 1

A career in retail banking

1 **a)** i **b)** ii **c)** i **d)** ii
2 **a)** T **b)** T **c)** T **d)** F **e)** F **f)** T **g)** T

Training on the job

1 1 f 2 d 3 a 4 b 5 e 6 c
2 **a)** Chief executive of BAE systems / member of the Apprenticeships Task Force
b) Up to £1m per year
c) Lower recruitment costs, lower staff turnover, and apprentices identify with company values more quickly
d) £1,300 per apprentice per year
e) In the later years of their apprenticeships
f) Because they understand company values and practices more quickly
g) They are a cost-effective way of replacing an ageing workforce and they ensure effective transfer of knowledge

Unit 2

Film deals online

1 1 h 2 c 3 f 4 d 5 b 6 e 7 i 8 g 9 a
2 **a)** T **b)** F **c)** T **d)** F **e)** T **f)** T
3 **a)** agree **b)** feature **c)** growth **d)** intention **e)** launch
f) speculate **g)** involve **h)** promotion

Online advertising

1 **a)** T **b)** F **c)** F **d)** T **e)** T **f)** T **g)** F **h)** F
2 **a)** ii **b)** i **c)** iii **d)** iii

Unit 3

Computer company success

1 1 h 2 i 3 k 4 f 5 b 6 e 7 d 8 g 9 c 10 a 11 j
2 **a)** from **b)** for **c)** on **d)** for **e)** of **f)** for **g)** from

Change for success

1 **a)** repair **b)** dying **c)** create **d)** declining **e)** modify
f) challenge **g)** recruit **h)** potential
2 **a)** F **b)** T **c)** F **d)** F **e)** T **f)** T **g)** F **h)** T **i)** F

Unit 4

Ideas from consumers

1 **a)** F **b)** F **c)** T **d)** F **e)** T **f)** T **g)** T **h)** T
2 **a)** i **b)** ii **c)** i **d)** ii **e)** i

Ideas from R&D departments

1 1 b 2 f 3 d 4 h 5 a 6 e 7 g 8 c
2 **a)** It covers 550 acres and employs 1,000 PhDs.
b) Jet engines, nuclear power stations, microwave ovens and wind turbines.
c) Light bulb, lasers and special glass for optical lenses
d) One of GE's forefathers
e) Research project for jet fighters led to an invention which revolutionised the way doctors recognise illnesses. Research into aircraft instrumentation led to digital X-ray machines.

Unit 5

Investing in stress-free companies

1 **a)** T **b)** F **c)** T **d)** F **e)** T **f)** T **g)** T **h)** F
2 **a)** 5 **b)** 2 **c)** 4 **d)** 1 **e)** 3

Technology – helpful or stressful?

1 **a)** F **b)** F **c)** F **d)** T **e)** T **f)** T **g)** T
2 **a)** relies **b)** touch **c)** capability **d)** Flexible working
e) portable **f)** device **g)** productivity **h)** morale

Unit 6

Entertain in style

1 1 d 2 e 3 a 4 b 5 c
2 **a)** T **b)** F **c)** T **d)** F **e)** F
3 **a)** incentive **b)** charter **c)** security **d)** resort
e) Amenities **f)** expertise **g)** presentation **h)** reward

Golf sponsorship

1 1 d 1 c 3 e 4 f 5 a 6 b
2 **a)** Asian; European **b)** profile **c)** worth **d)** wealthy
e) targets

Unit 7

Luxury brands

1 1 c 2 f 3 b,e 4 a 5 d
2 1 d 2 e 3 g 4 a 5 b 6 c 7 h 8 f

Food and drink companies

1 **a)** 4 **b)** 1 **c)** 5 **d)** 3 **e)** – **f)** 2 **g)** –
2 1 g 2 e 3 h 4 a 5 b 6 c 7 d 8 f

Text bank

Unit 8

Expansion plans

1 1c 2a 3d 4g 5e 6h 7f 8b
2 **a)** F **b)** F **c)** T **d)** F **e)** T **f)** T **g)** F

Survival plans

1 c, d, e, f, g
2 **a)** i **b)** ii **c)** i **d)** ii **e)** ii **f)** i **g)** i

Unit 9

Giving staff more freedom

1 **a)** T **b)** F **c)** T **d)** F **e)** T **f)** T **g)** T **h)** F **i)** T
2 **a)** ii **b)** i **c)** ii **d)** ii
3 **a)** to **b)** in **c)** for **d)** with

Improving the work environment

1 1c 2d 3b 4e 5a
2 **a)** T **b)** F **c)** T **d)** F **e)** T **f)** T **g)** T **h)** F

Unit 10

Better leadership

1 **a)** T **b)** T **c)** F **d)** T **e)** T **f)** T **g)** T **h)** F
2 **a)** ii **b)** i **c)** ii **d)** ii

Outsourcing conflict

1 c, d, e, f
2 **a)** reveal **b)** mature **c)** objectives **d)** assumption
  e) verify **f)** evolution **g)** tailored **h)** inadequate

Unit 11

Need for fast expansion

1 1c 2j 3g 4h 5b 6f 7d 8i 9e 10a
2 **a)** ii **b)** iii **c)** i **d)** ii **e)** iii **f)** ii

Problems of success

1 **a)** 1994 **b)** £20,000 **c)** £2.2m **d)** £10m **e)** £49.5m
  f) £110m
2 **a)** T **b)** F **c)** F **d)** T **e)** T **f)** F
3 1d 2e 3c 4g 5h 6a 7f 8b

Unit 12

Launching several new products

1 1f 2e 3g 4h 5b 6d 7a 8c
2 **a)** overboard **b)** manufacturing **c)** restructuring
  d) outsourcing **e)** expanding **f)** retire

Following new trends

1 **a)** T **b)** T **c)** F **d)** T **e)** F **f)** F **g)** F
2 **a)** i **b)** i **c)** ii **d)** i **e)** i **f)** ii **g)** ii

Text bank

Resource bank

Teacher's notes

Introduction

These Resource bank activities are designed to extend and develop the Skills sections in the Course Book. Each Resource bank unit begins with a language exercise that takes up and takes further the language points from the Course Book unit and then applies this language in one or more role-play activities.

What to give the students

You have permission to photocopy the Resource bank pages in this book. In some units, you will give each student a copy of the whole page. In others, there are role cards which need to be cut out and given to participants with particular roles. These activities are indicated in the unit-specific notes below.

The **language exercises** at the beginning of each Resource bank unit can be used to revise language from the Course Book unit, especially if you did the Skills section in another lesson. In any case, point out the connection with the Course Book Skills material. These language exercises are designed to prepare Ss for the role-play(s) that follow and in many cases can be done in a few minutes as a way of focusing Ss on the activity that will follow.

A typical two-person **role-play** might last five to ten minutes, followed by five minutes of praise and correction. An animated group discussion might last longer than you planned. In this case, drop one of your other planned activities and do it another time, rather than try to squeeze it in before the end of the lesson. If you then have five or ten minutes left over, you can always go over some language points from the lesson again or, better still, get Ss to say what they were. One way of doing this is to ask them what they've written in their notebooks during the lesson.

Revising and revisiting

Feel free to do an activity more than once. After one run-through, praise strong points, and then work on three or four things that need correcting or improving. Then you can get the Ss to change roles and do the activity again, or the parts of the activity where these points come up. Obviously, there will come a time when interest wanes, but the usual tendency in language teaching is not to revisit things enough, rather than the reverse.

Fluency and accuracy

Concentrate on different things in different activities. In some role-plays and discussions you may want to focus on *fluency*, with Ss interacting as spontaneously as possible. In others, you will want to concentrate on *accuracy*, with Ss working on getting specific forms correct. Rather than expect them to get everything correct, you could pick out, say, three or four forms that you want them to get right and focus on these.

Clear instructions

Be sure to give complete instructions *before* getting Ss to start. In role-plays, be very clear about who has which role, and give Ss time to absorb the information they need. Sometimes there are role cards that you hand out. The activities where this happens are indicated.

Parallel and public performances (PPP)

In pairwork or small-group situations, get all groups to do the activity at the same time. Go round the class and listen. When they have finished, praise strong points and deal with three or four problems that you have heard, especially problems that more than one group has been having. Then get individual groups to give public performances so that the whole class can listen. The performers should pay particular attention to these three or four points.

1 to 1

The pair activities can be done 1 to 1, with the teacher taking one of the roles. The activity can be done a second time, reversing the roles and getting the student to integrate your suggestions for improvement.

Unit 1 Careers

- This relates to the telephoning language on page 11 of the Course Book. Get your Ss to do this exercise as preparation for the role-play.

1 Can I talk <u>to</u> Beryl Yang, please?

2 I'<u>d</u> like to speak to Beryl Yang, please.

3 Just a moment. I'm putting you through.

4 Just a moment. I'll <u>connect</u> you.

5 <u>Is that</u> Beryl Yang?

6 Beryl Yang <u>speaking</u>.

7 Hello. <u>This is</u> Andres Solano, from Solano and Associates.

8 I'm phoning <u>about</u> the proposal you sent us.

9 The reason I'm <u>calling</u> is that we want to discuss it further.

10 We've lost your e-mail address. <u>Can</u> (or <u>Could</u>) you give it to me?

Ⓑ

- Divide the class into groups of three.

- Give each student a copy of the instructions to the telephone call.

- Get Ss to sit back-to-back to simulate the phone calls or, even better, get them to use real phone extensions.

- When the situation is clear, begin the role-play.

- Circulate and monitor. Note language points for praise and correction, especially in language used while making telephone calls.

- Bring the class to order. Praise strong language points and work on half a dozen points that need improving, getting Ss to say the correct forms.

- Get one or two of the groups to do their role-play for the whole class.

Model answer

A: Hello. Can I talk to Beryl Yang, please?

C: Just a moment. I'll connect you.

A: Thank you.

B: Hello.

A: Is that Beryl Yang?

B: Yes, Beryl Yang speaking.

A: I'm phoning about the proposal for a new office building that you sent us.

B: Right.

A: The reason I'm calling is that we want to discuss it further.

B: OK. We've lost your e-mail address. Could you give it to me?

(The situation is continued in Unit 7.)

Unit 2 Selling online

Ⓐ

- This allows Ss to revise the negotiating tips given on page 18 of the Course Book. The items a) to g) are the comments of a negotiator after a particular negotiation with a potential customer.

1 f 2 d 3 e 4 a 5 b 6 g 7 c

Ⓑ

- Divide the class into pairs. Give a role card to each student.

- Point out that Ss must negotiate the number of copies to be bought and the discount to be given. They do not have to negotiate anything else.

- When the situation is clear, begin the role-play.

- Circulate and monitor. Note language points for praise and correction, especially in the area of negotiation.

- Bring the class to order. Praise strong language points and work on half a dozen points that need improving, getting Ss to say the correct forms.

- Get one or two of the pairs to do their role-play for the whole class.

Unit 3 Companies

- This reminds Ss of the suggestions for making effective presentations given on page 27 of the Course Book. The items a) to f) are the thoughts of members of the audience at a presentation.

1 c 2 e 3 a 4 b 5 f 6 d

Ⓑ

- Divide the class into groups of three. Give each student a copy of the notes and tell them which company they are going to present.

- Give Ss time to prepare their presentations. Each student then gives their presentation to the other members of their group.

- Circulate and monitor. Note down language points for praise and correction afterwards, especially in relation to presentations language.

- Bring the class to order. Praise strong language points and work on half a dozen points that need improving, getting Ss to say the correct forms.

- Get one or two Ss to give their presentations to the whole class.

Unit 4 Great ideas

Ⓐ

- This allows Ss to revise the language used in meetings given on pages 38–39 of the Course Book.

Chairperson

1 Can we <u>start</u>, please? (Beginning the meeting)
2 The main <u>aim</u> of this meeting is to … (Stating the purpose of the meeting)
3 How do you <u>feel</u> about this? (Asking for comments)
4 Let's <u>move</u> on now to … (Changing the subject)
5 Sorry, I don't <u>quite</u> understand. (Clarifying)

Participants

6 I'm in <u>favour</u> of … (Giving opinions)
7 Perhaps <u>we</u> should … (Making suggestions)
8 I totally <u>agree</u>. (Agreeing)
9 I don't know <u>about</u> that. (Disagreeing)
10 <u>Hold</u> on a moment. (Interrupting)

 B

- Divide the class into groups of four. Explain the situation and hand out the role cards. Ask the owner of Flat A to chair the meeting, as well as give their own opinions.

- Circulate and assist if necessary.

- When the groups are ready, the discussions can begin. Circulate and monitor. Note down language points for praise and correction afterwards, especially in relation to language used in meetings.

- Bring the class to order. Praise strong language points and work on half a dozen points that need improving, getting Ss to say the correct forms.

- Ask the groups for the outcomes of their meetings.

Unit 5 Stress

A

- This allows Ss to revise the functional language on page 47 of the Course Book.

> 1 a, f, g, h 2 c, d 3 b 4 e

B

- Explain the situation. Divide the class into groups of three and hand out the role cards.

- Circulate and assist your Ss in preparing if necessary.

- Tell your Ss that this is an opportunity to use expressions for making suggestions, giving opinions, agreeing and disagreeing.

- Ask the Ss to start the role-play. Circulate and monitor. Note down language points for praise and correction afterwards, especially in relation to the language used for participating in discussions.

- When the groups have finished, praise strong language points and work on half a dozen points that need improving, getting Ss to say the correct forms.

- Ask one of the groups to redo all or part of the activity, incorporating the improvements.

Unit 6 Entertaining

A

- This revises the functional language on pages 54–55 of the Course Book.

- Make enough copies of the conversation for all Ss. Cut the copies up.

- Hand out the parts and get Ss to reconstruct the conversation. Then get them to read it in groups of three.

- With the whole class, work on intonation and pronunciation.

B

- Tell your Ss that this conversation is a continuation of the one in Exercise A.

- Ask your Ss to work in groups of three. Hand out the conversations. Give the groups time to prepare. Then get them to start the conversation, standing up as if on a stand at a trade show. Circulate and monitor. Note down language points for praise and correction afterwards.

- Bring the class to order. Praise strong language points and work on half a dozen points that need improving, getting Ss to say the correct forms.

- Get one or two of the groups to redo their conversation for the whole class, incorporating your corrections.

A	*to Barbara* Can you lend me your mobile so I can call my office? I'll come back after the call.
B	*to Carlos* Where are you staying?
C	At the Ritz. It's comfortable, but noise from nightclubs is a problem around 2 a.m.
B	I'm sorry to hear that. Would you like my business card?
C	Yes, please. Can I have some of your brochures?
B	Of course!
A	Thanks for the mobile, Barbara!
B	That's all right.
C	Would you both like to have dinner somewhere this evening?
B, C	That's a good idea.
C	Shall we meet in the lobby of my hotel at eight?
A, B	That sounds good.
C	Bye for now. See you later!
A, B	Bye!

Unit 7 Marketing

 A

- Do this exercise as a quick-fire activity with the whole class.

- Remind your Ss that groups within telephone numbers should be pronounced with rising intonation, except the last group in the number, which should have falling intonation.

- Point out the meanings of abbreviations 5, 6 and 7 if your Ss do not know them.

> 1 oh two oh – double seven oh nine – oh seven six five
> 2 oh one – double four – double one – two three – two three
> 3 oh two – nine two five oh – double seven double seven
> 4 two one two – seven three six – three one double oh.
> 5 aitch are
> 6 cee ee oh
> 7 are and dee
> 8 ay tee and tee
> 9 cee enn enn
> 10 aye bee emm

 (B)

- Point out that this is a continuation of the conversation in Unit 1 if your Ss have done it. It doesn't matter if they haven't.
- Get your Ss to work in pairs. Hand out a copy of the notes for the conversation to each student and give them time to prepare it.
- When the situation is clear, begin the role-play.
- Circulate and monitor. Note language points for praise and correction, especially in the area of telephoning.
- Bring the class to order. Praise strong language points and work on half a dozen points that need improving, getting Ss to say the correct forms.
- Get one or two of the pairs to do their role-play for the whole class, incorporating your improvements.

Unit 8 Planning

 (A)

- This activity revises the functional language on page 75 of the Course Book.
- Ask your Ss to work on these expressions in pairs. Circulate, monitor and assist if necessary.
- Go through the answers with the whole class.

> **Interrupting**
> 1 Could I just say something?
> 2 Could I just comment on that?
> 3 Hold on a minute.
> 4 Sorry to interrupt but ...
> **Clarifying**
> 5 How do you mean exactly?
> 6 What exactly do you mean by ... ?
> 7 Are you saying ... ?
> 8 So what you're saying is that ...

(B)

- Give the background to the role-play. Divide the class into groups of five. Hand out the roles, assigning the role of mayor to self-confident students. Tell the Ss that they should use the expressions from Exercise A whenever they can in the role-play.

- Give your Ss time to prepare. Circulate, monitor and assist if necessary.
- When they are ready, get the chair in each group to open the meeting.
- Circulate and monitor. Note down language points for praise and correction afterwards.
- Bring the class to order. Praise strong language points and work on half a dozen points that need improving, getting Ss to say the correct forms.
- Ask each group what the outcome of their meeting was. Contrast the different outcomes and encourage discussion.

Unit 9 Managing people

(A)

- Go through this exercise quickly with the whole class.

> 1 d 2 a 3 e 4 b 5 c

- Then get your Ss to discuss the visitor's questions in relation to their own country or countries.

(B)

- Explain the situation and then get a pair of Ss to read the example dialogue. Point out that this is part of a longer exchange. They should use the ideas in the table as inspiration and add their own ideas.
- Then get Ss to choose one of the people in the table. Working in pairs, they should have a conversation with someone else in the table.
- Circulate and monitor. Note down language points for praise and correction afterwards.
- Bring the class to order. Praise strong language points and work on half a dozen points that need improving, getting Ss to say the correct forms.
- Insist on idiomatic forms like *I watch a lot of sport on TV* or *I like going out to eat in restaurants.*
  Do not accept forms such as *I practise a lot of sport.*
- Get Ss to have other exchanges, incorporating your improvements.
- Then get two or three pairs to replay their exchanges for the whole class.

Unit 10 Conflict

 (A)

- Do this exercise in pairs or as a quick-fire activity with the whole class.

Calming down

1 I understand <u>what</u> you're saying.
2 I can see your point of <u>view</u>.
3 Why don't we <u>come</u> back to that later?
4 You don't have to <u>worry</u> about ...

Creating solutions

5 A compromise <u>could</u> be to ...
6 How <u>about</u> if ...
7 Let's look at this <u>another</u> way.
8 Another <u>possibility</u> is ...

Closing a negotiation

9 Let's see what we've <u>got</u>.
10 Can I go <u>over</u> what we've agreed?
11 I think that <u>covers</u> everything.
12 <u>We've</u> got a deal.

Ⓑ

- Give the background information and ask two Ss to read the initial exchange and one or two more exchanges based on the instructions given.
- Once they have got the idea, get your Ss to work in pairs.
- Circulate and monitor. Note down language points for praise and correction afterwards, especially in relation to the language of negotiation.
- Bring the class to order. Praise strong language points and work on half a dozen points that need improving, getting Ss to say the correct forms.
- Get one of the pairs to redo the activity, incorporating the correct forms you have suggested.

Unit 11 New business

Ⓐ

- Go round the class, asking individual Ss to say the sentences. Work on any problems.

1 A kilo is about two point two pounds.
2 An ounce is twenty-eight point three five grams. (not *thirty-five*)
3 An inch is two point five four centimetres.
4 A foot is thirty point four eight centimetres.
5 A mile is one point six oh nine three kilometres.
6 A UK pint is about three-fifths of a litre.
7 A hectare is about two and a half acres.
8 A second-class return train ticket from Paris to Marseille is a hundred and twenty-six euros twenty.
9 The average price of a house in England is ninety-six thousand, seven hundred and eighty-two pounds.
10 The Strahov sports stadium in Prague can hold two hundred and four thousand, one hundred and thirty-nine people.
11 The population of Istanbul at the last census was ten million, thirty-three thousand, four hundred and seventy-eight.
12 The GNP of Romania is thirty point six billion dollars.

Ⓑ

- The idea here is for Ss to exchange information about the economies of two countries.
- Ask your Ss to work in pairs. Hand out the information for each member of each pair.
- Start the activity. Circulate, monitor and assist if necessary. Note down language points for praise and correction later, especially in relation to numbers.
- Bring the class to order. Praise strong language points and work on half a dozen points that need improving, getting Ss to say the correct forms.
- Then get one student to read out the information they obtained about Brazil and another the information they obtained about Mexico.
- Check the answers with the whole class.

Unit 12 Products

Ⓐ

- Do the matching exercise as a quick-fire activity with the whole class. Resolve any problems.

1 f 2 g 3 d 4 a 5 b 6 c 7 e

Ⓑ

- Give your Ss the background to the task. They have to draw their product and then present it to their partner in a sales presentation.
- Give Ss time to draw their products and complete the other information.
- When your Ss are ready, the presentations can begin. Circulate and monitor. Note down language points for praise and correction afterwards, especially in relation to product presentation language.
- Bring the class to order. Praise strong language points and work on half a dozen points that need improving, getting Ss to say the correct forms.

UNIT 1   Careers

Telephoning: making contact

A Correct these telephoning expressions. One or two words are wrong in each expression 1–10. Replace the words that are wrong with the same number of words.

1   Can I talk on Beryl Yang, please?
2   I'll like to speak to Beryl Yang, please.
3   Just a moment. I'm putting you up.
4   Just a moment. I'll join you.
5   Are you Beryl Yang?
6   Beryl Yang talking.
7   Hello. I am Andres Solano, from Solano and Associates.
8   I'm phoning on the proposal you sent us.
9   The reason I'm call is that we want to discuss it further.
10 We've lost your e-mail address. May you give it to me?

B Student A is Andres Solano, Student B is Beryl Yang and Student C is the operator. Role-play this telephone conversation, using correct versions of the expressions above.

A: Say hello and say who you want to speak to.

C: Ask A to wait. Then say you will put A through.

A: Thank C.

B: Say hello, but don't give your name.

A: Ask who you are talking to.

B: Give your name.

A: Say why you are calling – about a proposal for a new office building.

B: Say you understand what A is talking about.

A: Say you want to discuss it further.

B: Agree. Say you have lost A's e-mail address. Ask A to give it to you.

(This situation is continued in Unit 7.)

UNIT 2   Selling online

Negotiating: reaching agreement

A A businesswoman is talking about a negotiation that she recently took part in. Match the negotiating tips (1–7) with the things she says (a–g).

1 Be friendly.
2 Prepare carefully before you negotiate.
3 Have a lot of options.
4 Never be the first to make an offer.
5 Ask a lot of questions.
6 Pay attention to the other side's body language.
7 Summarise often the points you agree on.

a) I waited for the other guy to name his price. I didn't tell him what my objective was.

b) I asked him exactly what his requirements were, who his current partners were and how long it would take him to reach a decision.

c) Every half hour, I tried to say what we had agreed on and what remained to be negotiated.

d) Before the negotiations, I spent days working on the figures.

e) I knew if he didn't accept my first option, we had two cheaper options to propose.

f) When the customer arrived, I asked if he'd had a good flight and offered juice and coffee.

g) I asked if that was his final offer and he went red in the face.

B Student A is a buyer for a large bookstore chain. Student B is the sales rep for a publisher. They negotiate the discount on a new thriller.

- A wants between 5,000 and 20,000 copies. The more copies A orders, the bigger the discount they want but, of course, B wants to limit the discount given.
- Negotiate the number of copies to be bought by A and the discount to be given.
- During the role-play, you should try to use all the expressions on your role card.

Student A	Student B
Discount objectives	**Discounts you can offer**
1,000–4,999 copies: 25% discount	1,000–4,999 copies: 20% discount
5,000–9,999 copies: 30% discount	5,000–9,999 copies: 25% discount
10,000–19,999 copies: 35% discount	10,000–19,999 copies: 30% discount
20,000 copies and above: 40% discount	20,000 copies and above: 35% discount

Student A

Expressions
- Do you agree to …
- As long as …
- How about …
- Absolutely.
- Maybe you're right.
- Agreed!

Student B

Expressions
- Mmm, I don't know.
- I can offer …
- That sounds reasonable.
- Will you agree to …
- We'd prefer …

Resource bank

UNIT 3 Companies

Presenting your company

A A company boss is presenting his company to potential investors. The presenter does *not* follow the usual tips for presentations and irritates the investors. Match the tips (1–6) that the presenter does not follow with the audience's reactions (a–f).

1 Find out about your audience and adapt your presentation accordingly.

2 Introduce yourself.

3 Use humour carefully.

4 Outline the structure of your talk.

5 Vary the tone of your voice.

6 Use clear visual aids.

a) This is no time for jokes.

b) Is he still in his introduction or is he on to the main part?

c) He's talking to us as if we were his customers, not potential investors.

d) His slides contain too much information – all those boring figures!

e) Who is this guy anyway?

f) I'm falling asleep. He talks in the same tone the whole time.

B Three human resources directors make presentations about their companies at a business school recruitment day. You are one of the HR directors. Use the notes below to make a presentation about your company.

	Futuropolis Parks	Austro Insurance	Smart-mart stores
Head office	Toulouse, France	Vienna, Austria	Peoria, Illinois
Activities	Theme parks about the future	All insurance products: life, property, car, etc.	Everything from food to clothing to furniture
Customers	Europeans, mainly middle class families with children aged 5 to 15	Businesses and consumers around the world	Consumers of all classes, all incomes
Annual turnover	€1 billion	€11 billion	€250 billion
Annual net profits	€250 million	€1.5 billion	€7 billion
Operations	2 parks in France, 1 each in Spain, Italy and Germany	Thousands of brokers (= independent insurance sellers) in Europe, the US and Asia	200 stores in the US, 55 in Europe, 30 in Latin America, 20 in Asia
Strengths	Good future for leisure industry in general, especially theme parks	Insurance has seen 10% growth a year over last ten years. Growth set to continue	Very low prices – other stores find it very hard to compete. 10–15% annual growth expected to continue
Future plans	Opening a park in Florida next year – English-speaking managers needed. Great career prospects!	Developing Latin American activities – Spanish- and Portuguese-speaking managers required. Great career prospects!	Developing further in Asia, especially China. Chinese- and English-speaking managers required. Great career prospects!

Photocopiable

UNIT 4   Great ideas

Successful meetings

A Correct the one word that is wrong in each of these useful expressions for meetings. The correct word begins with the same letter as the word that is wrong. (The headings in brackets are all correct.)

Chairperson

1 Can we state, please? (Beginning the meeting)

2 The main arm of this meeting is to ... (Stating the purpose of the meeting)

3 How do you fill about this? (Asking for comments)

4 Let's mobilise on now to ... (Changing the subject)

5 Sorry, I don't quiet understand. (Clarifying)

Participants

6 I'm in flavour of ... (Giving opinions)

7 Perhaps will should ... (Making suggestions)

8 I totally agreed. (Agreeing)

9 I don't know around that. (Disagreeing)

10 Held on a moment. (Interrupting)

B The neighbours in a block of four flats hold a meeting.

- They discuss repairs and improvements to the building – see the list below.
- They have already agreed to spend a maximum of €5,000 for the year.
- Chair or participate in the meeting, using the correct forms of the expressions above.
- Try to persuade your neighbours to agree to the repairs and improvements that you want.

---

1 Clean front of building – €2,000

2 Employ gardener to come once a week – €1,000

3 Install automatic gate to car park in order to limit access – €1,000

4 Paint common staircase to Flats C and D (The other two flats have their own entrances.) – €750

5 Repair roof that is leaking very slightly and affecting Flat D – €4,000

Owner of Flat A (ground floor)

- You want to sell your flat soon and you think improving the appearance of the building and the garden will increase its value.
- You do not care about the roof or the staircase.

Owner of Flat C (2nd floor)

- You had your car stolen recently and want the automatic gate to the car park to be installed as your top priority.
- You also want the staircase repainted.
- You do not care about the other improvements.

Owner of Flat B (1st floor)

- You are worried about the general state of the building.
- For example, you are willing to pay for the roof and painting the staircase to Flats C and D, even if you do not benefit directly.

Owner of Flat D (top floor)

- You want the roof repaired as your top priority.
- You also want the staircase repainted.
- You do not own a car and do not want to spend money on the car-park gate.

Resource bank

UNIT 5 Stress

Participating in discussions

A Three advertising agency managers are having a meeting about the problems of keeping their offices in London. Group the expressions (a–h) that they use under the headings (1–4).

1 Making suggestions **2** Giving opinions **3** Agreeing **4** Disagreeing

a) How about introducing special payments to help younger staff buy a house in London?

b) I agree with you when you say that London is a very expensive place to live.

c) I feel that we are not being as productive here as we could be in a quieter place.

d) I'm convinced that staying in London is absolutely necessary.

e) I'm not sure I agree. I think with e-mail and the Internet we can have enough contact with the outside world wherever we are.

f) We could offer to help staff with their travel costs.

g) What about asking all employees to vote on where they would like the company to be based?

h) Why don't we offer higher salaries to attract and keep the right people?

B Work in groups of three. You are one of the directors at the advertising agency meeting in Exercise A above. Your teacher will give you a role card to tell you who you are and what your opinions are. Use appropriate expressions from above, as well as others, to discuss the problems of keeping their offices in London.

Managing Director

- You think you should stay in London despite the cost.
- You will lose touch with the advertising industry and with customers if you go elsewhere.
- You listen to the suggestions about moving out of London, but politely disagree with them and say why.

Finance Director

- You are worried about the difficulty of recruiting new people to join the company. Young people cannot afford to live in London on the salaries the agency pays.
- Suggest moving to Newville, a small town about 100 km outside London.
- Talk about how the Internet means that it doesn't matter where the company is based.
- You happen to live in Newville and the move would be very convenient for you (no more commuting).

Human Resources Director

- You accept that the cost of living in London is becoming very high and that it is difficult to pay new recruits enough money to live there.
- But you also think that advertising agencies should stay in London if they want to expand and succeed.
- Personally, you like living in London because of its choice of activities, but you realise other people may not.

Resource bank

UNIT 6 Entertaining

Greetings and small talk

A This conversation takes place at a trade show. Rearrange the three parts into a logical conversation.

A: Hello again, Barbara. How are you? It's Alicia. We met in Paris last year.

B: Oh yes. I didn't recognise you. Your hair's different. I'm fine. What about you?

A: I'm very well, thanks.

B: And how's business, Alicia?

A: It's going well, especially in Spain.

B: Great.

A: Barbara, I'd like you to meet one of our best customers from there, Carlos González from Madrid.

B: Hello, Carlos. Nice to meet you. I've heard a lot about you.

C: Not all bad I hope!

B: Not at all. It's good to be able to put a face to a name.

C: Absolutely!

B This conversation is a continuation of the one in Exercise A. Use the words to make complete sentences. Each slash (/) indicates one missing word. Put the verbs in brackets into the correct form.

A: *to Barbara* Can / lend / your mobile so I / call / office? I (come back) after the call.

B: *to Carlos* Where / you (stay)?

C: At / Ritz. It / comfortable, / noise / nightclubs / a problem around 2 a.m.

B: I (be) sorry / hear that. Would / like / business card?

C: / please. Can / have some / your brochures?

B: / course!

A: Thanks / the mobile, Barbara!

B: That (be) all right.

C: Would / both like / have dinner somewhere / evening?

B, C: That's / good idea.

C: Shall / meet in / lobby / my hotel at eight?

A, B: / (sound) good.

C: Bye for now. See / later!

A, B: Bye!

Resource bank

UNIT 7 Marketing

Telephoning: exchanging information

A Say these telephone numbers, as in the example. (Use British English.)

1 Tower of London – 020 7709 0765
  oh two oh – double seven oh nine – oh seven six five

2 Eiffel Tower, Paris – 01 44 11 23 23

3 Sydney Opera House – 02 9250 7777

4 Empire State Building, New York – 212 736 3100

Say these abbreviations.

5 HR

6 CEO

7 R&D

8 AT&T

9 CNN

10 IBM

B Student A is Andres Solano, a client, and Student B is Beryl Yang, an architect. Role-play their telephone conversation. (This is a continuation of the conversation in Unit 1.)

A: Suggest meeting on Wednesday next week at 2.00 at your office.

B: Ask for the address.

A: 32nd floor, 625 Seventh Avenue. Tell B to ask for you at reception.

B: Agree.

A: Ask about the number of architects at Yang Associates.

B: 25 architects, including seven senior partners.

A: Ask about turnover last year.

B: Sales of €20 million in architects' fees.

A: Ask about important clients.

B: Clients: important companies such as JPG, AEI, KLQ and HRTZ. Say you can e-mail pictures of buildings you have designed for these companies.

A: Agree.

B: Ask for A's fax number in case there is a problem with e-mailing the pictures.

A: Your fax number is 212 563 9864. You are in a hurry. Say you look forward to seeing B on Wednesday at two. Say goodbye.

B: Confirm you look forward to seeing A. Say goodbye.

UNIT 8   Planning

Meetings: interrupting and clarifying

A Find the missing words in these expressions. There is one word missing in each of them.

Interrupting

1 Could just say something?
2 Could I just comment that?
3 Hold on minute.
4 Sorry interrupt but ...

Clarifying

5 How you mean exactly?
6 What exactly do mean by ... ?
7 Are saying ... ?
8 So you're saying is that ...

B Now use the correct forms of these expressions to role-play this meeting.

- There will be an important local festival in three months' time.
- The mayor of your city has asked the shopkeepers in the main street to attend a meeting.
- He wants the shopkeepers to contribute to paying for special street decorations. Some shopkeepers want to do this; others do not.

Mayor
- Announce that each shopkeeper should pay €1,000 towards the cost of the decorations – no matter what the size of their shop or their annual turnover.
- You do not own a shop yourself.
- You chair the meeting. Try to keep order when speakers interrupt each other.

Supermarket owner
- Annual turnover: €15 million. Shop area: large.
- The cost sounds very reasonable. People buy a lot of special expensive food on local festival days and the decorations will attract even more people than usual to your store.
- You do not mind if some of the small shopkeepers do not contribute. You know that some of them are not doing very well.
- In fact, you are willing to sponsor the decorations completely if other shops do not contribute. In this case, the name of your supermarket would be displayed often.

Hairdresser
- Annual turnover: €50,000. Shop area: very small.
- This festival does not change anything for you. People would have their hair cut anyway.
- You do not want to pay anything, however little.
- You don't mind if the supermarket owner sponsors the decorations, as the supermarket is not competing with you.

Women's clothing shop owner
- Annual turnover: €2 million. Shop area: medium.
- You think the decorations will be good for your business.
- However, you do not want to pay the full €1,000. You suggest that each shopkeeper contributes in relation to their turnover.
- You do not really want the supermarket owner to sponsor all the decorations. But if some of the other shopkeepers refuse to contribute, you will accept this.

Grocer
- Annual turnover: €1 million. Shop area: medium.
- You think the decorations will be good for your business.
- However, you do not want to pay the full €1,000. You suggest that each shopkeeper contributes in relation to the size of their shop.
- You do not want the supermarket owner to sponsor all the decorations, as the supermarket is a competitor. But if some of the other shopkeepers refuse to contribute, you will refuse, too.

UNIT 9 Managing people

Socialising and entertaining

A A business visitor from abroad has been invited to dinner at his host's house. Match the subjects (1–5) to the visitor's questions (a–e).

1 Being on time
2 The way people dress
3 How to address people
4 Giving gifts
5 Shaking hands / kissing / hugging / bowing

a) Should I wear a tie?
b) What should I take? Flowers, chocolates, a bottle of wine?
c) Should I shake hands with him again? We already shook hands this morning.
d) Should I arrive at the time I was given or should I get there 15 or even 30 minutes later?
e) Should I call their partner by their first name?

B You are one of the people below. You meet one of the other people, a business contact. Use the information given to make small talk about what you do in your spare time. Add your own ideas to the notes, as in this example.

Marie: What do you usually do after work, Ingvar?

Ingvar: I play a lot of tennis, indoors of course, and some evenings I go cross-country skiing just outside Stockholm, where I live. How about you, Marie?

Marie: Well, there's a lot to do in Paris, and I like to go to the theatre or go out for dinner somewhere. I have five weeks' holiday a year, so I take three weeks in August and go somewhere exotic. Last year, I went to Thailand.

Ingvar: Really!

	Winter	Summer
Ingvar – Stockholm	indoor tennis, cross-country skiing (just outside Stockholm)	house in the country, sailing (islands near Stockholm)
Marie – Paris	restaurants and theatre in Paris	travel abroad (five weeks' holiday a year, three in summer)
Len – London	sport on TV (most evenings)	play cricket (local team)
Raisa – Moscow	skating (lake near Moscow)	house in the country (100 km from Moscow)
Domenico – Milan	go to watch InterMilan play (every match, home and away)	sailing (lakes in the Alps)
Susan – Edinburgh	walking (Scottish highlands)	travel (June or July), go to Edinburgh festival (August)

UNIT 10 Conflict

Negotiating: dealing with conflict

(A) Correct these negotiating expressions. There is one wrong word in each expression.

Calming down

1 I understand that you're saying.
2 I can see your point of views.
3 Why don't we become back to that later?
4 You don't have to sorry about ...

Creating solutions

5 A compromise shall be to ...
6 How around if ...
7 Let's look at this other way.
8 Another possible is ...

Closing a negotiation

9 Let's see what we've get.
10 Can I go on what we've agreed?
11 I think that overs everything.
12 We's got a deal.

(B) Work in pairs. Student A is the customer; Student B is the supplier. You are negotiating the sale of some bricks. These are the negotiators' objectives in the beginning.

	Price per thousand bricks	Discount for bulk orders	Delivery	Payment currency
A: customer	€820	25 per cent	6 weeks	euros
B: supplier	€950	15 per cent	3 months	US dollars

- Start the negotiation using the sentences given. Then use the correct forms of the expressions above and other expressions to continue the negotiation, following the instructions.

  A: 'So you're offering a price of €950 per thousand bricks and, as I told you, I'm only willing to pay €820.'

  B: 'Yes. There seems to be quite a gap here.'
  Calm A down and suggest a compromise: a price of €855.

  A: Accept the solution.
  Move on to discount.

  B: You can only offer a higher discount if A accepts a longer delivery time.
  Suggest a specific discount and a delivery time.

  A: You can't accept B's proposal.
  Create another solution.

  B: Accept A's proposal.
  Move on to currency.

  A: Insist on paying in euros.

  B: Calm A down. Suggest half the payment in euros and half in dollars.

  A: Accept.
  Go over the agreement.

  B: Accept or disagree with A's summary. Clear up any disagreements.

  A: Close the negotiation.

  B: Reply.

UNIT 11 New business

Dealing with numbers

A Say these sentences.

1 A kilo is about 2.2 pounds.
2 An ounce is 28.35 grams.
3 An inch is 2.54 centimetres.
4 A foot is 30.48 centimetres.
5 A mile is 1.6093 kilometres.
6 A UK pint is about $\frac{3}{5}$ of a litre.
7 A hectare is about $2\frac{1}{2}$ acres.
8 A second-class return train ticket from Paris to Marseille is €126.20.
9 The average price of a house in England is £96,782.
10 The Strahov sports stadium in Prague can hold 204,139 people.
11 The population of Istanbul at the last census was 10,033,478.
12 The GNP of Romania is $30.6 billion.

B Work in pairs. Student A has information about Brazil. Student B has information about Mexico. Communicate this information to each other.

Student A

	Brazil	Mexico
Population	170,000,000	
Population of largest city	17,000,000 (São Paulo)	
GNP	$730 billion	
GNP per head	$4,350	
Inflation	4.9%	
Unemployment	7%	
Cars per 1,000 population	79	
Telephones per 1,000 population	149	

Student B

	Brazil	Mexico
Population		98,900,000
Population of largest city		26,000,000 (Mexico City)
GNP		$429 billion
GNP per head		$4,440
Inflation		16.6%
Unemployment		2%
Cars per 1,000 population		102
Telephones per 1,000 population		112

Resource bank

© Pearson Education Limited 2007 **Photocopiable**

Presenting a product

A Match the adjectives (1–7) to their definitions (a–g).

1	attractive	**a)**	made of good materials and put together well
2	fashionable	**b)**	always works and doesn't break down
3	robust	**c)**	can be used in different ways
4	high-quality	**d)**	strong and solid
5	reliable	**e)**	easy to use
6	flexible	**f)**	nice to look at
7	user-friendly	**g)**	looks modern and up-to-date

B Choose one of your company's products or a product you admire.

1   Make a drawing of your product and label it. Complete the technical information. You may want to mention:
   - dimensions
   - weight
   - available colours
   - power source
   - benefits for the user
   - how it compares to other products in the company's range
   - advantages over competing products
   - price
   - where to buy it

2   Work in pairs. Student A presents the product to a potential customer, Student B. Then Student B presents their product to Student A.

Photocopiable   © Pearson Education Limited 2007